Templewood

Chatfield

Ashfield

W. R. Inge

Gilbert Murray

Margery Fry

R. A. Gregory

L. P. Jacks

Frank O. Salisbury

Dawson

W. Beach Thomas

Seymour Hicks

Lewis Thomas

Margaret G. Bondfield

CROSBY HALL
RARY

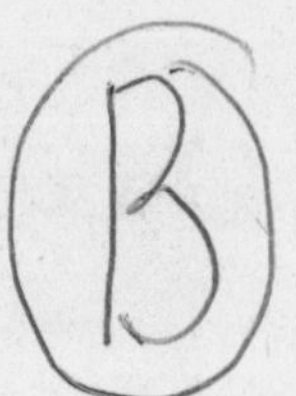
B

55 BROADWAY
WESTMINSTER, S.W. 1

Passengers, Sowest, London
Abbey 1234

With Lord Ashfield's compliments.

What Life has Taught Me

by

Twenty Five Distinguished Men & Women

Introduced by
GILBERT MURRAY, O.M.

Selected and Arranged by
SIR JAMES MARCHANT

ODHAMS PRESS LIMITED · LONG ACRE · LONDON

Published 1948
Made and Printed in Great Britain by Odhams (Watford) Ltd.
T.248.Q

CONTENTS

INTRODUCTION BY

CONTRIBUTORS

EDITOR

Sir James Marchant, K.B.E.

INTRODUCTION

BY

GILBERT MURRAY

SIR JAMES MARCHANT, as a collector of human specimens, is much to be congratulated on his present collection of individuals, so various in their views and experiences, but so similar in having successfully faced the trials and profited by the lessons of life. Human character is always an interesting subject, and merely from that point of view these papers are very good reading. Of course one must not expect of them what they do not profess to give. They are not autobiographies, not confessions, not words of advice to the young or cures for the corruption of the world, though elements of all these may be found in them.

I am struck by certain general points of agreement. Like most teachers, I have been occasionally afflicted by the type of Great Man who returns to the old school or university and boastfully explains how he was always at the bottom of the class or how he was "sent down" for idleness. In the present collection of Successful Livers the general tone is quite different. Nearly every writer lays stress on the importance of his upbringing; his debt to the pious home, the cultured home, the strict home; the affection and respect he felt for various teachers and friends who had helped or guided him. Had the writers belonged to an older generation I suspect we should have had much more direct edification and warnings against the errors that do, as a matter of fact, most widely spoil men's lives, against drink, gambling, loose living, extravagance and the like. But not only are such warnings unfashionable; the dangers themselves have probably not played any part in the life-problems of these writers. Miss Bondfield indeed does just mention her mother's admirable maxim, "Either pay cash or do without," and

Sir Bertrand Watson, speaking from exceptional experience, has some wise warnings on the tendencies of the time. The value of discipline, of course, is implied in many of the articles. For instance in Sir Miles Thomas's stress on the educational value of engineering. When an engine will not do what it ought there is no use in scolding or beating it, you have to find out what is wrong and set it right, and that is a wonderful piece of education. One cannot but be struck, also, by Lord Chatfield's account of the intense character-training involved in the discipline of a ship, and, in a less noticeable way, by Mr. Darwin's modest plea for the unconscious educational value of games or Sir George Dyson's remark on the great amount of latent knowledge and culture in our much abused public schools.

But how far does education or life itself alter what Miss Fry calls "the essential Me." It is clear that that varies greatly. Some of us are docile and some stubborn, some apt at learning and some not, some like Lord Horder, ready for anything, while of course some few are born with a special gift or genius. Bertrand Russell would have been a great mathematician, Sir George Dyson a musician, Father Martindale a saint and a mystic, Dr. Inge a scholar and theologian, Sir Beach Thomas a lover of rural monotony and happiness, whatever their schools or home circumstances. The maxim quoted by Sir Richard Gregory, "Find out what you want to do intensely; make sure that that's it; and then do it with all your might," is fine doctrine, but applies only to an exceptional and happy few.

The impress of religion and philosophy is strongly marked in many of the writers, from Dr. Jacks onward, which is not surprising considering how many of them belong to Dean Inge's profession of "Spectacle-makers, whose job is to help people with every degree of myopia to see the invisible." The call of science, as one would expect, is even more audible, that of public service more compelling still. This is an age of science, and most emphatically an age of great public trials and dangers making a call upon all good citizens, artists and musicians as well as the rest of us. To Lord Lytton high public service came as an obvious duty, to Bertrand Russell an "aristocratic liberalism" was almost as much part of his nature as mathematics; the same might be said of Miss

Fry's inspired philanthropy, and in all three cases, it may be noted, it was disinterested service uninfluenced by political ambitions. Public service was also the main interest of Miss Bondfield, whom I should count on the whole as the most triumphantly successful Liver of the whole list. Hers was a triumph of character. Starting from scratch, with no important home or school influences, rising steadily and winning friendship wherever she moved, she identified herself with a political cause which proved to be the winning cause, and was carried on without qualm or hesitation to the position of Cabinet minister, and, after retirement, to great peace of mind in religion. She had the strength that comes from a lack of "curiosity, criticism and introspection." I do not suppose that she ever lay awake, as Dean Inge did, haunted by "all the wrong and foolish things he had done in eighty years."

Few indeed of these successful Livers seem to have indulged in regrets or remorse. Such things no doubt are a waste of energy. But I am a little surprised that so few of them seem conscious of the ineradicable faults with which life has failed to deal, or which have grown upon them with age. The only writer who deals candidly with this subject is Mrs. Hamilton, and no doubt she hits the nail on the head in emphasizing the extreme egoism of youth. Babies, so I am informed by experts, are absolutely self-centred; certainly they have no other subject of conversation; and youth proceeds very slowly to escape from its prison, to extend its interest to others, and thereby to make a contented life much more possible. But, with the weakening of self-control which old age normally brings, there is another form of egoism less rapacious, but more grudging, peevish and tyrannical, that is often apt to set in. My wickeder self wonders what the secret comment of relatives and attendants might be on some of these successful contemporaries of mine who write such edifying words about Christian principles and consideration for others. The same deplorably cynical observer professes surprise that so few of the successful except Sir Seymour Hicks seem to think that they have owed much to mere luck. What would their unsuccessful competitors say?

I am sorry not to have had any word from these thoughtful and original-minded people, who have for the most part now passed into the latter days of life, on the tendency of the old towards Conservatism in thought and doings. In daily habits it is inevitable. One acts as one is accustomed to act unless there is some clear reason for changing. In thought, with the loss of mental vigour comes a loss of the power of adaptation to new circumstances and a resentment against new fashions. These are obvious weaknesses, but are they accompanied, or are they not, by a certain increase of wisdom? Experienced people are much less under the influence of catchwords and abstractions and cliques; more disposed to judge a thing by the way it really works than by its orthodoxy or its accord with some *a priori* principle. I half hoped to have some guidance here. Lastly, I am sure there is a question about which a great number of young people would be really grateful for guidance, if indeed guidance is possible. I mean the general problem of the relation of the sexes. I am not thinking of the mere avoidance of vice, on which, I imagine, our writers would be pretty well unanimous; but of the varied and delicate question of the suppression or control or guidance of the impulses of sympathy, love, and joy in beauty which the society of persons of the other sex often inspires, and which are by general consent harmless in themselves but "dangerous." The most useful remark on one part of this subject is Miss Fry's sentence about old maids, and her reminder that, even if love and motherhood are the high lights of a woman's life, a good third of life remains when they are over.

But all this is asking too much. The men and women who have been good enough to make these notes on what they believe life to have taught them, are not really, as Dr. Jacks puts it, attempting to answer Jehovah's tremendous question, "Adam, where art thou?" It is merely that, having made a good job of life themselves—for that must be the reason why Sir James Marchant selected them—they have been willing to put down some hints of what they think they have learnt by the way, a service for which we may well be grateful.

W. R. INGE

Born at Crayke, Yorkshire in 1860. Fellow and Tutor of Hertford College, Oxford, 1889–1904. After a few years as vicar of a London church and then as Lady Margaret Professor of Divinity, Cambridge, was appointed Dean of St. Pauls in 1911. Retired in 1934. Is author of some forty books, including several important volumes on the mystics and mysticism.

WHAT HAS life taught me? In eighty-seven years one ought to have learnt something. Marcus Aurelius says that an intelligent man of forty has seen enough of the world to understand all that he need know of the stage on which he has to act. Perhaps he is right. In middle age a sclerosis of the intellect, and too often of the conscience, begins to set in. I suppose these essays ought to be a kind of summary of a *Journal Intime*, like that of Amiel. But I have already said all about myself that I thought worth recording in the little book called *Vale* ("Good-bye") which I wrote for Messrs. Longman in 1934 when I resigned my Deanery. I think it is out of print, since the Germans burnt my publishers' warehouse, but I hope, if there is any demand for a record of my uninteresting life, that it will be reprinted, since no other memoir, except the obituary notice which the British Academy accords to its deceased members, will appear, by my request. I cannot avoid covering much of the same ground in what I am now writing.

One thing I have certainly learnt—not to have a good opinion of myself. When I lie awake at night, all the wrong and foolish things I have done in eighty years come trooping by and grinning at me. Most of these imps belong to the first half of my life. Count Keyserling thinks that we need not trouble ourselves about anything which we did more than fifteen years ago. I cannot let myself off so easily. When I think of all the loving care lavished upon me by my parents and others, and of the opportunities of friendship of which I took no advantage, I cannot acquit myself of coldness and ingratitude, and that is an unpardonable fault. But I fear that we remember most vividly faults that are no longer, and perhaps never were, part of our characters. Apart from what I have confessed, my memories are chiefly of innumerable stupidities and gaucheries, like the awful howler that I made in the Classical Tripos. That hideous secret shall die with me. It was not printed, like the great Professor Jebb's "he fell on his knees" for *submisit genas*, in *Cambridge Translations*, page 159. But there have been many worse slips, giving, I am afraid, the impression of bad manners and want of sympathy.

Ought we to apply the command "Judge not" to our own actions? St. Paul says, "I judge not mine own self." We pray for mercy, says Portia. We may be forgiven for faults of which we have sincerely repented, even when we cannot forgive ourselves, and possibly for some that we have forgotten, though this is not so certain.

But in a life which has been outwardly fairly successful, is there not much that I can remember with satisfaction? No, I think I have had much more than my share of good luck. The nineteenth-century parsonage, like the Scottish manse, was an ideal nursery of talent and character. Plain living and high thinking, "neither poverty nor riches," healthy and useful work—where else could these conditions be found more abundantly? My father, an Oxford cricket blue and a Fellow of his college, was one of the best and most unambitious of men. He was content to be curate-filial to my grandfather, Archdeacon Churton, till he was forty-five, and after a few years as Provost of Worcester College he declined, as a shock to his modesty, the very attractive bishopric of Salisbury. My mother was a highly cultivated woman. Instead of sending me to school my parents taught me admirably, and after only one term at a private school I was second on the list for college at Eton. My luck held. I had the best tutor at Eton, an enthusiast for the classics, Francis St. John Thackeray, a cousin of the novelist.

This was the golden age of Eton scholarship. In six years out of nine we swept the board in classical honours at Cambridge ; in one of the other years our best scholar went to Oxford. Even Shrewsbury under Kennedy, Samuel Butler's Dr. Skinner, never surpassed that record. But obviously the credit belonged to the school, not to the boy.

There was no vacant lectureship for me at King's, so I went to teach Latin and Greek to the little Eton boys, which was not my job. After four not very comfortable years the offer of a fellowship and tutorship at Oxford enabled me to retreat in good order. Fifteen years there passed very happily, and just when I was beginning to be rather tired of life in college rooms, my friend, Canon Henson, afterwards Bishop of Durham, gave me the West End living of All Saints, Ennismore Gardens. This change coincided with the greatest blessing that I have ever received—a perfect marriage. I do not think it is in bad taste to emphasize this, for I am asked to say what life has taught me. And this is the chief thing that I have learnt—that not only is a happy marriage the best thing in human life, but that love differs not only in degree but in kind from all other gifts of God. When St. John says "he that loveth not knoweth not God, for God is love," he expresses in the simplest language a profound truth, that love admits us into the heart of reality in a way that nothing else does. God reveals himself to us as perfect Goodness, Truth and Beauty. But these ultimate values, as we now call them, are like the Platonic Forms. They belong to the spiritual world, to which we have access by symbols, as in a mirror, as St. Paul says. In love God gives us himself, imperfectly but by direct communication. This truth is beautifully stated by St. Bernard of Clairvaux, who as might be expected applies it only to the love of God. But St. John warns us that he who loves not his brother whom he hath seen can hardly love God whom he hath not seen.

In addressing a bride and bridegroom at the altar I have often recited the sublime sonnet of Shakespeare, beginning "Let me not to the marriage of true minds admit impediments," one of the finest things that even he ever wrote. We must not be afraid of speaking out on this subject. The foul sin of adultery is not only increasingly practised but shamelessly condoned, especially by the upper class who ought to set a good example. There has been a lamentable falling off in public morality in the last fifty years.

Next to the supreme happiness and blessing of married love I should put the joys of parenthood. Our five children have brought us unmixed pleasure. But the two youngest have been taken from us. Our little daughter, one of God's saints if there ever was one, died at the Deanery after a long illness. I commemorated her in a short memoir which I know has helped to comfort very many who have had to bear the same sorrow. Our youngest son, educated at Eton and Magdalene College, Cambridge, after stroking his college boat at Henley, was ordained, and won all hearts in a Yorkshire curacy. He would have had a great career in the Church. I often thought of Hector in Homer taking the baby Astyanax in his arms and saying, "Some day people will say, this man is much better than his father." But it was not to be. When the war broke out he thought it his duty to enlist in the Air Force. He was appointed an instructor, with the dangerous duty of teaching novices to fly. There was a forced landing. Richard was seen walking away from the plane, and then turning back. The plane was on fire, and no doubt he hoped to rescue his companion. Both were suffocated.

We must beware of wishful thinking about another life. We can only picture it in terms of time and place. But if we believe that our Saviour "brought life and immortality to light," I think we may be assured that death is not what it seems to be. We may agree with the Quaker, William Penn: "They that love beyond the world cannot be separated by it. Death cannot kill what never dies, nor can spirits ever be divided that love and live in the same divine principle. They must needs be present that love and live in that which is omnipresent. In the divine glass they see face to face, and their converse is free as well as pure."

After less than three years in London I became, in 1907, Lady Margaret Professor of Divinity at Cambridge, where I was very happy, and expected to remain there till the end of my working life. But in 1911 the Crown, through Mr. Asquith, offered me, to my intense surprise, the Deanery of St. Paul's, and I thought I ought to accept it.

I will say very little here of my twenty-three years as Dean, which occupy the greater part of my little book of reminiscences. It was a very full and active life. Thanks partly, perhaps, to the newspapers, which chose to regard me as "good copy," a shy recluse became first a notoriety and then almost a celebrity. I was in great request as a preacher and lecturer, and my books had a large sale. The Prime Minister, when he appointed me, said that he hoped I would revive the traditions of the Deanery as the most scholarly post in the Church of England—he was thinking of such famous Deans as Colet, Donne, Tillotson, Milman, Mansel and Church. I believe I did my little best to follow in the footsteps of those great men ; it is not for me to judge how far I succeeded. Nor need I say much of the thirteen years which I have spent in retirement in a Berkshire village. Extreme old age is a strange experience. I do not feel things very deeply. Weeks and months glide by almost as in a dream. I do not find much to pray about, since the world, the flesh and the devil are only memories, and in this life there is nothing to hope and not much to fear. I can only commend my dear ones and my unhappy country into God's hands. The gradual loosening of the ties that bound me to life does not trouble me much. I do not lament like the Greek love-poet, Mimnermus, who prayed that he might die at sixty, nor like Horace, who seems to have aged very prematurely, that all his pleasures were being taken from him one by one. Tennyson's Ancient Sage says rather cruelly :—

> The years that made the stripling wise
> Undo their work again,
> And leave him blind in heart and eyes
> The last and least of men.

We may hope to be spared this humiliation, though we can hardly hope, with Sir Thomas Overbury, to "feel our old age rather by the strength of our soul than by the weakness of our body." I am not unhappy ; peace after a strenuous life is welcome, and if

Christianity is true, Lewis Nettleship was right in saying, "Death does not count." Our Lord, according to the Fourth Gospel, said, "He that liveth and believeth on me shall never die."

I ought to say something about the course of my religious opinions, for a man's real religion, which often differs from his professed creed, is what life has taught him. My parents, living in the depths of the country, were rather belated adherents of the old Tractarians, disciples of Pusey and Keble. It is an almost extinct type. They took no interest whatever in ecclesiastical millinery and fancy ritual, nor did they multiply church services. They believed in the verbal inspiration of Scripture, and very fervently in the unhistorical doctrine of apostolical succession. They were puritanical, spending very little on themselves, though generous in their charities. Sunday was observed severely ; no games or secular reading were allowed. For some odd reason the reading of novels with "yellow backs" was discouraged. Even Dickens and Thackeray were not put into our hands, though Shakespeare and Walter Scott were read aloud to us. It was a good education, with some queer inhibitions.

I soon began to rebel, and my mother, I fear, never quite forgave me. She was not at all pleased at my promotion in the Church. A Broad Churchman was quite outside the pale. But I did not begin to think much about theological problems till I became an Oxford don. At Eton we were not encouraged to think that life has many problems, and as an undergraduate I was too busy in circumventing the "riddling Sphinx," the university examiners. But at Oxford even a "Mods" tutor must be a philosopher.

The "conflict between religion and science," of which so much was heard in the last century, was conducted on both sides with what now seems amazing crudity. Orthodoxy relied mainly on the traditional arguments from prophecy and miracle. There is no reason to think that any human beings have been endowed with the gift of foretelling the future. Christ himself avowed his ignorance of the time of the expected "Day of the Lord." Examination of alleged fulfilments of prophecy reveals three expedients. Either the prophecies were delivered after the event, or they were twisted, to suit the event, into a meaning which they never had, or thirdly the event was invented to match the prophecy. This third method is almost certainly discernible in the Gospels. The birth at Bethlehem, the massacre of the innocents, and the flight into Egypt are probable examples. The earliest anti-Jewish Christian apologetic made great use of the argument from prophecy.

As for miracle, in the proper sense of a suspension of the natural order by the direct action of God, the traditional insistence upon it is not merely a desire to establish the factual occurrence of certain miraculous events in the past, for these, taken in isolation, do not prove anything of vital importance for religion. What Goethe means when he says that miracle is faith's dearest child is that men wish to be delivered from the rigid, meaningless and unspiritual rule of natural law. Special providences and answers to prayer are for many an integral part of their faith. The efficacy of prayer, it was suggested on the other side, may be tested mathematically in the same way as telepathy has recently been tested—some say proved—in the United States and in this country. The indignant repudiation of this experiment masked a complete want of confidence in the result of the trial. A God who "does nothing," it was felt, was either non-existent or a mere personification of natural law.

On the side of science the controversy was conducted with at least equal shallowness. Although the Victorian scientists disclaimed the name of materialists, they interpreted the world by mechanical and quantitative categories, and by disregarding what Bismarck called the imponderables, the whole realm of values, they arrived at what they hoped was a coherent and closed system. What they wrongly called the law of causality was really a law of unbroken continuity. The perfect science was mathematics, the clearest and emptiest of mental disciplines, which eliminates time, and will, of which time is the form, and makes every process reversible. It is not correct to say that they gave us facts without values, for truth is an absolute value, but they ignored the other ultimate values. They shut their eyes to the second law of thermodynamics, according to which the whole universe is running down irreversibly like a clock. They fell easy victims to the great superstition of the century, the supposed law of ineluctable progress. As for religion and idealism, Herbert Spencer claimed the knowable for science, and left the unknowable to religion. Leslie Stephen went a step further, and spoke of realities and dreams. The whole realm of values floated ineffectively like a mist over the real world of stars and atoms. Nevertheless, they had a strong case against supernaturalism, which claimed for miracle exactly that kind of actuality which science cannot allow it. If, as I said, an epidemic of cholera may be caused either by an infected water supply or by the blasphemies of an infidel mayor, there is an end of natural science.

Dogmatic materialism and materialistic dogmatism are brothers, like Cain and Abel. Their day is over ; both have crumbled from within. When I turned my attention to what William James called religious experience, and what used to be called the inner light or the testimony of the Holy Spirit, and resolved to devote myself to the study of the mystics and Platonists, I was only one of many who were embarking on the same quest. This is indeed the true foundation of faith. The testimony of the saints is decided, coherent, and almost unanimous. Those who have given all they have to find the pearl of great price have not come away empty handed. They have not all been Christians. The greatest of philosophical mystics, the third century Neoplatonist Plotinus, was a pagan. We are now beginning to realize that the Indians have something to teach us. It is a wise saying that both Christianity and Buddhism have suffered by their isolation from each other. Personally, I have had only faint glimmerings of the mystical vision ; I have not earned anything more. But, as I have said, if a dozen honest men tell me that they have climbed the Matterhorn, I am satisfied that the summit of that mountain is accessible, though I cannot hope to get there myself.

Christianity, as St. Augustine saw, is Platonism *plus* the all-important doctrine of the Incarnation. Almost all philosophies have offered to make man invulnerable. Christianity does not. God is love, and love often hurts. "God so loved the world that He gave His Son." Vicarious suffering, not vicarious punishment, is a law of life, to which all who are willing to follow their Divine Master are called. *No Cross no Crown* is the title of William Penn's best-known work. It will be seen that I think the Quakers have undoubtedly got the root of the matter in them.

On the Person of Christ my views have changed slightly. I was at one time much impressed by Seeley's *Ecce Homo*, Harnack's lectures on "What is Christianity?" and the writing of other German Protestants. I preached a furious university sermon against Loisy's words that we have to acknowledge "comme deux Christs," "the Galilean peasant of limited intelligence," and the object of the Church's worship. I am still convinced that the faith of the Apostles, which survived the crucifixion, can only be accounted for by the overwhelming impression which their Master made upon them while He was with them. "Never man spake like this man." Whatever view we take of the post-resurrection appearances, they would not have carried conviction and altered the whole lives of those who saw them, if Jesus had been such a one as Loisy supposes. The belief in the approaching "Parousia" was, in my opinion, a rationalization of an intense spiritual exaltation which men could not explain otherwise than as a great hope in a near future. Do we not see among ourselves visions of "a good time coming," which have not been extinguished by the fact that a very bad time has come?

But I have come to see that there is a danger in what has been called Jesus worship. St. Paul's words about no longer knowing Christ after the flesh have been too often explained away. St. Paul's own faith, so lamentably misunderstood by Martin Luther, was a Christ-mysticism, and the Christ who since his conversion had taken the place of the "old man" whom he had known, was "a quickening Spirit." The Christ of the Christian's worship is "He who is alive and was dead, and behold He is alive for evermore"—alive and "with us all the days, even to the end of the world."

I am more and more convinced that St. Paul's tripartite division of human nature into body, soul and spirit is psychologically true. We live mainly on the psychical level, and the soul is an "amphibious" entity, having affinities with what is above, and what is below itself. Our inner life should be a progressive transformation of soul into spirit. Spirit is the divine part of our nature, potentially but not actually ourselves. I think that modern philosophy since

Descartes and Leibnitz has tended to overemphasize the idea of personality as something fixed and permanent. We do not believe in the absorption of personality in an impersonal Absolute ; the "I and Thou" relationship remains to the end, otherwise love and worship would cease ; but we do look forward to a transformation which St. Paul says is nothing less than the "death" of the "old man" and the "renewal" of ourselves into a being who "after God is created in righteousness and true holiness."

This is the explanation of the necessity of symbolism in religion. While on earth we can see only "as in a mirror by means of symbols," and in passing, as we do every day, from the visible to the invisible, from time to eternity, from appearance to reality, we can hardly avoid intercalating our attempts to see the invisible into the world of space and time which we now inhabit. In one of my more successful after-dinner speeches, to the Worshipful Company of Spectacle Makers, I said that we clergy are spectacle makers, whose job it is to help people with every degree of myopia to see the invisible—a difficult business. If I am right, the less we talk about obscurantism and heresy, the better. All eschatology—doctrines about "the four last things"—must be frankly symbolical. Our Lord revealed nothing about it except in parables—"without a parable spake He not unto them"—and in language borrowed from the current beliefs of His time. His only argument against the Sadducees was "God is not the God of the dead but of the living, for all live unto Him," words which St. Augustine echoes very beautifully : "*Quod Deo non perit sibi non perit.*" I am not disposed to go much beyond this, but we may allow our imagination some freedom.

My chief interest has been in religion and philosophy, and I have allowed these subjects to take up most of my space. But of course, I have had other interests too. Under popular governments it is not only the right but the duty of every citizen to make up his mind on public affairs, and if he thinks he has anything to say which is worth saying, he may try to convince his neighbours that he is right. This applies to the clergy as well as to the laity. But a churchman, especially if he holds an official position, must not be guilty of the impertinence of speaking in the name of the

Church, when he knows that many men who are as sincere Christians as he is, and quite as intelligent, do not agree with him. There is a strong and permanent temptation for an organized religious body, especially if it is losing in popularity, to plunge into party politics on the winning side. It always comes out badly smirched ; for as Lord Acton said in words which are now often quoted, "Power tends to corrupt." The Church of England, in consequence of its privileged position, has been fairly free from this temptation ; there is no Church vote. But the ambitious ecclesiastic is always with us, and he knows, to use a vulgar phrase, on which side his bread is buttered.

My parents were of course Conservatives ; the association of the High Church party with Socialism began with Gore and Scott Holland. They only admitted regretfully that "Mr. Gladstone is a better churchman than Mr. Disraeli." For myself, it amuses me to remember that even as late as the Boer War I was a Tory imperialist of the school of Rudyard Kipling. That humiliating episode disillusioned me and many others. But as the new century advanced it became plain that the period of British expansion was at an end, and that we must resign ourselves to a period of contraction. All the nations bordering on the Atlantic have passed their zenith. Eastward, not westward, as Bishop Berkeley thought, the course of empire takes its way. I remember Lord Haldane saying during the first World War, "The Germans could have got all they wanted if they had kept the peace." They have twice thrown away the prize which was in their hands, and the day of the Slavs has come. The future belongs to nations with a larger area, a lower standard of living, and a greater aptitude for hard work than ourselves or the French.

As far as I can see, we are faced with three dangers. First, there is the inevitable result of universal suffrage, the certainty that politics will degenerate into an auction of the worldly goods of the unrepresented minority. I say unrepresented, for though numerically the professional and business class is perhaps entitled to a hundred seats, there is hardly a constituency, except the City of London and the Universities, in which they can return a member pledged to support their interests. The demoralization of the wage-earners has already gone so far that no nation in the world welcomes the British working man.

Next, there is the growth of bureaucracy, greatly stimulated by the two wars. In order to defeat Fascism we have had to fascise ourselves. Worship of the State is the worst kind of idolatry. Hitherto, we in England have given great power to society, but not to the State. Now the State is encroaching everywhere. As poor Laberius said when Julius Cæsar compelled him to act in one of his own mimes, "*Porro, Quirites! Libertatem perdimus.*"

Third, the new inventions, including the atomic bomb, have dangerously increased the power of governments, whether they are despotic or democratic. The mob is no longer to be feared. We have seen in Russia and in Germany how helpless the people are against a government which has violated all the laws of justice and humanity. We say sometimes, "Such things could not happen here." Well, perhaps not; but the danger exists. The middle class, which is the chief defender of individual liberty, is being everywhere destroyed, and the Liberal Party, once so proud and confident, is in a pitiable position. In my young days the Liberals used to call the Conservatives the stupid party. They were complacently cutting their own throats by advocating extensions of the franchise. Gladstone once said in conversation: "Depend upon it, sir, if Socialism ever gets a footing in this country, it will be the work of the Tory Party." This was Herbert Spencer's opinion, who called Socialism the new Toryism. But it was really the result of Liberal policy. "Peace, retrenchment, and liberty." They are bourgeois ideas, we are now told.

I have some hopes that the dethronement of Mammon, who has no longer any prizes to offer, may be a good thing for what used to be called the privileged classes. They are, I think, setting a good example. Unless it is more rotten than I hope ours is, the body politic generates anti-toxins as well as toxins. Almost everything depends on abolishing the supreme curse of war, and I cannot believe that this is impossible. St. Bernard says, "*Habet mundus noctes suas et non paucas.*" We may be at the beginning of another dark age; but where there is hope there is life, and the West has not given up hope. We have passed through the greatest calamity that has ever befallen the human race, but every challenge, unless it is absolutely crushing, evokes a response, and we have shown that we can stand severe punishment without flinching.

Well, let this suffice. Life has taught me, I suppose, what I was capable of learning. I have not been ambitious, and I have never said or written anything dishonest in order to please anybody. People call me a reactionary ; but a reactionary has enough spirit to be a rebel. It is the progressive who floats with the stream like a dead dog, and licks the hand of his master like a live one. The parrot-cries of today are the echo of the dreams of the day before yesterday. There is nothing so reactionary as being up to date. I hope my honesty will stand to my credit, however little good I have been able to do to my countrymen.

MARGARET G. BONDFIELD

Born in Somerset, became Assistant Secretary of Shop Assistants' Union in 1898 and rose to be the Chairman of the T.U.C. in 1923. Entered Parliament in the same year and in 1929 as Minister of Labour under Ramsay MacDonald became the first woman to achieve Cabinet rank.

MY LIFE has been nomadic—full of incidents and experiences; herein are set down a few of those decisions and events at the turn of the century, which built foundations and taught me lessons of life-long value. The extent to which I have succeeded in blazing a good trail is due to these countless influences and events which shaped my course. The decisive factors are not the big moments but the small everyday matters of choice.

I am glad I was born in Somersetshire—where children inherit the desire to leave home and see the world as soon as they get the chance.

For five years I was the youngest of a family of ten, most of whom had already "gone out," so two youngest brothers, too young for school, did thoroughly attend to my education. If they went to fetch the cows for milking, so did I, often fastened in an old three-wheeled pram. Following these boys around made me familiar with the use of gardening tools, pigs' swill, weeding out carrots, helping to gather fruit and vegetables, and watching my mother at the churn, the wash tub and the ironing board.

My youngest brother, Frank, was a born naturalist: we watched the ever-changing countryside—the first flowers in the hedgerows. He could imitate the birds and identify all life in the meadow and copse.

We had rollicking games; with me fastened in the old pram they would send it rattling down the hill, racing after and catching it before it plunged into a deep ditch. Sometimes I was allowed to "field" when the boys were practising at the wickets. Always I have been glad to have had the healthy companionship of these two boys at the beginning of life.

From mother we learned a fine code of conduct; with even-handed justice she required us to tell no lies, nor sneak, to play fair and enjoy life; she had a lovely sense of humour. In our almost self-contained homestead every child in turn shared the allotted tasks.

At five years of age my pilgrimage began. My parents were surprised by the coming of an eleventh child—a girl. I was sent to my maternal grandmother, widow of a Congregational Minister at Middle Lambrook; the Manse had been turned into a boarding school. The teachers were my eldest sister, Annie, and an aunt who was deaf. The most exciting event of my stay there was when my stately grandmother allowed me to brush her lovely white hair which cascaded down her back—she, too, was deaf, so we did not talk. These relations were all strangers to me.

I accepted this change of environment with interest. For the first time I was with other girls—with the adults all too busy to spare time for me. I much preferred my brothers' games and fun. I must have been nearly six when an illness from which it was thought I could not recover affected my memory.

The next clear recollection is of being at Stembridge for a few months in care of yet another stranger sister, a schoolmistress who lived at the school house—she, too, was busy and also socially inclined; she must have found me a severe handicap. I learned nothing I remember at this school, but passively soaked up impressions of a lot of little girls sitting on forms, one of whom had lovely golden-brown curls. I longed for curls! My hair was black and a mop, its one advantage after I had returned to my home was that, like my brothers, I could put my head under the pump for a shower and shake it like a dog on the way to school. I returned to a strange home, with the new fretful baby sister, Kate—the two brothers going off to school—an older brother, Allan, whom I had seen sometimes rushing off to work.

I became aware that we were a scattered family; Allan in Taunton and Herbert in London, Henry going as a missionary to China, Ernest planning to go to South Africa, John editing a paper in Brighton. The only ones with whom I felt a personal relation were my mother, Frank and Ernest. I had become uprooted. After a few months at home, with a label sewn to my coat, I travelled in care of the guard from Chard to Brighton, to my sister Annie, who with aunt had moved from Lambrook to keep house for John. Tragically John died almost before they had settled in. I went to school there for a year, during which my sister took me to see *Iolanthe*, the greatest experience of my young life; it shook me out of the passive state of acceptance—it dwarfed all previous delights—it was a new world. In those days, this sort of entertainment was an annual affair—and before the next became due I was returned home, this time really to go to school. I had lessons in music and deportment! Every day Frank and I walked about one and a half miles each way. That pleased me and he continued my real education. I was good at reading—fairly bad at everything else. In music I could play simple pieces, and my brother Ernest's accompaniment to voice and piccolo. Frank, too, had a good voice, but he preferred choir singing in which he could slide from tenor to bass, or alto or treble in the several parts. Ernest liked to rouse my temper when he wanted me at the piano. He said I always played better when annoyed—yet I could never refuse to play for him, even when he picked me up, as one would a kitten, and laid me out on the top of the privet hedge—then brought me to the piano stool and in the most cordial tones would say "Ready now Meg," my pride and temper dissolved in laughter. My first bitter grief was his death in South Africa during the Boer War.

It was in my eighth year that my father—after sixty years of faithful service in a lace factory, which he entered at the age of nine—was dismissed with a week's notice: I did not know him as the older children did. For them he was a great companion, but he was too old to be interested in my immaturity. One day, walking hand in hand, I said to him: "Look father—the train!" It was still a novelty which once a day passed up and down near our house; with his eyes still fixed on the road he replied: "Child, you will live to see men flying in the air and it will be such a common sight you will not lift your head to look at them."

That prophecy was fulfilled in 1915, but in 1881 it seemed unbelievable. I learnt later of the part he had played with Stringfellow and Henson in 1835-1865 in building the plane which laid down the principles of flight. He taught himself geology, astronomy, electricity. He made his contribution to the Reform Bill agitation in the 1830s and to the Repeal of the Corn Laws in the 1840s. He was a father to be proud of. I knew him only in his bitter hours of wounded pride and a sense of injustice inflicted on all the old men of the factory staff when the factory changed hands. Foreman and lace designer, he invented new designs for the Jaquard looms and many other inventions he gave to the firm without thought of reward. That "week's notice" planted in me the seeds of revolt.

We never knew poverty as the townsfolk knew it; we always had enough of good food from our own supplies, but for my mother the burden was great. Her pride of independence, such that the children—grown up and self supporting, had to be tactful about any help they offered. Her ruling principle was if you can't pay cash, go without. I have followed that principle throughout life.

I finished my schooling at the Chard Board School. Geography was not taught to girls and only headlines of history; we learnt knitting, sewing and cutting-out, writing, reciting, grammar and arithmetic. I had no need to learn to read. I read everything in print that came my way. At the age of thirteen I was in charge of a class of forty-eight infants in the boys' school, of whom thirty-eight passed in reading, writing and arithmetic. No one was more surprised than myself at this result, as in retrospect the classroom, to me, seemed like a continuous bedlam.

I spent the holiday with Annie in Brighton; her friend, Mrs. White offered me a place on the staff of her small shop in Hove. I did not want to train as teacher and this offer seemed to open a speedier way to independence, so I became apprenticed for three years to "ladies' outfitting."

Mrs. White's was not an ordinary shop; the counter trade was very small. She had a large Anglo-Indian connection and sent layettes and trousseaux to Calcutta, Simla and many other places in the East. She would buy from the wholesale good plain garments, which we made distinctive with smocking, embroidery or lace; a real old family business. I sat by the window encircled by a passion-flower vine. Incidentally, India became alive, as did Africa and China—as places where people lived whose lives touched mine and I learnt some more geography—in the way I had learnt about Middle Lambrook, Stembridge and Brighton and Chard schools, mainly through timetables and shop dispatches.

At Mrs. White's I first saw death. Her husband was an old man in his dotage and when he died she asked me if I would share a watch while she rested; she took me to his room flooded in sunshine and with many flowers. His face was peaceful and very beautiful. "You see, my dear," she said, "I lost my companion and husband when he lost his mind and I am glad his poor old body is at rest. It is no occasion for mourning." I watched for two hours. I felt happy to have had this rich experience which robbed death of its terrors for me.

Here I record with gratitude an influence which helped me when I was sixteen years of age. I had heard only the usual smudgy inaccuracies about sex that most children of my generation picked up from each other, all mixed up with a sense of shame. It was fortunate for me that a cultured woman discovered my state of mind and set herself to weed out the unwholesome patch and plant instead a clean, sane knowledge, both biological and social, on this question.

Mrs. White retired from business as my apprenticeship expired. I was not in the least prepared for shop life in general. My next job was in an Emporium, a huge place in Brighton, with many departments and hundreds of assistants, buyers and what not.

My sister was an ardent worker at Clifton Road Church. We were both in the choir and at sixteen I joined the Church as a matter of course, attended its services and prayer meetings. For three years life was divided into six days of hard work under horrible conditions and Sundays with my relations. It was a time of incubation. There came a day when I determined to break with

Brighton. I consulted no one and made the move in the slack season, a sharp sudden decision and a blunder for which I paid dearly. By rigid economy I had saved five pounds, which to me seemed great wealth, but the material side of life did not worry me then. I had reached a stage in the pilgrimage when I must travel alone. Religion had become something personal, to be accepted or rejected; at home it was like the air, it permeated our lives but was not discussed—I was experiencing the first shock in the realization of hypocrisy in commercialized religion—to which I applied the harsh judgments of the very young. I could no longer passively accept contemporary opinion on business morality and the visible sign of my protest was this move to London. It was a turning point in my career, but for which I might have become a successful business woman!

For the next three months I was nearer to starvation than at any time before or since. I learned the bitterness of a hopeless search for work. No labour exchanges, or unemployment benefit. I had introductions to a few of the well-known commercial travellers, and they showed goodwill, but by the time I had raced (on a horse bus!) from the warehouse to the address given the job was filled.

At last I got work in Tottenham Court Road. I still think of the line: "There is a Providence which shapes our end, rough hew them as we may," when memory roves over that period.

I had arranged a transfer from Clifton Road to King's Weigh House Church, and had personal introductions to Dr. and Mrs. Murrey. They were interested in a new club for shopworkers opened in Tottenham Court Road, and through their introduction I became a member, and found friends among stimulating and exciting people. We had a "St. Pancras Parliament." I became Member for Taunton. We were discussing the new plan to transform the old ecclesiastical vestries into borough councils with a mayor, aldermen and councillors, *with robes*, as that, the promoters said, will help to reconcile the vestrymen to the changing method of government while still giving even better pageantry.

R. C. Phillimore, G. B. Shaw, the Webbs, Lucy Fitzpatrick, afterwards Mrs. Phillimore, were all working on the bill carried into law. I remember most gratefully how they encouraged my interest in this strange new club life, where one could have physical drill, poetry classes, ethical discussions, dances and fun, all within five minutes' walk of my shop. Bernard Shaw was elected to the new St. Pancras Borough Council and one of the first of his reforms was to establish in the borough municipal lavatories for women. We at the club rejoiced at this reform, but my room-mates, living in, thought it not quite nice to talk about.

These same room-mates thought it most improper of me to wear knickers instead of three layers of petticoats, and suspenders instead of corsets. At the club I made life-long friends, notably Claire James, the drill instructor, famous now for her work on Canvey Island, who took me to her adopted home with Mrs. Amie Hicks. It became my adopted home on Sundays.

An apparently trivial thing opened the door to new adventures. Being hungry one night I bought "a penn'oth of fish and a ha'poth of chips," that great standby of the very poor. It was wrapped in a bit of newspaper which I read while munching the food sauntering around Fitzroy Square. It contained a letter from James Macpherson, Secretary of the National Union of Shop Assistants, Warehousemen and Clerks, urging all shop workers to join up and fight for better conditions in their trade. My conversion was instantaneous and for three years my scanty leisure was given to my union. We had about six campaigns running, viz.: For more wages, against fines and deductions, against the living-in system, against secret references, against radius agreements, above all, for more leisure. Ah! they were splendid days!

To me at that time the denial of privacy was my greatest trial. I was enrolled in the company of pioneers in what was generally regarded as a forlorn hope—our union numbered 2,500 out of a possible million. Joseph Chamberlain had said shop workers would never organize—but we had faith.

My hours of work were from 7.30 a.m. to 8.30 or 9 p.m. with three breaks for breakfast, dinner and tea. Supper was served after the shop closed. My wage: £25 per annum paid monthly. A rush at closing time to get to the union branch meeting usually meant a fish and chip supper out of the scanty wage; often, too, a rush to get back again before one got locked out at 10.30 p.m.—lights out at 11 p.m. We slept four in a room.

Under the pen name of Grace Dare I was enlisted to write for the union journal. Waiting till my room-mates were asleep, with a towel draped over a chair to hide the halfpenny dip, I wrestled with words far into the small hours to deliver my monthly article. If my room-mates knew what I was doing they never reported me.

The intimate disclosures my shopmates impressed upon me revealed their determination to "get out of the trap" of shop life, and the most respectable way was by marriage. They were frank about this man-hunt, which so disgusted me that I decided it was not going to be my way out of the trap. In 1896 the Women's Industrial Council decided to make an investigation into conditions of shop life, and I eagerly accepted their invitation to be the investigator under a substantial guarantee. It meant the more successful my work the more certain I should not be able to return to the distributive trade. I enjoyed the spice of danger; this was my way out of the trap.

The investigation lasted two years, and formed the basis of evidence submitted to the Departmental Commission and of a series of articles in the *Daily Chronicle* by Vaughan Nash. By 1908 public opinion, together with the constant campaigning of the union, had got the worst evils mitigated; the living-in system ceased to be a compulsory condition of employment. My work as investigator also led in 1898 to my appointment as a full-time official of my union.

During the ten years of service in that capacity I had an intensive education such as few people have known. A vast indulgence in reading and access to books included those of the Webbs, Shaw, William Morris, John Bains Reade and Winwood Reade, detective and cowboy stories—Walt Whitman, Browning, Tennyson and the Fabian Tracts—Tolstoy, the Hammonds, the Brôntes, Jane Austen. Members of the union included H. G. Wells, W. C. Anderson, J. J. Mallon, Mary Macarthur, T. Spencer Jones and dozens of others since distinguished for high public service. As member of first the S.D.F. and later of the I.L.P. I worked with Hyndman, Keir Hardie, G. B. Shaw, Bruce and Katherine Glasier,

Mrs. Despard, Enid Stacey, Blatchford, Annie Besant. I learnt from all of them and became a Socialist. We lobbied for a succession of Bills pioneered by Sir Charles Dilke. My union appointed me to represent it on the Women's Trade Union League, whose chairman was Lady Dilke, and on whose executive were also Arthur Henderson, David Shackleton, Gertrude Tuckwell, Julia Varley, Sophie Sanger and others helping practically in the organization of women in all trades. The union nominated me for the Trade Unions Congress Parliamentary Committee (now called General Council) and generally urged me into the front ranks of trade union leaders.

Under the chairmanship of Keir Hardie and with Jimmy Maxton, Margaret Macmillan, Dick Wallhead and other notable Socialists, I served on the I.L.P. National Administrative Council. We also took part as members in the Women's Co-operative Guild campaigns under the leadership of Margaret Llewlyn Davies.

I was in at the birth of the Labour Party in 1898 when it was decided at the Plymouth Trades Union Congress to set up the Labour Representation Committee. I remember with gratitude the help and guidance given me so freely by all these great companions who gave me an international outlook. What a decade! What a school! I learnt about people—but there was more to learn.

My Sundays were the heaviest work days. Quite early in this decade most of the union executive meetings were held on Sundays—an all-day sitting with two nights of travelling for provincial members. To me they were heroes to give up their leisure in this voluntary service to the union.

One Sunday a deacon of my church said he had missed me from the choir. I told him I had attended my trade union branch meeting and at least once a month my absence would recur. He was genuinely shocked and said in effect that such conduct was incompatible with church membership. I was shocked at this, for I felt God was with us; the choice was made and I did not join a church again for nearly twenty years.

This decision did not disturb my faith in the reality of religion or in the existence of God. It did, however, bring me into a whole series of new relationships—a new world of surging economic and political controversy. In trade union and political work I have been spared the pain of indecision and have hardly ever felt the impulse to turn away from larger responsibilities, because the road I travelled just naturally led into wider fields of service ; of course this illustrates my own limitations of which I am very conscious. The valuable qualities of curiosity, criticism and introspection are almost entirely lacking ; I have a natural inclination for teamwork, so that, when, for example, I am asked if I felt nervous on becoming a Cabinet Minister, I can truthfully say "No," because it presented itself as only another and rather wider aspect of the work I had been doing for thirty years, and largely with the same team.

I can only plead that to forget oneself, not to be too critical of others, does give one a chance to do a job of work with whole heart and undivided attention, and that in itself brings deep satisfaction.

Then came another sudden decision. My effective work for the union was done—and it was necessary for me to broaden out. My services were in great demand as a lecturer from all aspects of the triple movement. I resigned as officer of the union and became a free lance. Since leaving home I had no real home life or domestic experience. Now I was to learn about that aspect of the worker's life from the inside.

At that period paid lecturers for the movement depended upon hospitality, and while I often had most comfortable quarters and a considerate hostess, there were many housewives and families whose contribution to the movement consisted of entertaining the speaker. They gave the best they had; but it was touchingly inadequate to sustain the strength of an overworked lecturer leading such a rackety life all over the United Kingdom.

I shared rooms in London with another free-lance lecturer, M. M. A. Ward, an adventurous spirit, and when we got an invitation from Mrs. Glendower Evans to come to the U.S.A. we were ready to make a break. We had enough to pay for second-class fares and hoped to get enough paid lecture work to cover expenses of a stay for six months.

Life had already taught me that change of work gave the finest form of rest. Despite a bad crossing we were ready, when we arrived in Boston, for whatever came our way. It came, before we finished tea, in a telephone invitation to speak that night to a big women's club, about two hours' journey from Boston. Lack of space forbids more about that wonderful six months, beyond saying that now I look upon America as a second homeland. We had adventured through Connecticut, Massachusetts, Maine, New York, Tennessee, Georgia and Chicago. We met and loved Jane Addams at Hull House, Lillian Wald at Henry Street Settlement, Paul Kellog of the Survey. We were able to discuss problems of excessive wealth and poverty—the go-getter, the immigrant, the Poor White Trash—the negro.

We sampled the fine hospitality of women's clubland. We saw our country through critical eyes and found we loved her all the more—indeed, it was a great adventure and an enrichment of our lives. Fees covered our expenses.

On my return to England I was drawn back into teamwork. I was asked to join in the Women's Co-operative Guild's Campaign for Maternity and Child Welfare, and this brought me into touch with some of the best of our people, the artisan mothers and housewives. I stayed in hundreds of small houses, and saw much of the real heroism and nobility of conduct of these self-respecting working women—real home builders ; of their needless suffering due to ignorance and the lack of medical and surgical attention, of their unselfish neighbourliness, and of their determination to get things altered for mothers and babies.

This experience deepened my reverence for motherhood, and strengthened the conviction which I have always had, that, whatever else a woman may do (and I would not bar her from any form of service), her highest contribution to civilization will be in the quality of her motherhood and of the influence with which she surrounds the young life.

All of us who are called to do public work must strive to give the home-maker the help she needs from the community and in the equipment of her workshop—the home, so that she, too, will have her quota of leisure, and exercise her share of civic responsibility as a well-informed citizen.

I have never been able to approach the question of suffrage from the standpoint of *women's rights.* In those early days of struggle, in fact, I opposed the idea of a limited franchise on a property basis, because it seemed to me that it was tipping the scales against the workers by strengthening the political power of the privileged classes. I wanted full enfranchisement of all women, largely because there was a wide area of public life in which the service of women was needed, and in which that service could only be given under the obligation of full citizenship. So we formed our small group of Adult Suffragists in criticism of the policy of the larger Suffrage movement. We were never strong enough to obstruct their policy, but I think we may have performed a useful service in keeping to the fore a particular point of view.

I have been privileged to help in the building up of the three great organizations of the workers—the Trade Union Movement, the Labour Party, and the Co-operative Movement. I have taken part in the campaign for Old Age Pensions and for the break-up of the Poor Law ; in the fight for the improvement of the Factory Acts ; in the crusade for the abolition of the living-in system, and the regulation of hours of work in shops ; to establish Trade Boards for the sweated industries ; to develop the Health and Unemployment Insurance services and to improve the opportunities for the physical and mental development of children.

I remember the thrills of triumph when, as a result either of crusades in the country or of lobbying in the House of Commons, we secured even one step toward our objective. All these matters sink into their right perspective when one takes a long enough view, but on the day when the first women factory inspectors were appointed the Women's Trade Union League Executive felt that a new page was added to the history of our country! When an Act to establish a legal minimum wage for sweated industries was finally put upon the Statute Book, we felt we had broken the back of one of the horrors of industrialism.

The younger generation of today have their own conquests to make ; I have no doubt that they are repeating the thrills which we experienced in connection with victories in other spheres, but our generation travelled over particularly rough ground where, when a path was made, it was very visible, and certainly made travelling easier for those who came after.

Finally, let me try to describe the foundation without which the others here referred to are but temporary props.

In 1915 another chance conversation led me into the deeps of spiritual experience. On two successive Sundays, free from Labour meetings, I had sampled two churches. The preacher at each church had spoken against some heresy committed by the other ; on the way home I met a casual acquaintance to whom I spoke scornfully about this exhibition of Christian charity. I was told of a series of lectures being given at the King's Weigh House Church. "You'll find charity there," said my friend.

These lectures opened up a new world of adventure, a spiritual world—an introduction to the mystery and dynamic force of prayer. Unlike other turns in the road of life, this experience was of slow growth—full of retreat, of backsliding, to use an old evangelical word. I do not think it possible to exaggerate the importance of the discoveries I made about life, and the relation of the self to the unseen world of the Spirit, and yet I find it hard to speak about ; these are matters that cannot be taken on trust, they must be individually experienced and have no validity otherwise. In my case, a course of reading brought to me a sense of the *quality* of service given to the world by people like the Lady Julian of Norwich, Catherine of Sienna, the Quaker Saints, Josephine Butler, and that great host of dedicated lives. My everyday trade union work took on a deeper significance. The doing of ordinary everyday things became lit up with that inner light of the Spirit which gave one strength and effectiveness ; strength to meet defeat with a smile ; to face success with a sense of responsibility ; to be willing to do one's best without thought of reward ; to bear misrepresentation without giving way to futile bitterness. Saint Theresa declared that: "There are only two duties required of us—the love of God and the love of our neighbour, and the surest sign of discovering whether we observe these duties is the love of our neighbour"; and a great scholar has asserted that this love of God is not an emotion, although that may be experienced, it is a *principle of action*—it reinforces effort, it demands that we *do* something, not merely talk or feel sympathetic, we've got to use the new strength or it will break us.

That is the vital difference between those who drift with the stream, as I did at first, and those who, like the great souls down the ages, inspire, revive, and strengthen the corporate life of their generation. Most of them are treated by their contemporaries as dangerous—and they are to systems outworn and hampering.

Another lesson I learned was that the intensity of prayer is not measured by time, but by the reality and depth of one's awareness of unity with God. I learned to look on prayer not as a means of influencing the Creator in my favour, but as an awareness of the presence of God—everywhere.

I also learned a few helpful ideas about sin. Broadly speaking, I learned to recognize sin as the refusal to live up to the enlightenment we possess. To know the right order of values and deliberately to choose the lower ones. To know that, however much these values may differ with different people at different stages of spiritual growth, for one's self there must be no compromise with that which one *knows* to be the lower value.

I learned, too, that to condemn others is a grave mistake, since hatred, and even the wrong kind of criticism, is an evil which recoils upon its author and poisons every human relationship.

That does not mean we should be blind to the weaknesses or wickednesses of others, any more than to our own, but that we should learn to look on them as the limitations of birth and circumstance, limitations which it is our duty to help them to rise above. In this I have found that example and service are more helpful than advice or preaching.

It has enabled me to get some little glimpse of the meaning behind that great truth—that all the living are as one, in the Great Life of the Universe.

And it carries with it a deep sense of rest. It gives a meaning to life, and a happiness which nothing else can give and no one but ourselves can take away. It is a road to be travelled with a shout of joy—a most exciting road!

BERTRAND RUSSELL

Born in 1872 at Trelleck, Monmouthshire. Educated privately and at Trinity College, Cambridge. Became first known for his work in mathematical logic, but is now equally famous as a philosopher, as an educationalist, as a writer of popular expositions of science, and for his incursions into the realm of politics. A grandson of Lord John Russell, he succeeded to the title in 1931.

WHEN I UNDERTOOK to write on this subject, I did not realize how difficult I should find it. Of the things which I now believe, some spring from my own temperament, some from reading and reasoning, and some from experience ; it is only these last that can be said to have been taught me by life. But to separate them from the others is a matter of hazardous psychological conjecture.

When I was young, if I had heard of an elderly man writing on this subject, I should have had very definite expectations. I should have looked for a collection of moralistic platitudes explaining his success, such as : "Good habits cannot be acquired too early in life. Such modest achievements as may have been mine I attribute to early rising, cold baths, abstinence from tobacco, moderation in alcohol, but above all regular work, day in, day out, with occasional holidays devoted to healthful exercise in the Alps or on Highland grouse moors." But the splendid certainties of those days are gone, and I cannot speak to the young of this time with the same hope of imposing on their credulity.

For my part, a large proportion of my activities has been devoted to logic and mathematics, and to the more abstract aspects of the empirical world, such as space and time. On such matters life has nothing to teach ; on the contrary, it has always seemed to me that the spirit of impartiality and detachment which they demand has an important part to play in teaching how life should be lived. Perhaps as a result of these pre-occupations I have learnt less from life than most old men have ; I have sought rather, in a platonic spirit, to mould life to a pattern than to mould the pattern to what life would have suggested as the line of least resistance.

But in saying this I am thinking of my adult life. The pattern that has influenced me was, of course, formed by early influences, and might have been very different if I had grown up in a different environment. The Jesuits used to say that the first seven years are decisive ; psycho-analysts sometimes speak as though character were determined by what happens to a child during its first three years. However that may be, I recognize that, in my own case, my character, tastes, and ideals were, in the main, fixed by the time I reached the age of sixteen. Of course many things then were only in embryo, but the seed had been sown, and could only produce a growth of a certain species.

In practical matters I was brought up in the creed of nineteenth-century aristocratic liberalism, involving toleration, democracy, freedom of opinion, and respect for the individual. I have never seen any reason to abandon any part of this creed, though I have been more conscious at some times than at others of its apparent or temporary limitations. Until 1914 I shared the optimism which then seemed reasonable. Parliamentary institutions were firmly established in America and Western Europe ; the German Reichstag was a vigorous body which had every prospect of increasing its power ; Japan had a Diet, Russia acquired its Duma in 1905, and China attempted to adopt democracy in 1912. No reason appeared for doubting that all the world, before long, would be governed by democratic representative institutions.

Toleration, equally, seemed assured of victory. The days when Bradlaugh had been prevented from taking his seat were in the past ; the vindication of Dreyfus led to a Liberal era in France. In Germany, it is true, men who made fun of the Kaiser suffered a few months' imprisonment, but I doubt if there is now any country outside Great Britain and the Dominions where the penalties for political heresy are as slight as they were in Germany between 1900 and 1914. The intolerance and cruelty of the Tsarist government, which shocked enlightened opinion throughout the world, was provoking a revolutionary opposition from which something infinitely better was to be expected before long.

There was always the possibility of war, but Hague Conferences and the Concert of the Powers gave grounds for hope that an explosion could be deferred until the probably not distant date when the Social Democrats acquired control in Germany. And surely, in an epoch of sane progress, men could not be so mad as to jeopardize everything in the gamble of a world conflict. So I, in common with most others of liberal outlook, thought and felt in the years before 1914.

The experience of subsequent years, while it has not changed my views as to what would be desirable, has shown that the road to the realization of nineteenth-century hopes is much longer and more arduous than it had seemed. The forces of obscurantism, irrationality, cruelty, and ruthless strife have shown themselves (temporarily, we may hope) capable of defeating the movement towards ordered progress. A war in defence of freedom, even when victorious, inevitably involves the sacrifice of some part of what is being fought for. The world in which we find ourselves is nearer to the world of Hitler's dreams than it was before 1933 ; in this impersonal sense, some part of the victory was his. To take only one instance : there is far more anti-Semitism, both in England and in America, than there was before Hitler's persecution of the Jews began. The First World War, we were told, was a war to end war, and for a moment it seemed as if it might achieve this object ; but no one dares to maintain that the Second World War can have any such outcome. Instead, the menace of the atomic bomb suggests the futility of all hopes for the immediate future of mankind.

This gloomy situation may be met in various ways. The easiest, and perhaps the most natural, is "let us eat and drink, for tomorrow we die." If this attitude is widely adopted, there is no doubt that tomorrow we shall die, and not only we, but the whole civilized way of life gradually built up by the Greeks and Romans, Christianity and science. Perhaps it is now too late ; perhaps the seeds of death, nourished in the soil of the unbridled lust for power which moralists have never succeeded in curbing, cannot now be prevented from bearing their dreadful fruit ; perhaps the discipline of a dark age is necessary before a saner civilization can arise. If so, those who say "let us eat and drink" are in the right : forethought is folly, and intoxication—alcoholic or spiritual—the only possible alleviation of despair.

But while there remains any chance that this utter pessimism is excessive, I shall refuse to adopt it. There is still a chance of averting disaster, and to increasing that chance all the efforts of those who feel a responsibility towards the world should be directed.

The lessons that life has taught me during the present century are not cheerful ones. I have had to admit that sheer cruelty plays a much larger part than I thought in the make-up of a large proportion of mankind. I have had to admit that, when the present is painful, men, for the most part, will seek alleviation, not in rational measures which might produce gradual amelioration, but in myths inspired by hatred and phantasies of power, leading to outbursts of violence which intensify the evils by which they are caused. I have had to admit that when suffering is intense and widespread it generates callousness : large-scale atrocities and cruelties which, fifty years ago, would have caused a universal outcry, now pass almost unnoticed unless they can be used to incite to war. I have had to admit that gains are never secure, and that benefits to which men have grown accustomed are liable to be carelessly tossed aside in moments of excitement. I have had to face the possibility that perhaps knowledge is a misfortune, and only ignorance can preserve human beings from mutual extermination.

These facts, and others like them, are to be assimilated, but afford no argument against the desirability of what they prove to be difficult. We know that democracy is possible, since there are countries where it exists ; we know that tolerance is possible, for the same reason. If there are populations incapable of the compromise and mutual forbearance upon which tolerance and the success of democracy depend, that is no reason for not valuing these things, but only for not attempting to approach them by short cuts, and for studying the conditions which, hitherto, have made them possible where they were possible. There is a type of person, all too common in the world of practical affairs, who is determined to be effective at all costs, and who, if he cannot do good, is content to do harm. If he knows how to make dynamite but not how to build houses, he will blow up existing buildings, causing a greater racket and a quicker change than any architect could hope to cause. And so, when democracy proves difficult, dictators arise, and take pride in the multiplicity of the hopes that they have brought to ruin. If I had to make up moral maxims for the young, my first would be : "It is better to do a little good than much harm."

Respect for the individual—a very essential part of the Liberal creed—is a less definite matter than democracy or legal toleration, and more hedged about with limitations and provisos. What I mean by it is rather a state of feeling than a definite precept. It is not always possible, in practice, to treat an individual with respect, for example, if he is a homicidal maniac. But I will try first to indicate what I mean, and only then consider what life has taught me as to its practicability.

Human beings impinge upon each other in many ways. Where there is food for one, and ten people to eat it, there will be conflict. Where two rivals each desire to be supreme in one community, at least one of them must be disappointed. Where there are many religions, each claiming to be the unique repository of absolute truth and the sole means of eternal salvation, it is difficult for them to live in peace with one another. In the present day, those who believe in State trading and those who believe in private capitalism are finding it very hard to adjust their differences. It is certainly not always possible for conscientious men to avoid violent conflict, since two creeds, both impersonal and both held with perfect sincerity, may be mutually incompatible.

But much the greater part of the violence in human relations would be prevented if men could feel and practise the virtue which I am calling "respect for the individual." Primarily, this consists in a great reluctance to inflict humiliation. In former times hardly anyone (except King Lear when he was mad) saw any harm in this. The stocks and the pillory were opportunities for the jeers of hostile crowds ; criminals were branded so that their disgrace became indelible ; children were not only flogged, but unmercifully mocked. This sort of thing was dying out during the nineteenth century, but has been revived in recent times. The Nazis, in their milder moods, dressed Jews in ridiculous costumes, and drove them through the streets wearing placards saying "I am a Jew." After the liberation of France, female collaborators, shorn of their hair, were exhibited to the execration of their neighbours. In all totalitarian countries, punishment has consisted partly of making its victims, under the influence of torture, behave in ways that destroyed their self-respect; confession, begging for mercy, and betraying comrades were the commonest of these ways.

To anyone possessed of sympathy and psychological imagination, this sort of thing is infinitely painful. When a human being has been humiliated beyond a point, something of value in him has been irreparably destroyed. The Stoics maintained that a man could always avoid this damage by the exercise of his own willpower, but we now know that this is false. There is no one whose will cannot be broken by torture which is sufficiently severe and sufficiently prolonged, but apparently the ancients were less ingenious in these ways than the governmental fiends of our day. The knowledge of these dark facts saps most men's resistance at an early point, since they are aware that it will give way sooner or later. Consider a German who was a Communist till 1933, then a Nazi till 1945, and now (in the Russian Zone) is again a Communist. What self-respect can such a man have retained? What crimes will he refuse to perform, and in what atrocities will he be unwilling to bear a part? And almost the whole of the Continent of Europe is full of such men, many of them in positions of some authority.

Aristocratic pride was formerly regarded as a virtue, in part with justice, and in part not ; it was a virtue in so far as it consisted in self-respect, but a vice when it involved contempt for inferior mortals. In Spanish peasants I have found the good element of pride without the bad ; so I have in all classes in China. But in Western urban communities, and among those who have submitted to dictatorships, whether of the German or the Russian variety, not only is the good kind of pride usually absent, but there is no willingness to admit that it is a virtue. This is due, I think, to the diminution of economic, social, and political independence. It has been revived, to some degree, among Western wage-earners, by the growth of trade unionism. But it is hardly to be expected where success depends upon currying favour with official superiors, or where unguarded candour may lead to execution or the concentration camp. To preserve it should be one of the aims of a good social system. In economic and political relations, and above all in education, self-respect should be carefully guarded, and humiliation avoided to the utmost extent that practical necessities permit.

The problem of combining the greatest practicable degree of respect for the individual with the indispensable controls required for public order, economic justice, and technical efficiency, is one of immense difficulty and complexity, requiring hazardous conjectures as to social consequences and a doubtful balancing of one set of ethical values against another.

In the province of education, respect for the child demands that instruction shall, as far as possible, be a matter of co-operation between teacher and pupil, not of a discipline imposed by force without the child's inward assent. It demands also that the beliefs and precepts instilled into the child's mind shall be such as are genuinely believed to be for his good, and not merely such as are convenient to the powers that be and calculated to make him die quietly whenever a predatory government can further its ends by having him killed. These considerations led me to believe in "progressive" education. At the same time, I am compelled to acknowledge that many "progressive" educators, in their zeal for individualism, neglect things that are of great importance. We are not only individuals, but also members one of another ; education should make a man not only an upstanding individual, but a useful member of society. This requires, on the one hand, adequate instruction, and on the other hand a social ethic. Everything possible should be done to make children enjoy learning, but learn they must, if they are to play their part in a civilized community. And in a world where organization has created great forces—churches, political parties, industrial corporations, and above all, armed States—a man who never thinks of himself as a unit in a group is impotent unless he is a great creative artist. It is necessary to find a cohesive force as powerful as patriotism, but without the limitations that make patriotism inadequate. Education must take account of the need for collective sentiments, with the correlative concept of social duty.

We need, and should teach in schools, loyalty to something greater than our own nation. It is nationalism that has brought the world to its present terrifying condition, and that is making an acceptable solution of international problems so hard to find. The loyalty that is needed is loyalty to Man, and not to Man merely as a biological species, but as the sole embodiment, so far as our knowledge extends, of certain values. Man is capable of creating and appreciating beautiful things, he is capable (within limits) of knowledge, he can experience love and admiration and ecstasy. It is true that he exemplifies also the opposites of these goods: the creation of hideous squalor, wilful ignorance, hatred and envy and anguish. But in spite of all that is horrible and all the insistent incitements to despair, I retain the belief that Man is capable of developing his better potentialities and gradually lessening the intensity of his evil passions. It is this belief, not a narrow nationalism, that should be taught in schools and made the basis of social obligation. It is this belief—so at least it seems to me—that alone supplies an antidote to despair that is rational, and not based upon some comforting myth that invites men to abrogate the primary duty of a sober search for what is true.

For the man who values individual liberty, perhaps the most perplexing of all problems is that of economic organization. The case for Socialism, broadly speaking, is derived from the concept of justice, not from that of liberty. But its opponents argue that justice may be too dearly bought if it involves the sacrifice of freedom. This is one of the matters as to which life has taught me most, but unfortunately, its lessons have been mutually contradictory, and have left me somewhat bewildered. Until 1914 I was a Liberal, and felt hesitations about Socialism because I feared that it would diminish freedom. The First World War made me a Socialist, because I thought that Socialist States would be less warlike than States inspired by predatory capitalism. But the Soviet régime, which I have always abominated as ruthless and dictatorial, showed how easy it is for a nominal Socialism to develop an oligarchical tyranny more thoroughgoing and disastrous than any that is possible under capitalism. In the substitution of bureaucracy for big business I see no cause for rejoicing.

If Socialism is to be a boon and not a disaster, it must fulfil certain conditions. It must be democratic, in the Western sense, not in the perverted sense that the Soviet Government is endeavouring to popularize. And it is not enough that it should be democratic as a whole ; there must be democracy in the various parts, as was suggested by guild socialism. Take, say, the iron and steel industry. If this industry is in the hands of the State, and its governing officials are appointed by the Government, they will have at least as much power as now belongs to the great capitalists who control the industry. Indeed, they are pretty certain to have more, since strikes against a democratically elected government will win less sympathy than strikes do at present. Clearly the solution lies in extending, rather than in curtailing, the functions of trade unions. Every great industry should be controlled, so far as its internal affairs are concerned, by a trade union co-extensive with the industry. The general public, which is represented by the State, is interested in the amount and price of the product, but the mode of production and the appointment of managers concerns the industry itself, and should be in its hands—subject to an ultimate control by the State in the event of gross evils being established by a public inquiry.

Not only the industry as a whole, but each factory, should have a measure of self-government. If Socialism is not to stifle individual energy and initiative, it must be accompanied by an immense extension of federalism. The general principle that should govern all federal institutions is clear : whatever mainly concerns a subordinate group should be managed by that group, while what concerns its external relations should be managed by a federal authority. Thus there are matters concerning a single factory, matters concerning the national iron and steel industry as a whole, matters concerning its relations to the rest of the nation, and matters concerning its relations to the industry in foreign countries. Each of these should have its own democratically elected authority, with suitably limited powers. Short of some such system, Socialism will merely introduce a new tyranny, the tyranny of officials. And this will not long remain merely a matter of inequality of power ; it will soon become—as the development of the U.S.S.R. has shown—a matter of inequality of income also. All the old privileges will reappear, without the exceptions and loopholes and irregularities that, in the old system, enabled men like Shelley and Darwin to do valuable work of which the community did not see the value.

All the questions that I have considered hitherto are overshadowed —and have been overshadowed ever since 1914—by the supreme problem of the abolition of war. If this can be solved, it is reasonable to hope that others will be solved in due course ; but if it cannot be solved within the next few years, the outlook is one of utter and unmitigated disaster, at any rate for Western Europe, including Great Britain. And even if our complex social organization could survive one more great war, it could not survive a series, each worse than the last, combining continually more destructive forms of atomic energy with bacteriological warfare. Somehow the habit of war must be ended, and ended soon.

The atomic bomb, while it has made the problem more urgent, has also made its solution much less difficult. The American Government has proffered what would probably develop into an adequate system, but Russia has refused to accept the offer. The atomic bomb is such a terrible weapon that, if it were controlled by an international authority, that authority would be able to make aggressive war hopeless. This requires that all nations should submit to inspection by officials representing the international authority, and that any attempt to resist or obstruct their work should be treated as a *casus belli*. The United States, in spite of its initial advantage, is willing to submit to these conditions, but the Soviet Government has rejected the necessary limitation of the veto on the ground that it involves infringement of sovereignty. Without infringement of sovereignty human life, as we have known it, cannot long continue, unless some one nation succeeds in conquering the world.

What the world needs is the elimination of wars between nations by the creation of an international authority, possessed of irresistible force, and using that force in accordance with an agreed body of international law. The first and most urgent step towards this end is the international control of atomic energy. To this step the Soviet Government is now the only serious obstacle.

Ever since the dawn of history, communities have oscillated between the opposite poles of dictatorship and anarchy, involving the opposite dangers of ossification and dissolution or foreign conquest. Through science the world has become one community, which has to choose between common prosperity and common ruin. But it is as yet an anarchic community, destitute of government, filled with hatred and suspicion, profoundly obsessed with the archaic belief that one man's gain must be another man's loss. Under the stress of misfortune passions have grown more violent, and fear has increased mutual suspicion. Jews and Arabs, Hindus and Muslims, Chinese Communists and Chinese nationalists, carry on their little wrangles, while the dispute between Washington and Moscow threatens to reconcile them all in a common grave. The new danger is so vast and so terrible that men shrink from allowing themselves to realize it; they shrink still more from admitting that ancient enmities, burning controversies, and passionate shibboleths have all become absurd, pathetic and trivial, like sailors quarrelling over a sixpence while their ship is sinking.

What mankind needs is not law alone, or liberty alone, but each in its own province: law to control impulses of aggression and tyranny, freedom for impulses that are creative or for the common benefit. Various obstacles stand in the way, partly institutional, partly psychological. Of the institutional obstacles the most serious and the most dangerous is national armaments. If this were overcome, the resulting prosperity and relief from fear would gradually promote sanity, and lead to the discovery of methods of diminishing the psychological obstacles of cruelty, envy, greed, and lust for power—methods which would be partly psychological, partly educational, and partly economic. The problem of creating a happy world is not insoluble, provided the will to solve it existed. Will men prefer disaster, or will they acquiesce, however reluctantly, in their own salvation?

LORD HORDER

Born in 1871 and studied at the University of London and St. Bartholomew's Hospital. Was knighted in 1918; created a Baronet in 1923; and raised to the Peerage in 1933. In 1936 was appointed Physician to H.M. King George VI, having been Physician to King Edward VIII as Prince of Wales and as King (1923-1936). He is a keen gardener, and in addition to being Consulting Physician to St. Bartholomew's Hospital, is President or Chairman of many strictly medical organizations, and holds a similar position with the Empire Rheumatism Council, the Cremation Society, the Noise Abatement League, the Marriage Guidance Council, the Family Planning Association, etc.

I THINK I AM responsible for changing the Editor's original title of this symposium from "What I have learned from life" to the one which the book actually bears. I felt that the chief operating factor was not myself but life. Even then the title does not seem to me to connote what really happens to us by way of schooling during our existence on this planet ; what really happens is the result of the interaction between ourselves and what goes by the name of our environment. This result is a moulded, modified self, an evolution of the personality inherent in me "from the word go." Both elements participate, but the dominant one, as it seems to me, is "life" rather than myself. And so I feel that I am taught—with a certain degree of willy-nilly—rather than that I learn, as I go along.

All this may seem to be somewhat of a quibble, but there is a difference in the approach to the subject implicit in my point of view and one which, I feel at the outset, will probably govern most of what I am likely to say.

INHERITED QUALITIES

I have failed to get any guide from the Editor on the question how near to a "potted" autobiography an essay with this particular title is expected to be. Nor, indeed, any hint as to its approximation to what authors have variously called "confessions" or "apology." In his wisdom he has probably left us all to interpret his title in our own way, and there seems to be a collusion between us which is well calculated to enable him to achieve his object.

Let me glance at these two basic elements in the interaction which is my life. As a eugenist I attach great importance to inherited qualities, both physical and mental. But, unlike the Emperor Marcus Aurelius, I find it very difficult to trace my temperament directly to that of either or even to those of both of my parents—not a surprising thing, of course—though it is not difficult to recognize particular characteristics of theirs, repeated in myself and modified by different contacts and a different training. Both my parents were of yeoman stock, gifted with good "constitutions," which they never abused. They were what is termed "simple" folk, hard working, honest and God fearing. They spent a lot of time and thought over an ample provision of plain living for their children, but they left high thinking to develop, if it might, from some inherent gene to which, if they made a contribution to it, this was indirect and not direct. "Self-expression" was, fortunately, denied us whilst there was as yet no self to express, but so soon as there was, the world did, literally, lie all before us, where to choose.

Of love and comfort in times of stress we could place infinite reliance upon a mother's "brooding care," but a queer shyness and detachment seemed to inhibit paternal guidance, and discussion about a vocation, however carefully engineered by the maternal parent, never aroused more than the mildest interest in her partner. I have appreciated this same inhibition in myself : the psychologists probably have a name for it : I have struggled to overcome it and have tried to help a good many fathers to do the same.

In my own case the situation was not helped by the fact that I "didn't know from Adam" what I "wanted to be." However, looking back, I realize that the lessons I was taught by my father were of a sort that helped me in life generally and irrespective of my future business or profession. They were hard work until hard work became a pleasant habit, obedience, economy and the simple courtesies towards others. I was taught how to use the more common tools of the garden and the workshop and to find close contact with the earth a pleasant occupation. Holidays spent with a string of farmer uncles (my mother was one of fourteen children) were weeks of hard toil and discipline in Richard Jefferies's county, with the satisfying experience of "harvest home" hand in hand with a steadily developing love of the countryside. It was a natural evolution from all this to that familiarity with one's fellow human beings which Medicine brings, a familiarity which in my case bred respect and affection and not contempt. The link was the lure of science, through biology, chemistry and what in those days was quaintly termed "mental and moral science."

The impact of temperament with environment was a very naked one in my case. Warnings which might act as buffers were singularly few. This very direct contact had its dangers, but it also had its educational advantages and there was certainly no parental "complex" or "fixation" to warp the result. Life has taught me that when Emerson says that temperament "shuts us in a prison of glass which we cannot see," that we "resist the conclusion in the morning, but adopt it as the evening wears on, that temper prevails over everything of time, place and condition and is inconsumable in the flame of religion," that "the individual texture holds its dominion, if not to bias the moral judgments yet to fix the measure of activity and of enjoyment,"—my own experience tells me that this is no overstatement but harmonizes with fact.

The lack of anything like a "call" to a vocation caused me no little shame. I passed from "pure" science to Medicine partly in order to resolve this difficulty, and partly because the "pre-clinical" studies enabled me to continue what had become very attractive without committing myself to the final step. Contrary to the general view, Oliver Cromwell thought that a man never rose so high as when he knew not whither he was going. Certainly the fact that my future career was for so long undetermined did not lead to anxiety. This unconcern is a part of the temperament which I have conceded to be so fundamental. At its best it accounts for staying power, resilience and poise ; at its worst it spells unawareness of impending troubles and lack of purpose in providing against them. Allowed its natural drift, a state of mental inertia is liable to set in and life tends to become more passive than active. But it is "in the will" that men are enjoined to "work and acquire," and the will is the dynamic, not the static, part of our being.

One phase of this drift shows itself in procrastination, and against this life has taught me the need for constant effort. How many times have I written in my diary, "do the next thing," and, "do it now," and how many times have I left the next thing undone! What is the meaning of that almost uncontrollable distaste which seizes the mind when faced with certain clearly recognized duties—a letter to answer, a visit to pay, an article to write? And why, having yielded once and passed to the pleasanter task, does the distaste grow yet stronger? What is it that manacles the mind at such moments? And yet who has not experienced many times how great is the satisfaction which results from facing these repelling duties and disposing of them? In his "Ode to Duty" Wordsworth declares that :

> "There are who ask not if thine eye
> "Be on them. . . .
> "Who do thy work, and know it not."

I have met such people and have recognized that they are the salt of the earth.

To procrastinate is not only to steal time—as the old adage reminds us—it is, again and again, to let people down. The very converse is seen when we obey the generous impulse as soon as possible after it arises and before it has passed "into the light of common day." The one exception to "haste not" is the doing of a kindly act ; here expedition is not only called for, it is part of the virtue of the act itself : he gives twice who gives quickly. This carrying out of a generous impulse is a matter that transcends mere duty. It is the stretching out of the spirit of man after the divine. The habit is learnt as the result of three things: close contact with our fellows, observation of their difficulties, their strivings and their hopes, and the vision which enables us to put ourselves in their shoes—in imagination suffering with them and rejoicing with them. I can never get quite into another man's mind because he is a different personality, but there is a common denominator between him and myself—a lust to live and be happy, a desire to be fulfilled, an ambition to be achieved. It is on the basis of this common denominator that I can help him and he me. But to help him I must be patient and tolerant ; I must let him express himself ; I must not dominate the situation.

I have done a lot of teaching in my time and I am painfully aware today that, though I have usually been careful to be at close quarters with my subject—an essential ingredient in good teaching—I have not always taken the same pains with regard to my pupils—an equally essential desideratum. Impatience with indolence may be justified and a gentle sarcasm is a wholesome corrective for pretentiousness. One of my best teachers, knowing his man, once asked a student at the bedside of a patient suffering from a malady of (as then) unknown causation, "Let me see, Mr. Smith, *what* is the cause of this disease?" "I am sorry, sir," said Mr. Smith, "I *did* know but I have forgotten." "That's a pity, Mr. Smith," said the professor, "for now nobody knows." For the oleaginous and the sanctimonious there are also appropriate methods of treatment. But a cutting retort to the student whose only fault is ignorance, especially if it be made in the presence of others, creates an attitude in him which is resistant because it becomes hostile. The scorching tongue sears the surface of the pupil's mind and it is no longer receptive. To be fair to myself I was never half such a sinner in this respect as some of my own teachers, and yet, despite my own bitter experiences, I am conscious of not sufficiently appreciating the sensitiveness of some minds whilst under instruction.

This essay threatens to develop into a catalogue of vicious trends in temperament and the efforts that life has made to eliminate them. But the more I think of it the more certain I am that this disciplining and developing of the self does lie at the very root of life's teaching and that all the other things learnt are incidental. So I shall pursue my theme.

Acquisitiveness has been a tiresome element in my make-up and one that is very difficult to eradicate. It has in it a competitive feature that is perhaps not altogether bad but taken by and large it is a vice akin to that of the miser, and definitely anti-social. As a student I was a "pot hunter." Even then, and still more later, I accumulated books (*what* books!) which I did not read. This vice is akin to the vanity of knowing something about everything and being sought after because of being a repository of what is really pseudo-knowledge. Thank God I learnt the evil of all this before I was tempted to join the Brains Trust, and so saved Society, in one person at all events, from confusing nimbleness of mind with wisdom. The Press has much to answer for in this matter. Life has taught me the folly of diffuseness of effort, for it has become clear to me that the men and women who really matter are those who can say, with Paul, "this one thing I do," who can say "no" and can sit quietly at home when all the world says "come out and help us." The Oxford Groupers are right in their insistence upon "sharing," but I think they would do well to stress more the sharing of their goods, their chattels and their honours, and less the sharing of their spiritual experiences. There is perhaps an element of exhibitionism in both, but one is the act of an extravert and the other of an introvert, and the difference between these is all the difference in the world.

The joy of giving should be learnt, and practised, early rather than late, for it is a type of joy which is constructive, both to the giver and to the receiver. If it is left too late there may be little remaining of life in which to construct. Indeed, many leave giving until life ceases and the gifts, of whatever sort, are no longer theirs to give.

Like many doctors my hobby has been gardening. In addition to its providing complete mental distraction it possesses the inestimable advantages of fresh air, early rising and sound sleep. I probably owe my love of it and much of my knowledge of gardening technique to my forbears and my early upbringing.

I suppose I have made most of the mistakes that gardeners are prone to make when they begin: planting too thickly; planting established "subjects" (as the catalogues call plants and trees) rather than young ones; dotting things about instead of massing them; interrupting natural vistas when forbearance should be exercised in preserving them; leaving out of the reckoning that the sun can kill as cruelly as the frost; and seeking to acquire every known specimen instead of specializing in those that say "thank you" when grown in my particular soil and in my particular aspect—acquisitiveness again.

My hobby has done its best to teach me what a virtue is thoroughness and what an evil is procrastination. In this way it has probably helped to render less noxious than they might otherwise have been a couple of weaknesses to which, as these notes make clear, I have found addiction all too easy.

Since Nature's way with the plant is much the same as with the human being, gardening has also, I think, confirmed me in the lesson which clinical observation of my fellows has taught me—that you cannot, unless you sacrifice their dignity and their satisfaction, live other folk's lives for them. You can keep the ring for them so that they get a good chance of success, you can teach them the rules, you can even be a "sparring partner," but it is their fight, not yours.

And now comes this business of growing old, concerning which there seems to be, on the part of most of those engaged in it, a conspiracy of silence. But I think there are lessons that life teaches us here, too, if we are willing to learn. There are all manner of pitfalls in regard to senescence, and a man becomes more and more dependent upon his friends, both for warning and for indulgence. I think we should learn first of all to avoid vanity and attempts to conceal the inevitable. An old fellow came into my consulting room the other day, obviously got up to look much younger than he was—moustache waxed, tie, handkerchief and socks all matching, etc. After getting a few symptoms I asked his age. "Well, doctor," with an air of confidence, "what age do you think I am?" "That's a challenge," I said. "Well," said the patient, "what age?" "Eighty," I said. "No," said the old chap, terribly crestfallen, "not till next week." Then there was another who used to come to see me yearly on his birthday. There was never anything the matter, and it was an easy job for me. After telling me how well this organ worked and how fit another was, and so on, he used to conclude by saying, "Ah, doctor, but that's not the best: all my faculties unimpaired, eh what?" I shouted my congratulations, for he was very deaf, and the interview ended.

Then there is inanity; that should be avoided also. I remember the shock it gave me many years ago when I saw one of my old teachers walking slowly and aimlessly down Harley Street, stopping anon at some open area and watching the boy delivering the milk and the cat lapping some that had been spilt: shocking, as I said. But perhaps unawareness is the most subtle, as it is perhaps also the most inescapable, of all the troubles of oncoming age. It is a question whether it is better to be aware or to be ignorant. Is it better to feel with Andrew Marvell that:

"At my back I always hear
Time's wingèd chariot hurrying near,"

or to be like the old man whom I vetted on his ninetieth birthday and who, when I said, "It's all right, your bronchitis has cleared up, you can go downstairs," said, "But that's not what's worrying me, Sir Thomas." "What *is* worrying you?" I asked. "This," he said, pointing to a truss he was wearing. "Why, doesn't it fit?" I said. "Yes, it fits alright," said the old fellow, "but what do you think the doctor says? He says I've got to wear the damned thing for the rest of my life."

I am afraid awareness is my lot, after all, awareness of a fearful lot of things that go to make up old age, physical things that never get into the textbooks, and, in the moral sphere, things that Cicero never experienced, perhaps because he wrote his famous essay at the relatively youthful age of sixty-three! But how to adjust one's behaviour is very difficult, so ingrained are people's notions about age. I have to smile and seem to appreciate the deference of others—some of whom are not very young either—and all the time I'd willingly exchange it for that experience I thought so odd many years ago, when a pupil of mine signalized his passing his final examination by calling me Horder for the first time. The old man is reported to be testy, irascible, intolerant; but if he warns himself against these things and observes a bland and generous demeanour folk speak of it as the fatuous benevolence of old age! It really is very difficult.

It should not be regarded as egregious to hint that the fact that "knowledge comes but wisdom lingers" suggests that the old may still retain a function:

> "Men must endure
> Their going hence, even as their coming hither:
> Ripeness is all."

I have more than once referred to the fact that man is still half savage and half babe. Glancing through these notes I am troubled by the thought that most of life's lessons have been directed towards taming the former and training the latter. I am humbled still more by the realization of how little life has been able to do for me in either case, so resistant has been the pupil to both instruction and control. And yet somehow it has seemed good to have been in this school. The system of education has appealed to my logical sense, though this was not so at first. Someone has said that in Nature there are neither rewards nor punishments—there are consequences; and the laws of cause and effect have aptly been called the Chancellors of God. To observe them at work, and, at long last, to accept their wise control, this is the only road along which, rough and steep though it sometimes is, we can attain that

> ". . . central peace, subsisting at the heart
> Of endless agitation."

This does not mean that we should shun the factory and the mart and other places where men congregate and work and live out their lives. The "agitation" is not an evil to be avoided, it is the natural human hive. After all, "the end of life is not knowledge but action," and it is in the sphere of action that we must be ready to learn. If life were only theory most of us could put up quite a good show. Nor does it help to be meticulous; what matters is that we are basically sincere. "Nature comes eating and drinking and sinning. The mid-world is best. The wise, through excess of wisdom, is made a fool."

As I said just now, though there are regrets on account of dilatoriness towards life, there are no regrets for having lived. Even the fact that most of life's lessons have been learnt too late is not wholly depressing, since the very learning of them has been worth while. The very fact that there is "no end to learning" is stimulating. Provided "health and a day" remain to us we can still "make the pomp of emperors ridiculous." So it is: "Up again, old heart! Never mind the ridicule, never mind the defeat; patience and patience, we shall win at the last. We must be very suspicious of the deceptions of the element of time. It takes a good deal of time to eat or to sleep, or to earn a hundred dollars, and a very little time to entertain a hope or an insight which becomes the light of our life. We dress our garden, eat our dinners, discuss the household with our wives, and these things make no impression, are forgotten next week; but in the solitude to which every man is always returning, he has a sanity and revelations which in his passage into new worlds he will carry with him."

Life has taught me that living has been worth while. I am aware that this may not apply to everyone. There are, alas, people who cannot say, "I have a goodly heritage." But for most of us the exhortation to "fight the good fight" is not ironical. Two of our greatest poets join in the call. Tennyson urges us to be: "Strong in will. To strive, to seek, to find and not to yield." And old Chaucer says:

> "Forth, pilgrim, forth! Forth beast, out of thy stall!
> Know thy country, look up, thank God for all;
> Waive thy lust, and let thy ghost thee lead,
> And truth shall deliver, it is no dread."

MARGERY FRY

Born in 1874. Educated privately and at Roedean and Oxford. Was Librarian at Somerville College, Oxford, from 1898–1904 and then Warden of University House, Birmingham, until the outbreak of the First World War during which she worked with the Quakers' War Victims Relief Mission in France. Principal of Somerville College 1926–31, and Governor of the B.B.C. 1937–39.

I HAVE BEEN walking up and down the pathways of one of the loveliest districts of France, and while my feet followed the familiar tracks I have sent my mind strolling back through the years of my life, seeking an answer to the question posed by the title of this book.

I doubt whether it is possible to make a formal map of either set of wanderings, since both lack any exact or logical form. Life does not give its lessons on dissected subjects in the squared periods of a school time-table : to formalize one's experiences would be, in a way, to falsify them.

But I shall try, throughout these wandering notes, to suggest that the lessons of life can be looked on as the slow learning of skill in the management of a kind of general respiration, a breathing in and out, inclusions alternating with exclusions, the exclusions sometimes wholly involuntary, neither perhaps ever wholly voluntary. Such skill can never be perfectly achieved, but the extent to which one gains it is a measure of one's progress in the art of living.

Frankly I am a little troubled at the small harvest I bring from a long life. With a bad memory and a habit of living much in the moment, I have been too like a careless child, gathering blackberries into an untrustworthy basket, spilling them as I went.

Even of the few remembered lessons most are probably those imperfectly learnt. "What life *should* have taught me" might be an apter title. I suppose everyone is conscious of faults recurrently bringing them into collision with the outer world, hurting both themselves and others. These clashes are the lessons one remembers, re-enforced often by regret. But it is probably an illusion to think that they really alter the essential "me" very much. They moderate action rather than modify character.

Altogether I am far more conscious of the continuity of personality than of its changes, and feel myself essentially very much the same as I was at the dawn of memory—a creature of two and a half staggering down to the beach through a little gate, with my father behind me, going to discover the truth about an incredible statement made by "The Others" (that tribe of friendly brothers and sisters) that the sea was salt. That is how life opens for me—with a question: it will probably close with a vaster and less answerable query mark.

But to go back only to two and a half is not quite fair. I must have learnt more strange things in the years before that than in the seventy that have followed. Personal consciousness, the existence of others, the use of language, and its limitations (those first cries which seemed to work a magic played false too often, and the first steps had to be taken in that hardest of all lessons—that the world is by no means conformed to every desire). Besides, there was the strange art of interpreting the sensations of touch, taste and hearing, the multiplicity of images on the retina, into an exciting world of external solids. Not quite all the art was gained so young: on that same seaside visit "The Others," bathing in the sea, seemed strangely placed in the sky, perspective being still a half-learnt lesson.

These are the universal elements of baby-learning—but what individual forms are imposed on our already so diverse personalities by the circumstances, the very atmosphere of our infancy! With its mother's milk, or at any rate from her intimate handling, the child gets its first intimations of human relations. The study of baby behaviour in the very earliest days is already yielding clues of immense importance to the later development of character. The child's relation to the world of other people grows first in the sensitive tendrils by which it clings to its mother, and through her to the larger circle of the family. If those tendrils are bruised or broken the opening personality may be irretrievably damaged.

Our mother was an apprehensive person and I think almost all her children got this from her, probably more from these first impressions on the suggestible material of babyhood than from any direct heredity. But she had also a great and expressive tenderness towards the very young, and none of her children grew up with any shrinking from human contacts. Even where shyness intervened we have *wanted* people.

So the inclusive phase of that inevitable pulse of life, that breathing rhythm of acceptance and rejection, started well for me with a confident expectation of loving-kindness. Perhaps the exclusive phase had less happy features. For if it is true that our manner of thinking—the very axioms on which we work—are largely the result of the economic status of our youth—it is probably in very early childhood that the bent is given. When I see the children of small American towns running in bands in and out of each others' houses I regret the segregation of our own home. Children in the country we met on a definite basis of patronage, of Sunday school and treats and soup for the sick, but the cheerful mob of Highgate brats seemed almost more remote from us than the Zanzibar boys for whose conversion we saved rather unwilling pennies and sewed marble bags. Definitely, by the nursery code "dirty people" and particularly "dirty men" must be avoided.

I must have been between six and seven when the first shock which began to reverse this lesson came. It was a time of tragic unemployment, and the "out of works" paraded the country with a lamentable "band," seeking, I suppose, sympathy and half-crowns. But the beat of their drum approaching the house seemed to me like a threat of revolution and then the sight of the sorry, discouraged crowd gave me a violent sense of social injustice. The clearness with which the scene comes back assures me that I do not exaggerate its significance.

All friendship implies exclusions, but it seems to me now a senseless impoverishment of life that choice should be limited by economic accident. A real democracy must be based on an education uniting, not separating people in the impressionable years of childhood, yet it must be such that the most intelligent parents can gladly accept it for their children. I am none too sure that our new Act is capable of ensuring this.

From another aspect our earlier education was also somewhat exclusive. Whilst neither of my parents were very active in the Quaker community, its traditions were strong in the atmosphere that surrounded us ; and we were certainly conscious of being members of a small body, of shutting out, and of being shut out from, many aspects of the social life of other middle-class people. We neither learnt to dance, nor were we allowed to play cards or go to the theatre. We inherited from my father an intense dislike of all sports that involved killing. Of course, anything in the nature of betting or race-going would have been unthinkable. These abstentions certainly made ordinary social conversation difficult for us, made us seem odd and priggish to casual acquaintances, but I do not find myself regretting this influence. It is not a bad thing to get used to being in a minority, to saying uncomfortable things in the interests of honesty, even if the occasion is trivial. What is, of course, regrettable, is the over-sensitiveness, the self-righteousness of the people who feel they can never quite "belong." I doubt whether it is possible entirely to avoid these by-products of a minority upbringing.

The dominant influence in our education was undoubtedly the personality of my father. He was a somewhat austere man, his pleasures were almost entirely intellectual, his friendships few, his mind powerful, and rather intimidating. I have never known anyone with a more sensitive feeling for honour, truth, and scrupulous justice—that "most unpopular of the virtues" as he used to call it. He tried to give us his own high standards, he hated inaccuracy and sloppy thinking. He had come far, perhaps he himself hardly realized how far, from the orthodoxies of his youth (the generation for whom Darwin was the great revealer of new thought) but he held, as the one vital element of faith, to a profound belief in the spiritual meaning of the universe.

I am not one of the people who are always saying "nowadays" as the preface to a disparaging remark ("then-a-daysers" is a convenient name for them)—but I do feel that some of the scrupulosities, the controls by which such men as my father lived are neglected over-much today.

From my formal education I seem to have gained painfully little. So little that, even as I write, I feel ashamed to allow my name to stand among the distinguished gathering in this book.

I comfort myself by the reflection that an anthology of experiences—to be of any use—must include that of all sorts of people. That vague thing which we call civilization is the sum of an enormous number of personal experiences, an atmosphere of whose pressure we are barely conscious, and perhaps an individual experience is of most use to other people by its contribution to this sum.

We are all tempted to overvalue our own reminiscences as guidance to others. Those who appeal to past experience to sustain prophecies of the future often forget that experiments depend for their prediction value on a rigid similarity of circumstance. The French with their one word "*expérience*" (covering experiment as well) may plausibly accept a confusion, for which we have no excuse. To deduce from one's own youth precepts for the young is so universal a fault of age that one cannot hope to avoid it, but it is certainly riskier than ever now, when one generation has lived through changes of world circumstance, hitherto unimaginable. Two earthquakes have nearly shattered the social structure of the world in this century, and the crash which has brought down nations has shaken the slighter structures of personal lives in every continent. Even our comparatively untouched England has changed on a revolutionary scale. And for all of us the world picture has grown very grim. The limits of nobility and baseness possible to human beings are driven far wider apart than we believed possible in my peacetime youth. It is not of these vast transformations that I can write in this brief chapter. Only I must make it clear that I realize how unsafe it is to argue directly from a nineteenth-century youth to twentieth-century ones. But recorded experience even if not very useful can still give some pleasure, in particular the amusement of discovering common impressions, disclosing the oneness of human nature underlying differences of time, space and tradition. When a Chinese poet of the eighth century describes the three successive tastes of a lichee, the remote reader gets, even through a translation, a little stab of satisfaction at an observation shared! I like to feel that I may have such a slender link with some unknown mind.

To return without further apology to my own schoolroom education. It was mainly imparted by a series of governesses, two of whom were real teachers, the others unwilling earners, who for the most part kissed the rod of their poverty humbly enough. But the first of the series to practise upon me was more inclined to turn the rod on her pupils. She hated her profession, poor woman, and despised us visibly as stupid, which we were not, and as a troop of dowdy little dissenters, which we were. Every day my music lesson ended in tears—a "G" in the bass of "Long, long ago" eluded my little finger unfailingly; it could only fumble in anxiety till her bony one crushed it down on the note. The conviction that music was not for me lasted half a lifetime, till I discovered that, all ungifted for it as I am, it holds a revelation of things beyond other expression. I know only too well that education must select—and so must exclude, but I hold it vital, that the exclusiveness should come as late as possible. As a baby's skull remains elastic round the developing brain, the scholastic structure must allow room on all sides to the growing personality.

Perhaps it is because I have had to do with many people in the later stages of their education that I feel strongly about this.

For many years of my life, as student, librarian and Principal of Somerville (the college at Oxford to which my loyalty and my affection both belong for all it has given to me), and also at the university of my adoption, Birmingham, I have lived in closest contact with university students. So my thoughts turn naturally to people at this stage of life when I think of that often tedious, but always important subject, education.

For most of my lifetime there has been very little choice open to the unprivileged classes of society. Boys and girls left school at twelve or thirteen—the cleverer the child the quicker the standards were passed, and wage earning began. I remember watching my nephew, about nine years old, walking with a country boy of twelve. My nephew was the taller of the two, and looked the more mature, but he was just about to begin his serious schooling whilst the other boy had just ended his. The child whose education was so early finished was pitchforked into whatever job offered. Even today things are not much better, though a larger number of children *do* get secondary schooling, and far more will now have extra years for finding themselves. This haphazard and premature employment has meant a loss of capacity to the community which we shall only be able to measure when we reach a genuinely universal system of education. But for many, at least, of the children of the middle class the question of a career has long been deferred till sixteen or seventeen, or for university students, till later. Whilst this is as it should be, it does in some ways make the choice more difficult. So many doors have been half opened, of literature and the arts, of science and of administration, of adventure or devotion, that the moment of inevitable exclusion is a very searching one. It brings a realization, which is apt to hurt, that the question is no longer, as in the cared-for course of education, "what is best for you," not even, unfortunately "how could you best serve the common good?" but "what have you got to offer that the world will buy." This hard option often comes at the moment when people of any æsthetic sensibility, who have been exposed to the arts, are in the full flush of delight in them. (I should like to see a poll taken to determine how many people have, at some time of their lives, dreamt of a career as painter, poet, actor or musician.) I do not think older people always remember that this moment of decision, of choice, of exclusion—this discovery that one can't have all the toys in the shop, is a critical and difficult one in the lives of (perhaps pampered!) young people. Alas, what seem, and perhaps are, the highest activities of which one is capable are rarely those of which the community has need. And far more people feel a vague desire for self-expression through the arts than have anything profound or new to express. Nor do they realize what a lot of dumb drudgery, even the more artistic or more intellectual pursuits claim. Madame Curie, in a shabby shed, working through tons of pitch-blende, is typical of most discoverers. (On a humble scale, what social reform doesn't at the bottom rest on hours of envelope addressing?) So the choice of a practical career often seems to involve a denial of the qualities most precious to oneself, and too often the half loaf of unprofessional activity is rather bitterly rejected. I believe this to be a great mistake. "Hobbies" have a tiresome, arty-crafty sound, amateur painting lost half its *raison d'être* when photography became universal, amateur music is shamed by gramophone and wireless, plays and films have largely ousted "theatricals." But the person who is not afraid of looking foolish in using these arts, not to inflict torture on his friends (or only a minimum of torture!) but frankly, in order to maintain the balance of his own life and to nourish his powers of appreciation, has an extra window on to the world. Some minor creative skill, or even some small-scale scientific observation, not for livelihood but for the interest of living is a very real, if minor, insurance of contentment.

The trouble is that today the average person lives longer than he is "meant to" (to use a phrase which always covers a tangle of confused thought); or, more exactly, longer than the uncomprehended force driving on through the individual for the survival of the race demands. As far as that force is concerned, those who procreate their kind are unwanted as soon as their progeny can fend for themselves, whilst those who fail to produce young have never any value for it.

> So careful of the type she seems
> So careless of the single life.

Man, alone of Earth's creatures, has consciously revolted against this evaluation. The animal, too, lives and loves its individual life, enjoys it and protects itself. Man, as self-consciousness emerges, turns round and proclaims other things to be as good as the instinctive life. Modern psychology has shown us that he has often damaged himself in the struggle, the slighted underground forces of his nature have exploded under repression. But the challenge has been made, man asserts himself as more than the temporary vehicle of genes, he defies Nature—or does he, perhaps better than her other children, divine the secret meaning behind his own slow emergence? Beyond the maintenance of life he demands an ever wider range of satisfactions in living, and in their exercise he has extended life itself far beyond the needs of racial survival. The strong instincts, those of sex and parenthood, which to many young people seem to enfold the whole meaning of existence, dwindle, and perhaps a third of life is left over to be lived uncoloured by their intensity.

The cultivation of other sides of the mind and spirit seems a remote and unnecessary pedantry just at the age when it should be begun. The people who by nature have in youth other than instinctive interests have a much higher chance of contentment in the latter part of life, and even in the earlier if, as inevitably sometimes happens, the instinctive satisfactions prove elusive.

Here is the answer to the argument, perhaps hardly obsolete even yet, that women's education should be "for the home." The bitter virgins of Victorian fiction, the mothers we have all known who cling like leeches to their grown-up sons, because they have been prepared for no independent life, are there to refute it.

And here, since this is to be a faithful confession, must come a digression on old maids.

It may be that in this, as in other matters, my "lessons" are rather out of date. The greater freedom of friendship between men and women, and perhaps the less strict sex morals of the present day may to some extent have eased what was, in my generation, a grave hardship to many women. But the grim fact that in our grown-up population women seriously outnumber men has meant, and means still, that between one and two million must go without a normal home with husband and children. And somehow the reflection that many marriages are failures and that many children bring anxiety rather than happiness is cold comfort. Old maids' children are proverbially perfect, old maids' husbands are prodigies of faithfulness and brilliance. It is natural to feel regret for all the unlived lives which have beckoned, but the regrets for having missed these basic social relations, which seem to belong of right to every woman, have a power of wounding beyond those of abilities unused or careers untried.

Now since this has been an aching lack in my life, on the whole an unusually pleasant one, it seems only fair to write of it here, since no one else is likely to do so. Most old maids shirk discussion of the subject, lest they should be thought embittered. Other people, regarding their condition as a sign either of coldness or of failure, do often unconsciously make harder what is by no means an easy situation, but some, with a more generous spirit, are ready to make for the unmarried friend a real place in their own homes, and to give her a share in the hopes and fears and triumphs of a rising family. Nothing can compensate for love and motherhood foregone, but my own experience is that in opening one's heart to friendships of very varied kinds, and above all, to those with younger people, a real compensation comes for the good things missed. The happiness this brings has never the passionate instinctive satisfaction given to the young wife and mother. It is to the end, lonelier, more diffused, but it can be very real. In such friendships one must be ready to accept people with their imperfections, to meet them along certain facets of their and your personalities. Nature forces lovers to the illusion of complete acceptance, friends have to be more aware of forbearance. To expect to find one's every principle or prejudice, one's interests and admirations completely mirrored in friendship, to give play to censoriousness or snobbishness or even too much fastidiousness of taste is to miss relationships which might enhance others' lives as well as one's own. This would degenerate into a mere squashy good nature, if one did not insist that anything to call a friendship must have at least *some* links of appreciation and admiration. Mere propinquity intimacies (for which a new name is sorely needed) are not enough.

I have already suggested that our wretched class education limits disastrously the field of friendships; national divisions are also far too rarely bridged by them. We *must* increase personal contacts between people of different races and cultures. These contacts seem to me like the Lilliputian threads which bound Gulliver to the ground, almost the only way of holding down the spirit of war. For myself, friendships of this type, which singular good fortune has made me rich in, have brought so much happiness that I long to see infinitely greater chances given for their formation. There is a peculiar tang or satisfaction (like that of appreciation of the lichee!) in finding affection and agreement on fundamentals in spite of different cultural settings, and to be able in intimate sympathy to enter into lives very different from one's own is to multiply the adventure of the spirit.

I suggested earlier that in education one should keep many branches growing ; when some are cut off the wise liver will put forth others. And this is immensely true of the people who have suffered some great deprivation : either they become lop-sided and unstable, or they compensate by a more vigorous output on other lines. Two of the finest characters I have known (they will forgive my referring to them here) are respectively quite blind and quite deaf. Like trees trimmed by a skilful forester they have attained a new nobility of form by their acceptance, but not a purely *passive* acceptance, of loss and limitation. Such lives are outstanding instances of what I have called the rhythm of respiration, the voluntary compensation by inclusions for exclusions compelled by circumstances.

But it is not only in the development of the mind and character that this rhythm occurs, it is the very foundation of our thinking. Whether we hold or not, that thought can exist without language, the basis of all logical thinking is the division of its objects into classes which can be united in the bond of a single definition. Such a union is also for the moment, an exclusion from our thought of all their individual differences. And it is these excluded qualities which, creeping back, as it were, into our general statements and opinions make them often so lamentably false. I like to put this for myself—inaccurately but shortly thus: "Whenever we say 'they' we tell a lie." This is, of course, most flagrantly true of our judgments of nations: The English are . . . The French are not . . . The Chinese always . . . Here not only do unincluded qualities creep in, the very definitions which should give a unity to the subjects of our rash generalizations are lacking. You can define an ellipse accurately, a cat fairly accurately, but how do you define an Englishman? Of course, the pedantry of never making a statement unjustifiable by the rules of an absolute logic is neither to be expected nor wished for. The Quaker who, in his desire for truthfulness, finished a sentence with "perhaps I ought to have said 'perhaps' " would have been an easy conversationalist in comparison with anyone who tried to dance in such fetters. But I have learnt the immense importance of, as it were, changing focus frequently to keep attention not only on the specific characteristics but on individual ones.

This has come home to me very much in connection with penal questions—a subject into which I got plunged, a good deal against my inclinations, by a series of impulsions. (How odd it is that whilst we are usually moved by a number of re-enforcing causes it seems weak to give several reasons for an action. Though you probably break an engagement for a dozen cumulative hindrances, one overwhelming excuse will be much politer than recounting them truthfully.) But having got, as I say, plunged into this subject I discover continually that the objection to reform comes mainly from people who insist on believing that "criminals" are all alike. They are actually rather badly classified together for most purposes by the fact of having broken one or other of our laws. For their legal position, as having forfeited certain rights of citizenship, they are conveniently and accurately so grouped, and certain more or less scientifically definable types of person are *perhaps* more likely to be found amongst them than others (though this is a matter which greatly needs statistical investigation).

Moreover, the unnatural life of prison does tend to set its mark upon the man or woman who has spent long periods in it, so that habitual criminals may tend to have an exceptionally large number of common characteristics. But for the prevention of crime the most urgent matter is the recognition at the earliest possible moment, after the determination of the specific quality of having broken the law, of all those other individual traits which indicate the possibilities of checking an anti-social trend.

This watchfulness against the dangers of classification, this alertness to detect life in the individual instead of accepting things in the mass, is one of the things I learnt to appreciate most keenly by contact with my brother Roger. I remember strolling with him through one of the dreariest galleries of the British Museum, where rows of late Græco-Roman nonentities, destined obviously for the purchaser who "had to have" statuary for the decoration of his villa or the perpetuation of his features, drag out an almost invisited existence. Suddenly he pounced upon one head in which a spark of sensitive vitality made itself felt through the traditional exterior, and the long-dead nameless sculptor made direct contact with the artist of the twentieth century. And if many of us are apt to reject real merit in unloved surroundings, how easy it is to accept mediocrity in goodly company. In my youth whatever came from the primitive Florentine painters seemed adorable, all the painters after Raphael were to be shunned like the devil, and Raphael himself regarded with mingled suspicion and unwilling admiration. The other day I looked at three pictures by a modern artist, hung together in an exhibition, and ventured to express, to a French woman, my dislike of one in comparison with the others. "Ah," she assured me, "you do not understand, all the artists in Paris are painting like that now." In fact, the idea that one could make any selection of personal preference in what was the mode was incomprehensible to her. You must swallow the fashionable school, as a whale welcomes a shoal of little fish into his belly, provided they are all of standard size.

But, if one is honest, how hard it is to recognize with any certainty, not only in the arts, but in thought, in action, in people, this spark of authentic spirit. Slowly, as generations pass, the works of art, the lives of men warmed by it, glow more and more brightly, and perhaps this power of survival, of burning again in the hearts of later generations, is the one sure test of greatness either æsthetic or moral, just as the inspired guesses of philosophers or men of science illuminate discoveries they never dreamt of.

I think this is really what Dr. Schweitzer means when in one of his books he describes himself as trying as he steamed down a great African river, to find a phrase to sum up his own creed. And, with the sight of a great herd of hippopotami, it flashed into his mind. (The introduction of the hippopotami here is magnificent. It undoubtedly must be a matter of biographical fact, but it gives all the delightful, half comic, surprise that Mozart gets by his use of the bassoon.) And the creed that came was simply "reverence for life"—I myself have never found one more worth struggling for.

Here, in accepting this very simple phrase, I am aware that if I am to complete honestly this sketch of my life's development, I must say something of the things I have had to renounce, often with great regret, amongst those which are very dear to many people. It would be easier to leave this unsaid, for it is painful to give pain. But I suspect that, in fear of disturbing those who feel their feet firmly set on a rock we sometimes neglect those who, like myself, find it hard to keep more than a small, and perhaps shifting footing on the uncertain sands. My father's phrase, when I made confession of "doubts"—"You will not go far wrong if you can hold to the spiritual meaning of the Universe"—comforts me often, after half a century. It is hard to know how many people today cling strongly and confidently to the orthodox tenets of religion. They are probably fewer but more ardent than when such orthodoxy was almost a matter of course. Of the rest, a good many people seem to slip through life without asking much of the meaning of things, governed more or less by customary rules of behaviour reinforced by the sanctions of popular opinion. But there are others who, whilst holding to the hope of a "spiritual meaning in the Universe," yet cannot seize upon what seem to them the wish-fulfilment comforts of religious faith. Perhaps just for the reason that each feels the loneliness of their position they often go without that sense of human fellowship which might assuage it. And so it becomes something of a duty, in a confession such as this, to indicate one's own position.

To those who accept "revelation" the question of how far the human mind can grasp anything of the nature of things hardly presents itself. To others it must seem doubtful whether the forms of thinking developed in that marvellous instrument for survival, the human brain, are not conditioned by the story of its slow formation as an essentially practical instrument. There are not wanting those who say that, if we can make no statement which can hope to approach the inner meaning of things we may just as well content ourselves with accepting any traditional version which has served its purpose for generations—the difference can be but infinitesimal between one inadequacy and another. To take this view seems to me to sin against another fundamental principle, fit to stand beside that of reverence for life, reverence for truth.

That these two principles *are* fundamental, are binding, is impossible of proof. For one's philosophy, as for geometry, the fewest, simplest, most apparently self-evident axioms must be taken; and, as for geometry, the self-evident axiom of one generation may be a highly debatable hypothesis for the next. But I do not think the principle of reverence for life would be shaken if next year a chemist produced protoplasm from inorganic matter in his laboratory. I should say rather that whatever links up the dreary inorganic universe of gases punctuated by a few spots of solids and liquids with even the humblest life irradiates the whole with new meaning.

Intimations of a spiritual reality reach different people in a multitude of ways. Where the promptings of our hungers are evident, where vanity, cowardice or even the need for a mother's breast show through we must be watchful of their genuineness. But if honesty compels us for ourselves to rule out many statements, many hopes, many assurances which others can accept, let us still keep ourselves ready to recognize the intimations however they may come. The orthodoxy of unbelief may be as arid as that of belief. Reverence for life in whatever form must illuminate reverence for truth :

> The lust after life in the chills of its lust
> Claims a passport of death.
> The lover of life sees the flame in our dust
> And a gift in our breath.

E. V. KNOX

Born in 1881, the eldest son of the late Bishop Knox. Educated at Rugby and Oxford. Served throughout the First World War and was wounded at Passchendaele. Joined the staff of "Punch" in 1921 and succeeded Sir Owen Seaman as Editor in 1932.

IS THIS an autobiography? It would seem so. Yet have I not for many years from long ago been publishing fragments of my life, and the bitter lessons it has taught me? For instance there are the lines:

I used to be a fearful lad
The things I did were downright bad;
And worst of all was what I done
From seventeen to twenty-one
On all the railways far and wide
From sinfulness and shameful pride.

For several years I was so wicked
I used to go without a ticket,
And travelled underneath the seat
Down in the dust of people's feet,
Or else I sat as bold as brass
And told them "Season" in first-class.
In 1921 at Harwich
I smoked in a non-smoking carriage:
I never knew what life nor art meant,
I wrote "Reserved" on my compartment,
And once (I was a guilty man)
I swapped the labels in guard's van.

A bad beginning. Yet I made no secret about it.

From 1922 to 4
I leant against the carriage door
Without a-looking at the latch ;
And once, a-leaving Colney Hatch,
I put a huge and heavy parcel
Which I were taking to Newcastle
Up on the rack above my head ;
And when it tumbled down, Oh Lord!
I pulled communication cord
The guard came round and said, "You mule!
What have you done, you dirty fool?"
I simply sat and smiled, and said
"Is this train right for Holyhead?"
He said, "You blinking, blasted swine
You'll have to pay the five-pound fine."

You might have supposed that here was lesson enough. But did it teach me anything? No. I gave a fake name and address. Puffed up with my vain-gloriousness. I was in fact almost incorrigible. And as time went on I became worse.

At Bickershaw and Strood and Staines
I've often got on moving trains,
And once alit at Norwood West
Before my coach had come to rest.
A window and a lamp I broke
At Chipping Sodbury and Stoke,
And worse I did at Whissendine :
I threw out bottles on the line
And other articles as be
Likely to cause grave injury
To persons working on the line—
That's what I did at Whissendine.
I grew so careless what I'd do
Throwing things out and dangerous too,

prison house begin to close about the
that King Herod or some even mor
would be a great benefactor to the

Or he would take Coleridge's *A*
great lesson of this poem is that if y
any question arises of shooting an
are the man who does it. For this
the only man of the whole crew w
All his dear companions, like those
were drowned or destroyed. What
humbug was not only shrived of his
dwelt in a wood, but had the subse
be appreciated by any raconteur) of
a man who was going to a weddin
including no doubt the bridegroom
them far more unhappy than himself.
anecdote for the rest of his life. 'Her
sea' people would say in taverns. 'G
about the albatross that he once found
that would mean another quart of bee

Or he would read Gray's verses abou
in a bowl of gold fish, with its conc

> Not all that tempts your
> And heedless hearts is lawf
> Nor all that glisters

and he would remark upon it:

"The proper moral of this poem is
the poet. The cat didn't want gold
fish. If she had succeeded in catching
were not fish, but gold, she would l
appointed. But fish they were, and s
thing) of knowing that she had no busi
she could have learned, if she had surv
is a slippery substance which gives no
No more illogical or nonsensical lesso
the poet could be imagined by the mi

> That, last and worst of all I'd done
> I threw a great sultana bun
> Out of the train at Pontypridd—
> It hit a plate-layer, it did.
> I thought that I should have to swing
> And never hear the sweet birds sing.
> The jury recommended mercy,
> And that's how grace was given to Percy.

Not, of course, now I come to think of it, that Percy is my true name, and it may be that the events recorded here are coloured a little by fantasy. Yet take the confession to a psychiatrist. Let him eliminate the truth from the falsehood. He will have plenty to tell you, I feel sure. It is only because the last line may seem unduly optimistic that I cease to re-quote myself in verse and begin again.

I know a man who whenever he is asked to write anything personal about himself, and has promised to do so, can never fulfil the pledge without being seized by a frenzy of self-pity and despair. Why had he bound himself to this odious task? Has it not all been written down by other and better men? Or if not, was it worth writing down at all? He bound himself once to say in what age of history he would have most liked to live, and when the time drew near for the fulfilment of his vow, he was scarcely fit to live in any age that the world has ever seen.

"How do I know," he cried, stamping madly about his study, "when I should have liked to live, without knowing whether I should be I, what is my outlook, what is my rank, when I project myself into another period of time, and whether I carry into it with me any of the me-ness that is really me." He compromised in the end by saying that he would have liked to be an Elizabethan pot-man in the Mermaid Tavern, and listen to the stuff that Shakespeare talked when he really let himself go. "Either that," he said, "or a fighting Prince Bishop of the Middle Ages, who could commit as many murders as he liked in a day, and order himself to be forgiven." I know that man fairly well, but not so well as I ought to know him, for I am he. And even though this

Or yet again he might call our attention to Rudyard Kipling's perpetually quoted poem called *If*. "Here," he would tell us, "the poet, after reciting a long series of almost impossible virtues, ends by saying what? That if you can do all these things:

Yours is the world and everything that's in it
And what is more you'll be a man, my son.

Supposing that there were a few hundred out of every million human beings capable of reaching this pitch of perfection, each of them would possess the world, which would cause infinite confusion, quarrelling and bloodshed, and each of them, moreover, could attain to the triumph of being what every other male being presumably is—namely a man."

I do not think that this lecturer was really a cynic. He was dealing with a lot of rather "tough" students, and he argued that we should like a little amusement (mixed with logic) at the end of our dose of literature. And I recall him thus clearly, because if I had read and learned all the notes that I didn't take at his lectures, and those of his colleagues, I might at this moment be a retired Indian civil servant, which would have been of little use to India, and none at all to me.

This reminiscence, however, seems to bring me rather more near to myself. How hard it is in an essay about one's life to keep away from the character that one most wishes to avoid! I was never a good pupil at all. It seemed to me that lessons were always thrust upon me, and that they were never the things I cared about or wanted to know. Yet I suppose Life was there (at the desk) all the time, and saying quietly, "Well, if I don't teach you, nothing will." (Though even that may not be orthodox theology.) I had to make experiments, of course. I fancy I am right in saying that if Life taught one nothing we would not be able to see or stand or walk or speak. But how disappointing many of the experiments were. Consider for instance one of the most elementary laws of dynamics. A small boy, not more than ten years old, who came to live in a large industrial town, I was much impressed by the way that men or larger boys jumped off trams (we are back on the rails again) before they had stopped. We had steam trams in those days, towed by a little engine in a sort of square box, the only kind of trams that have seemed to have any romance for me. I have never found any spiritual exaltation in electric trams.

I thought to myself, I, too, will leap off a moving tram, and going to the platform with my back to the conductor, and summoning up all my courage I did so. I immediately fell on my back in the mud. There must be something wrong here, I reflected. The next time I kept my eyes on the conductor, and jumped off backwards. I immediately fell face forward in the mud. You need not think that I was daunted. Afterwards by patience, perseverance, practice (though not, I suppose, in any spirit of jesting) I learned to be very good at jumping off a moving tram (they did not go very fast) and I think I could still do it, if we still used steam trams. Time has taken away the value of that lesson, as it has taken away the pride I felt in my earliest bicycle, and the lessons I learned from it, one of which was that if you go fast enough down a long country lane, and hit a cow, you may find yourself in a field on the other side of the hedge. I could write many things also about the riding of horses at this point, and about Flanders in 1917, but I shall forbear.

It is rather of moral lessons that, I think, I am compelled to speak, and diffidence falls again about me like a dark robe.

I remember one.

About ten years after the first event of which I have spoken, I was supposed to be reading, or beginning to read for one of those examinations which seem to have been invented for me to avoid. I was staying at a country vicarage, and the daughter of the house, finding me in a day-dream with my book on political economy on the floor, said to me: "I know what is the matter with you. You have no ambition."

"By that sin fell the angels," I told her. (You see I had been reading something or other.)

"It is the last infirmity of noble minds."

She considered this, and then, "I think," she went on, "that you will always be able to find an excuse for not doing what you don't want to do."

It struck me that she was an amazingly wise and clever girl, and I asked her to marry me. I have always been glad that her refusal was so firm. If there is no lesson to be learned from this, Life must be a very bad schoolmaster indeed.

What I should have liked to say about life is that it had taught me how to write, but alas! it would not be true. If it is my "occupational activity" (I believe that is the correct and fearful phrase), it has always caused me infinite annoyance and pain. I did not wish to begin and I did not wish to go on. I do not wish to go on now. At the age of three (I fancy) John Stuart Mill could write in Greek ; at the age of seven Lord Macaulay wrote a *Compendium of Universal History* and three cantos of "The Battle of Cheviot." I refrained. What strange disinclination it was that with-held me from these exercises I cannot now recall. But most probably then, even as now, I clearly perceived that my own thoughts and fancies were far more beautiful to me, far more intensely true, than they could ever be, set down on paper with pen and ink ; and that so set down they would be ruined for evermore. They come to me almost always in the bathroom before breakfast. And when breakfast is over they are gone. They appear to be the product of soap and water and steam, and (short of thinking aloud, and having a dictaphone in the bathroom) I do not see how they could be preserved. But they have existed for me, and I have had great pleasure in them. The loss is the world's, not mine.

Moreover, taxing my memory, I find that I did not write the first thing I wrote at all. The first thing, I mean, that I was not compelled to write : I had it in my head (it was a piece of verse) and I repeated it to a friend. I think I was about nineteen years old at the time. He said, "You ought to have that printed," but I demurred. I did not like it well enough, and repeating it again I wanted to alter it. But he said, "If you don't have it printed, I shall. I shall send it to a paper under your name." And this in fact was what he did. I don't exactly owe him a grudge, for in other ways he was a good man. But his action greatly influenced my life, and I rather resented it at the time. I also feel that if he had not behaved in this impetuous fashion, I might have brought the words more nearly into the shape I wanted—they might have been almost ready for publication now.

Into a sort of life then I drifted or was driven, where I mimicked other men's words and examined with a faint curiosity other men's minds. No doubt I have learned a great deal. I have learned, for instance, that beyond fame and riches, adventure and piety, beyond wit and science and wisdom the people of this country value their sense of humour. That is the one thing that they take seriously. They boast of it, when they would not dream of boasting that they were good or brave. I must suppose that even in the wreck of their fortunes they often cry, "All is lost save humour." The husbands leaving their wives and hurrying to their clubs are wont to murmur, "I could not love thee dear so much, loved I not humour more," and that a day may come during a great international crisis when a statesman will be pelted with roses for crying, "I have brought back peace with humour."

The great men of the Brains Trusts who gather to talk to us on the air have sometimes said that a sense of humour is the greatest gift of all. They should know. Yet I find that everybody has it. Demosthenes, searching London with an arc-light, would not discover a humourless man. That is why on the same day I open one letter which begins :

Sir,

I flatter myself on my sense of humour, but neither I nor any of my friends can see any point in the joke at the bottom of page 173. We are still trying hard, but if we do not succeed in a few days, we shall give up the attempt in disgust.

and another which says :

Dear Sir,

I can boast that I know a good joke when I see one, and as soon as I looked at the bottom of page 173 I burst into such a roar of merriment that the whole house shook. When my friends had seen it we made such a noise that the neighbours threatened us with violence, and the police were called in.

I often wonder that the insurance companies do not take the matter up.

There was, for instance, the terrible affair of the two hippopotami. This was a picture in which two of these creatures were shown in an African swamp, and one was saying to the other, "I keep thinking it's Tuesday." This wrecked many a home.

One day, when I thought the storm had blown over I heard a loud puffing on the stairs, and a very large red-faced man with eyes bulging from his head, came into my room. He made a few remarks about the weather, and then said: "There was one thing that I particularly wished to see you about. You had a picture about two hippopotamuses."

"Hippopotami," I said nervously to gain time.

"What was the point of it all?"

I shifted in my chair. I took up a ruler and put it down. I gazed at the windows, the walls.

"Well, you see," I said, "it's like this. Here are these two animals out there in an African swamp far away from civilization, wallowing, if you understand what I mean——"

"Precisely."

"And one of them says to the other, as I might say to you, or you to me here in London—here in this room, 'I keep thinking it's Tuesday'—the sort of thing one *does* say at times, and——"

"I see. But why hippopotamuses?"

"Oh well. I don't know. But——"

"And why Tuesday?"

"I can't tell you," I said desperately. "I think they must have got into the paper by accident."

"Ah," he said with great satisfaction, "I thought so. That's all I wanted to know." And he went, puffing, away.

Next to their sense of humour, I have learned, people value their dogs. So many have sent me poems about their dogs, that I once determined to take up the whole subject scientifically, and in a way which suited the age in which we live. I called my work *The Problems of Doghood*, and began:

We have surely got past the old bad days when correction

and chastisement could be employed with advantage on the dog-child, and begin to realize that a system of obsolete and meaningless taboos must end by establishing morbid and troubling fixatures in the dog-soul, such as transferred rat-suspicions, illusory parasite complexes and bone sepulture. Psycho-pathology is what the dog-soul needs.

I soon found the topic was one on which I could write both convincingly and well.

We want the dogs of this generation to become different and better sires and dams, producing broader-minded and less irrational puppies in the next. There is an urgent need of a body of sympathetic cynoanalysts who will study the individual members of a given litter with kindness, reason and understanding. . . .

I went on to discuss particular cases, as for instance that of A, an Airedale terrier who contracted a habit of pursuing sheep, and even began to snarl at X, a frequent visitor to the house, who had a face amazingly like that of a sheep.

A's attitude towards X, I wrote, was a clear case of "ambivalent" love-hate, X being identified with the object of A's repressed libido, i.e. a sheep. The proper course was to have taken out A for several walks, on a strong lead, accompanied by a sheep, which could have been borrowed for the purpose, attached to another strong lead . . . and subsequently X should have been introduced as a fourth member of the party, either with or without a lead, and treated conversationally in such a manner that A began to distinguish him clearly and continually from a sheep, so that both complexes would have been finally resolved.

Too many dog-owners, I concluded, are influenced by the old and tyrannical superstition which regards the dog-soul as a possession-object rather than a responsibility-motive, or by the equally abominable idea of dog-idolatry, which substitutes the pet-wish and the pauper-love for a true realization of the dog-dog's moral and spiritual good.

The result of this little essay was very gratifying. Several people wrote to congratulate me and say how heartily they agreed with my theories, and two of them enclosed photographs of their dogs.

It was only when I passed on from dog-owners to the difficulty of people who could not decide what dog to own, and said:

> They can be obtained in any size from roughly (or even smoothly) four foot six inches by one foot, to eleven inches by five . . . on the whole a medium size and a neutral colour without pattern are advisable, with both ends slightly blunted, and the legs, which should number four in all, should be of sufficient strength to carry the body without fatigue,

that I began to get into difficulties with the Kennel Club. And one lady wrote to tell me that it was not silly but in bad taste to jest on a serious theme.

It should be obvious from what I have said that to deal intensively and almost exclusively with such matters, is a very responsible task, and does not lead to any lightness of heart.

I was always impressed by the very old story that used to appear in advertisements of a famous effervescent saline. It ran something like this:

A very woe-begone man once came to visit Dr. Abernethy, the famous physician.

"You should take more recreation from your work," he was told. "Why don't you go and see Grimaldi the great clown?'

"I am Grimaldi," replied the visitor.

But I like to tell it the other way round.

A very woe-begone man sat through a whole performance by Grimaldi, the great clown, without a smile on his face.

Meeting him afterwards, Grimaldi said: "There must be something wrong with your health. Why don't you go and see Dr. Abernethy the famous physician?"

"I am Dr. Abernethy," was the reply.

It comes to the same thing in the end. And if what I have written does not seem to be a full and candid recital of my life and character, and the morals to be drawn from it, you must take the whole essay, as I suggested at the very beginning, to one of Dr. Abernethy's successors. You will be surprised.

SIR RICHARD GREGORY

Born in Bristol in 1864. Leaving day school at the age of twelve he afterwards gained a scholarship to the Royal College of Science in 1886 and rose to become a Fellow of the Royal Society and President of the British Association for the Advancement of Science from 1940–46. For many years Editor of "Nature"—the weekly journal of international science.

EVERY CHILD comes into the world with animal instincts common to the offspring of all human parents. By birth it is given the right to live and grow through the use of the powers with which it is endowed. The two factors involved in this process are Nature and Nurture : one represented by inborn abilities: the other by the means available for the exercise of them.

A new-born babe has not to learn how to obtain the nourishment necessary to keep alive, any more than have the young of other living creatures. It knows by instinct what it wants, "And with no language but a cry," seeks to satisfy its natural needs. All its actions are determined by these needs and the way in which they are supplied. There can be training in habits, just as other animals train their young, but learning from life begins when thought and instinct are combined in purposeful action.

The primary needs of human life are food, shelter and clothing, all of which have, under primitive conditions, to be obtained from natural surroundings. What there is to learn under such conditions, and how to acquire the knowledge necessary for survival, constitute the elements of the practical education of young people. The training for this kind of existence is comparable with that given to animals maintained for the service of man; and when the primary wants of life are provided as the result, there is similar contentment.

When a child has learned to stand upright on its two feet and to walk instead of crawl it represents a stage of evolution at which the human race emerged from its purely animal ancestry. With his head high in the air, a man became able to free himself from the limitations imposed upon him by Nature and to create a world of his own. He has thus superimposed an artificial life upon his natural life, and introduced a process of cultural evolution which is independent of natural conditions, except in so far as they can be used for his own ends. Like other creatures, he inherits certain instincts as "action patterns," but every human being has to acquire knowledge and wisdom for himself.

By the exercise of these instincts, such social insects as bees and ants carry on their marvellous communal work from one generation to another, but always in the same natural way, and only where natural conditions are favourable for their existence. Each new generation of insects can survive only if it is born under these conditions ; and the children of mankind are no better provided for in their infancy. In civilized communities they come into being in circumstances which are biologically and morally artificial, while their instincts are purely of an animal kind.

The basic characters of civilized man are the same as they were thousands of years ago, in spite of all individual and social attainments. Each generation starts with the same natural instincts, yet each has to learn afresh to adapt itself to an unnatural environment, and to acquire a new consciousness of what is good or evil. The social and cultural conditions change in place and time, but human nature remains in most respects unaltered, except perhaps in the capacity to learn and the means of passing on wisdom and knowledge to succeeding generations. The only sense in which we can truly say that we stand on the shoulders of our ancestors is that we can see more of their achievements and are provided with more powerful weapons to control or subdue forces of Nature.

The kind of start given to life depends upon the circumstances in which it is shaped, both materially and spiritually. What is first taught, and what has to be learnt in early years, is a way of life which conforms to the ideas of the class or community in which the growing human organism is placed. The food thus provided for body, mind and spirit is what is regarded as suitable and right in the established social order. Sacred worship as well as secular works are the elements of adaptation to this order, though their forms vary greatly, according to geographical divisions and conditions of life in them.

All these influences give trend to what are conceived to be right ways of living by doing. As such they are enduring forces in the formation of character, which in man implies action guided by a will conscious of moral or ethical standards. Human conduct is determined by actions in this sense. It may thus be distinguished from the instinctive or unconscious impulse which, in other creatures, represents purely biological reaction to a stimulus.

Where anyone is born and begins to live as a member of a community determine, therefore, what there is to learn in particular surroundings and the kind of training imparted. To acquire knowledge or skill by deliberate exercise of hand and brain is the way of learning : the simple desire to know is curiosity and is an instinctive attribute not peculiar to human beings. Inquisitiveness may combine curiosity with intelligent inquiry and need not be confounded with impertinence or irreverence.

Interest in a subject is the main motive of learning from the stage of casual curiosity in things and phenomena to that of concentrated thought and inquiry into meanings. At the dawn of intelligence in infancy, the reactions to what is seen, heard or felt are wonders. Then comes the ability to identify objects and to learn the sounds or names by which things are called. In general, this psychological stage, when the question "What is it?" is asked of everything brought before the young mind, lasts to the age of about ten or eleven years. Then, and for four years or so, comes the question, especially in boys, "How does it work?" or "How is it made?" With the full advent of adolescence the mind is ready to be interested in the "Why" and the "Wherefore" of things and to understand principles derived from acquired knowledge of their properties and actions.

The presence and activity of these three phases of mental development indicate common attitudes of response of human senses to natural objects and phenomena. Though young minds experience the urge of all three motives, yet each becomes dominant during certain periods of normal growth, and each varies in strength and duration according to individual inclinations.

In these respects there are as many variations as there are in the physical forms and faces of human beings. The stock from which a child springs implants the power of attaining a certain stature, and the fertility of the soil is a measure of opportunity to grow. There are thus limitations of natural capacities to learn, whatever nurturing influences may be available. All that can reasonably be asked of a social community by a member of it is opportunity to grow to the limits of inborn capacities, and to live a full and progressive life in his surroundings.

The American Declaration of Independence announced as "self-evident truths: that all men are created equal; that they are endowed by their Creator with certain inalienable rights; that among these are life, liberty, and the pursuit of happiness." The characteristic of Nature, from the lowest forms of life to the highest is, however, not equality but diversity. What is regarded as the right kind of life to live, and what means are provided to pursue it, are decided by prevailing social conditions, with freedom of choice to accept them or fight against them in the attainment of high ideals.

Everyone of us has to "Learn to live, and live to learn." We all learn by experience, but this often leads to injurious consequences which can be avoided by learning from the experience of others. This is the substance of the process of training, whether the guidance is afforded by reading or by word of mouth. In literature it may be found as real or imaginary experiences and emotions aroused by them, and in history as narratives of repercussions between new and old ideas about human rights and duties and the structure of society.

H. G. Wells's works—novels, fantastic and imaginative romances and books upon social, religious and political questions—describe a wide range of experiences of life and what he learnt from them. In the two volumes of his *Experiment in Autobiography* which run into more than eight hundred pages, he dealt frankly and broadly with life as it was given to him and what he learnt from it. The subtitle of the work is "Discoveries and Conclusions of a Very Ordinary Brain," by which he meant to imply that he was like other men in his feelings and in his attitude towards life as a whole. He was far from being strong in body, and had several serious breakdowns in health when a young man, yet he overcame these bodily weaknesses by the power of his mind and the desire to learn and to express his reactions to knowledge right unto the last.

It is given to very few even to approach his genius, or to have so many adventures in different walks of life, yet everyone shares in similar experiences, and can learn from them that they need not submit, like a creature of the field, to be a victim of circumstances. In one of Wells's books, he makes a character say : "Find the thing you want to do intensely, make sure that's it, and do it with all your might. If you live, well and good ; if you die, well and good. Your purpose is done." That is the spirit in which life should be lived, with "well-being" and "well-doing" as the guiding principles and mastery of yourself as the driving force against circumstances which oppose their fulfilment.

These with other principles already referred to relate to the art of living, or the philosophy of life. They are generalizations arrived at as the result of studies of human nature in its impulses and reactions, as recorded in lives lived and things thought and done. They show what can be learnt from life as well as what has been learnt in societies by individual members of them.

Every living person exercises an influence upon others and is influenced by them. At all stages of civilization certain basic codes of human conduct have existed as elements of survival. These rules are formulated to bind people together in particular kinds of social structure and are expected to be known, whether they are observed or not. They always include standards of moral goodness, using this term in its widest sense, as well as of physical fitness. To attain any standard above that of the lower animals demands the control of inherited instincts by the force of thought. The higher the aim of individual life the more difficult are the lessons which have to be learnt to reach it, but the struggles strengthen the discipline by which the human race has separated itself from its animal ancestry through a long and painful history.

Civilization is essentially distinguished from barbarism, and man from other creatures, by the effects of high ethical ideals upon human conduct. Many of these ideals are common to all peoples and all religious faiths. They are taught as guiding principles of Buddhism, Confucianism and Hinduism as well as in Hebraism and the less ancient religions of Christianity and Islam; and they all include the Golden Rule : "Hurt not others with that which pains yourself," or as laid down by Jesus of Nazareth in the Sermon on the Mount : "All things therefore whatsoever ye would that men should do unto you, even so do ye also unto them."

That such a rule should be a universal standard of ethics is an impressive testimony to a force, working within ourselves, which makes for righteousness of life. In everyday life and affairs of individuals, classes or nations, it is expressed in the phrase : Consideration for Others. This principle promotes qualities of brotherly kindness, care for the weak and suffering, mercy, regard for justice and other virtues by which men become other than animals only. Though it is "More honoured in the breach than in the observance," yet there is an upward trend towards its fulfilment, otherwise there would be no noble meaning in life or in civilization.

The present position of the civilized world may represent only incipient stages of growth of human aspirations so sublime that they may be said to approach the divine. Only by belief in the possibility of continuing this upward trend towards the light, and action in the spirit of it, can our race be saved from degradation and destruction. That is the lesson which has now urgently to be learnt, with expectation associated with hope as the stimulus to high endeavour.

Poets and philosophers, as well as founders and interpreters of religious faiths, have shown in their lives and teachings both real and ideal conceptions of a world worthy of the trusteeship of it given to the human race. Whether the world was created for man or man for the world is a question which cannot be answered by positive knowledge, but we do know that every member of our race possesses, in varying degrees, certain inherent powers of body, mind and spirit which have to be exercised in order to develop. Whatever beliefs are held about the meaning and purpose of man's existence, he finds himself upon a globe which can provide every human being with the primary needs of life in full abundance, and also with a mind which can appreciate such abstract qualities as beauty and love, goodness, justice and mercy.

Though our planet be only a particle in a universe of thousands of millions of visible and invisible material bodies, it is probably unique in a particular combination of physical conditions which have led to the evolution of human life upon it. There may be living organisms on other globes but they would not be cast in exactly the same mould of circumstances. If there are intelligent beings in the heavens around us, to them we are in their celestial regions, with powers to make this world of ours an exalted dwelling-place by service to high ideals.

There is a beautiful legend among the primitive natives of Australia : that a conspicuous dark patch of the Milky Way in the constellation of the Southern Cross, and known to mariners as the "coal-sack," is the entrance into the star-lit dome of their heaven. The trail of a shooting star is believed to be the rope which a blackfellow climbs when he dies. He carries the loose end of the rope with him as he moves upward, and when he reaches the roof he throws the rope down again as the streak of a shooting star to be grasped by another blackfellow whom it touches. It is a long climb to the top of the dome and difficult to get through the hole in it, but even after this has been done, another journey just as long has to be made over the roof to come back again to the flat earth, this time as a black ancestor bleached by age into a whitefellow.

The story is symbolic of human life and its immortal spirit. Everyone has to climb up the rope and must throw the loose end down again for another to use. How high our heavens are above our earthly selves depends upon our own conceptions of them, and the efforts made to reach them. The value of these efforts should not, however, be measured in terms of self-help but of service to others, and thus be given truly humanistic standards. This does not mean that every undertaking in life can or should be based only on altruistic principles, but that personal goodness or fitness of mind or body ought not to be gained by depriving others of the powers or opportunities to attain similar advantages.

The world is made up of many sorts of people and degrees of class and moral consciousness which direct desires and determine opportunities. The start in life has the same diversities of powers and equipment to walk steadfastly along the way towards the light. Long before this way was shown on scripts for the guidance of men it was known in their hearts. It is expressed in the proverbial folk-lore of peoples of all tribes and races as unwritten laws of conduct and ethics and is found in all religions and philosophies of life. The lives and works of revered teachers of this gospel represent the fervent spirit by which the light of the lamp has been increased in its range throughout the ages. Though made up of many colours, the composite beam is white to all who look for it and use it to guide their courses on the sea of life.

With this beacon to guide the way, charts to show the rocks and currents by which many lives have been wrecked, and a compass which always gives true bearings, every mariner has the power and means to make his voyage a worthy and successful adventure. He cannot, however, reach the right port unless he first learns how to plot a true course and steers his own ship along it.

"A community," wrote Henrik Ibsen, "is like a ship ; every one ought to be prepared to take the helm." Our parents and relatives form the master, crew and passengers of the ship in the book of which each one of us is entered as a child. The discipline of this ship has strong influences upon the development of character in early years. When the apprenticeship stage is reached we are being taught how to live, and it depends upon ourselves what exertions we make to learn to pass from the stage of ordinary seaman, to mate or master mariner. The higher the aim, the longer and more intense are the efforts needed to attain it. It is given to every one to qualify to take the helm of his own life in whatever seas he may have to sail. The spirit should be that of the familiar couplet from W. E. Henley's "Invictus" :

> I am the master of my fate.
> I am the captain of my soul.

We all have to make the voyage of life, however long or short this may be or varied our horizons. Each has, therefore, a story to tell of places and people, of scenes and experiences, hopes and frustrations, belonging especially to himself and worth relating to others. Depth and extent of knowledge afford no measure of "goodness" of life : neither does the acquisition of power or of riches. Nobility of character is not the exclusive possession of any class or age ; it is to be found in all social ranks from the lowest to the highest : from those with little book-knowledge to peers in worlds of learning. The basic principles of life are the same for the whole human race : communities and individual members of them may be said truly to give the word civilization a worthy meaning when they really put these principles into practice.

The sum and substance of what can be learnt from life must be stated in principles, whether as essential elements of religious faiths or as philosophic conclusions.

In their appeal to the throbbing human heart, the messages embodied in the sacred literature of the world may well be said to be of such exalted excellence as to approach the divine. Some philosophies of life suggest ideal aims of man and conditions of society, with the pursuit of knowledge as a virtue and virtue its own reward. Other standards of uprightness common to all religions and ethical systems are those of Love and Charity, Justice and Mercy, Truth and Wisdom, Humility and Purity. It is by aspiring towards these ideals that the human race differs from other animate groups and expresses its intrinsic soul.

There is in the Collection of Babylonian and Assyrian Antiquities of the British Museum a fragment of a tablet containing a number of moral precepts of this kind, which are said to include instructions given to the first man and woman to be created. They were included in the great Code of Laws of Hammurabi four thousand years ago, as rules to be observed by all classes of society in Babylon at that time. They appear with laws concerning religion, justice, private and social rights and duties as physical and moral principles of the Mosaic code, as they do in rules of right ways of living laid down in the ancient civilizations of Egypt, India and China. Though everywhere the giver of moral laws is believed to be a supreme deity, responsibility for their observance is placed upon the peoples who are subject to them.

The existence of this moral background, and the persistence with which exhortations have been made to paint inspiring pictures upon it, are the most significant factors in the history of civilization. The canvas may differ in time and place, but there are certain eternal values by which work upon it during life can be judged, and consciousness of them is a distinctive characteristic of human life. Whether attained or attainable, high ideals of worthy ways of living have been taught by saints and sages throughout civilized times and approached in varying degrees by their followers. They are concerned with conduct of life upon earth ; and East and West are united in their principles.

In the sixth century B.C., Gautama Buddha taught his first monks that the right or middle way of life was between the two extremes of excessive gratification and mortification of the flesh. This is the path which leads to insight, knowledge and wisdom and conduces to calm :

> It is the noble eightfold path, namely : right view, right intention, right speech, right action, right livelihood, right endeavour, right mindfulness, right meditation.

To the Western world, St. Paul, as an Apostle of the founder of Christianity, gave a similar message in his Epistle to the Corinthians when he said :

> Whatsoever things are true, whatsoever things are honourable, whatsoever things are just, whatsoever things are pure, whatsoever things are lovely, whatsoever things are of good report ; if there be any virtue, and if there be any praise, think on these things.

There are as many Buddhists in the geographical world as there are Christians ; and the two faiths together are taught to more than half the total human population of two thousand million. Humanity has, however, still far to go before ways of life anywhere approach through works the ideals presented by its spiritual leaders.

All that has been said so far in this article relates to what can be learnt by anyone about principles and practices of life as responses of human nature to external conditions, whether real or ideal. It is an outline of powers and possibilities of cultural development, using this phrase in the sense of growth of body and mind for the purposes of the spirit. It represents the views of many people on the nature of man and the structure of society by wise and practical service towards a goal of general goodness. Where, how and why these conclusions have been reached by a particular individual after eighty-three years of contact with other lives, from the poorest to the richest in every quality, have, therefore, now to be included in a reply to the specific question of what I, personally, have learnt from life.

It is only because this article would not be complete without a sketch of my own life that I am induced now to draw it. I came into being in a room of a house in a mean street of the City of Bristol. My father was a boot-finisher by trade but a poet by nature, and he produced during his life several volumes of beautiful verse. His father was for sixty years a lay preacher of the Wesleyan Society at Bideford, Devon, where a tablet is erected to his revered memory.

After leaving school at twelve years of age, I became in succession a newspaper boy, a machine boy at a printers, and an apprentice to "clicking," or cutting-out uppers of boots and shoes, in a factory in Bristol. Before this stage, I had read many books, including all that I could get hold of by Captain Marryat and Dickens, followed by Scott and Thackeray. When I was about fifteen years of age I began to attend a night school to renew my acquaintance with arithmetic and other subjects for which I had no need in my daily work. While an apprentice also, I attended the Latin class at what is now the Merchant Venturers College, Bristol, and managed to gain the prize in it at the end of the year. My working hours in the factory were from 8 a.m. to 6.30 or 7 p.m., but I was keen to learn and studied for at least an hour before going to the factory and also in the evenings as a recreation for the body and mind after standing all day at a bench.

I had served more than four years of my five-year apprenticeship when the headmaster at Clifton College, Canon J. M. Wilson, who was an admirer of the personality and poems of my beloved father, invited me to see him at his house and to bring my Smith's *Principia Latina* with me. The result of the interview gave me much encouragement and led a few months later to my being offered the post of what is commonly known as "bottle-washer" in the science department of the College. I am sure that there were many youths in Bristol at the time better qualified than I was to become a laboratory assistant, and that the chief reason why Canon Wilson offered me this minor post was that I should have much more time to continue my general studies and to work especially at science and mathematics.

As I had not completed my term of apprenticeship when I received this offer, my employer's consent to the cancelling of the indentures had to be obtained. He agreed to set me free on the payment of £5, which was kindly advanced to me by the chief science master at the College out of my first term's salary of about £15.

A new world of knowledge was thus opened to me and my heart and pursuits have been in it from that beginning. As laboratory assistant I had the care of instruments and materials required for the teaching of elementary physics and chemistry and was able to listen to the lessons given as well as to prepare the practical demonstrations of them. I had the great particular advantage of being able to use the equipment by myself in experiments and to have access to good textbooks of science and mathematics. I was also fortunate in being associated with the use of instruments in a small astronomical observatory at the College.

After about three years of this kind of work and study, I learnt that the Science and Art Department held examinations in these subjects every May, and I entered my name for several of them. The examinations were held throughout England, and from the results a few candidates were selected annually to take courses of training as science teachers at the Royal College of Science, South Kensington. I was fortunate in being one of these successful candidates, with the result that I received free education at the college for two years with a maintenance grant of one guinea a week in the terms. During the long vacation from June to

October, I did coaching and other jobs to earn means of living, including in one year the taking sole charge, for two months or so, of the sale of cameras and photographic materials at a small shop in Mortimer Street, off Oxford Street.

In the year 1885, when I left my native city for London, Ramsay MacDonald went there as a guide to a boys' and young men's club. At that time he thought of taking up science teaching as a career, and during his stay of nearly two years in Bristol he made a good collection of fossils by excursions to places of interest in the surrounding district. There was then a fine group of social and labour leaders in the city and Ramsay lodged in the house of one of them. Under this influence he joined a branch of the Social Democratic Federation. My father was one of this pioneer band of social reformers ; and from its school came Ben Tillett, who, like myself, was apprenticed to a bootmaker ; Jim O'Grady, who afterwards became Sir James O'Grady and High Commissioner in the Commonwealth of Australia ; and later, the present great statesman and Foreign Secretary, Ernest Bevin.

Each of these lives is an example of mastery of circumstances instead of passive acceptance of them, by choosing independently the road to follow. Ramsay MacDonald's early ambition was to become a science teacher and he retained his interest in scientific subjects throughout his life. It was almost by accident that he entered the field of the social sciences through the Labour Movement, but it was through his own personality and powers that he became the head of the movement as Prime Minister of the first Labour Government.

My own youth was lived in the same atmosphere as that which inspired Ramsay, and I still like to breathe it, but again almost by accident I entered another domain in which the air was different in its nurtural elements and was found by me congenial to growth. I do not suppose for a moment that Ramsay regretted devoting himself to a political career instead of to science, but he learnt in his later years how unstable is a reputation in it ; and on one occasion he said to me, in recollection of our early hopes and intentions : "You chose the better path."

While at the Royal College of Science I first came into contact with H. G. Wells, who was then also a science teacher in training there. He was my closest and dearest friend for more than sixty years afterwards, and he is as alive to me today in spirit as he has always been though his heart ceased to beat in the month of August, 1946. After leaving the college, each of us became engaged in science teaching, he first in private schools and then at a coaching institution in London, while I first became a science demonstrator at H.M. Dockyard School, Portsmouth, to return two years later to the college as a research assistant in astronomical physics under Sir Norman Lockyer.

Wells's career as a professional teacher came to an end in 1893, through a breakdown in health, and he then began to earn his living by writing reviews and articles for the periodical Press. Two years later, when his first book, *The Time Machine*, was published, he was recognized as a new star coming above the horizon of the world of letters, soon to reach the first magnitude in an international constellation. His life and mine came very close together in that period, and we continued to travel along parallel lines from much the same starting-point but always on my part with deep admiration of the brightness and power of his being. What we had in common was a training in powers of observation and experiment as ways and means of acquiring knowledge at first-hand and arriving at correct judgments from the evidence obtained. As teachers we had the experience of explaining to students what had been seen, done and found out, and that work had to be undertaken personally in order to understand its meaning.

Before our tracks in life became parallel and yet in the same direction, Wells had shown his genius of expression in contributions to educational and other periodicals. His *Textbook of Biology*, published in 1893, enabled many thousands of medical students and others—Lord Horder among them—to pass certain qualifying examinations successfully. Before that date, I had written three textbooks of Physiography, which means the study of natural things, properties and events on the earth and in the sky, and is now known as Everyday Science. I had also done a fair amount of abstracting scientific papers and writing articles for various journals, not so much for payment or other form of reward but because of the urge within us to learn and express ourselves, just as artists and poets do in their own fields.

When I became assistant editor of the weekly journal of science, *Nature*, in 1893, Wells also entered upon what became his life's work in another international field. We had found for ourselves conditions in which we could grow without restrictions placed upon us by the state of life to which we had been called by birth and early circumstances. Whether conditions of development are favourable or unfavourable, work has to be done in one way or another in order to live, with working well in what we have the capacity to do as the aim.

More satisfaction is found in this way of life than living mainly for pleasure. In whatever kind of daily labour anyone may be engaged, most people in modern communities have sufficient hours of leisure to express themselves in other constructive ways, not necessarily to change their everyday occupations but to cultivate their particular gifts and to find enjoyment in doing so. The greater the opportunities afforded for the development of these creative motives in association with other humanistic attributes, the higher will become the quality of civilized society. Many kinds of work are necessary to build such a structure, whether done willingly or unwillingly and with or without pride in what is done. The differences are illustrated in the following parable of three men engaged in everyday occupations and what they thought of their labours.

"Three stonecutters were at work, and a passer-by said to each in turn 'What are you doing?'

One said, 'I am cutting stone.'

The next replied, 'I am earning my living.'

The answer of the third was, 'I am building a cathedral.' "

This story may appropriately conclude what I have learnt from life : that work is a necessity and may be done in a mechanical way or to earn payment in one form or another, or with high ideals as its spirit. It is possible to combine all three purposes in shaping the structure of both life and society, each generation contributing its part to add strength and beauty to inspired designs.

MARY AGNES HAMILTON

Educated at Glasgow Girls' High School and Newnham College, Cambridge. Author of a score of books, of which the best known are biographies of leading figures in the Labour Movement. Represented Blackburn in the House of Commons from 1929–31 and was a Governor of the B.B.C. from 1933–37.

FIRST REACTION to this searching question is apt to be the unflattering suspicion that a longish opportunity of learning has not, in fact, taught one much. In my own case, I am painfully aware of the gap that separates the person that, in youth, I wanted to be and, at times, dreamed of one day becoming, from the person that today I am. There are aspects in which I have changed, and not for the better : others in which, alas, I have not changed, but remain what I then was.

This, though true, is not, however, the whole truth. The years have not taught me all they might, and certainly far less than I could have wished. Yet they have taught me something. The deposit is not grandiose. It is, rather, trite and lamentably simple. One merit, however, it has. It can be passed on. Others may make better use of it than I have been able to do. And it is, I am sure, quite fundamental.

It is connected, this deposit, with the backward look that carries regret for missed opportunities. The regret is there, for much that is gone; yet a definite admixture of relief accompanies it. The process we call growing up carries its compensations; indeed, to me, they are so significant that I find existence at once more tolerable and far more interesting now than I did when I was young. Disadvantages there are; I am not going to pretend that the physical decline that one notices in one's contemporaries if not always in oneself, while they certainly do notice it, is anything but very unpleasant. Lines on the face, grey in the hair, spectacles on the nose and so on are distressing to more than the vanity; the tendency of eyes, ears, feet to be, if still serviceable, not either as quick or as apt as they once were, is unmistakable and vexing. Worse is it to have to ask oneself: Is this outward deterioration the signal of inward decay?

That can happen. Sometimes it does happen. But it need not do so. One may be more readily tired. One need not be more readily bored. On that, my own answer is unequivocal. I find "the great globe itself" and the people who dwell in it more fascinating, not less. Interest in the whole business of being alive can be more acute for the adult, for the middle-aged, and even, low be it spoken, for the elderly, than for the young. It is an interest with a difference, of course; but that difference can make interest more sustained, more constant, and more vivid: not less. Experience enlivens, rather than deadens the mind, whatever it does to the body. This heightening of interest happens, I am convinced, because of, and in proportion to, a shift in the centre of interest itself which is, in turn, the signal of achieved adult status. When it occurs—and its doing so is in large degree a matter of normal experience—it brings with it "abundant recompense" for whatever is lost through the sheer passage of time. This shift I want to track down and describe.

On the threshold of that enterprise stands a robust lion. This is the inclination we all have to romanticize our own youth and even youth as such. It is, perhaps, as part of the price of war, an exceptionally active lion, at the present hour. Youth is, today, extolled, even worshipped. It is not, in part as a result of this attitude, understood. One element in this lack of understanding derives from a want of precision in dating. Since I want, for the sake of my argument, to draw the contrast between the state of being young and that of being adult, I need to get a little more precision than is common; thus, I am going to take youth, in the sense in which I shall use the term, as ending somewhere in the twenties. In my own case, I can mark the passage from being young to being grown-up as occurring when I was about twenty-three. I am quite aware than any such demarcation is most unlikely to find favour. The contemporary rating of youth carries far into the thirties. Once, J. M. Barrie said, "The stalls are full of twenty-nine"; today, for twenty-nine one would have to read at least thirty-nine, and confine the dictum neither to the stalls, nor to their feminine occupants. Since, with us, and, to an even more marked extent, in America, the "accent is on youth," a great many people take a great deal of trouble both to "feel young" and to be counted among the young by their acquaintances. There is something almost amounting to a cult of youth. The views of the young, as such, are sought for; to have "somebody young" on this or that body is now rated as important: second only to having "a woman." There is, in either case, much the same careless lumping together: all the young and all the females are put in one assimilated group, as though youth, like sex, carried such distinct differentiating characteristics as obliterate individual variety. This crude assimilation goes on although we have, after all, every one of us been young, and ought therefore to remember something about it.

Of course, on the physical side, the cult has useful aspects. It certainly is no bad thing that as many of us as possible should, if we can do so without being ridiculous, remain sensitive, active, energetic, athletic and slim as long as we can. It is a definitely good thing, for us and for the community, that we should go on working, and should hold off any slackening or hardening of the arteries of body and mind for as long as we can. Let us dance and swim; let us keep our windows open, in every sense. But it does also matter that we should realize what we are doing and not fancy that it is either possible or desirable to have the still healthy body enclose a mind which retains the special characteristics of youth. Alertness, zest, readiness to receive new impressions, the tolerance and candour which permit, nay compel, reversal of earlier judgment—these things are not the characteristic attributes of mental youth; they belong to mental maturity. Mental youth has characteristics which distinguish it and set it apart as a defined period in mental experience.

We are likely to be unfair to the young themselves, as well as mistaken in our interpretation of existence as a whole, unless we try to recapture, without romantic illusions about it, what that period felt like, while we were actually passing through it. Youth seen through the golden film of memory is one thing: youth as lived is, at any rate in one respect and that a respect which seems to me to be of vital significance, another. An incident comes back to me, from my childhood, on which I have often pondered since, and always found revealing. In the garden of our old home, my mother and my Aunt Jane were sitting under the great walnut tree, with their sewing; I lay flat on the grass beside them, reading. Across my absorption broke the voice of my aunt. Hers was a pleasing voice: deep, resonant, the voice of a natural singer; she always maintained that she might have been a great singer, but. . . I did not, as a matter of fact, often hear from that voice anything I wanted to hear; I did not, on this occasion.

"I do not see why she should go. After all, she's young. Going or not going won't matter to her. Being young is enjoyment enough in itself."

Her voice sharpened, as she spoke; it had, on the last phrase, an edge—a strange edge, since it was sharpened by envy. Envy of me, simply because I was young.

What the party of pleasure was of which she was anxious to have me deprived I have forgotten; I daresay I knew, at the time, that my mother would let me go, whatever my aunt said, if I much desired to do so. Instinctively, even then, I registered the deep difference between the two sisters and realized that my mother did not share in the envy animating my aunt, or take her position that to be young is, of itself, to be happy—so happy that no more is needed. What I did find odd was that my aunt, otherwise an intelligent person, could take this view, and, seeing youth as a time of carefree happiness, resented it in me because it was over for her. I have often met this resentment since; still more often, the error from which it derives.

In a sense, of course, the error is inevitable. By a merciful, but misleading dispensation, our minds are so constituted that pleasure holds, in retrospect, a sharper and more enduring stamp than pain. As incidents recede, the good colours come out while the less good tend to fade. So, in the past, summers were invariably sunny, at its parties the company was always well adjusted and agreeable, personally one felt well and never failed to shine. There were other occasions; they are blurred. With no conscious sense of re-arrangement of recollected facts, we see our young days as a period in which the grim fact of the world as we now know it did not press upon us but, pleased with others and above all with ourselves, we knew nothing of the defeated hopes, frustrated expectations, and disappointments, internal and external, which make up the normal texture of adult experience from day to day.

A resolute and objective inspection of personal experience will, in nine cases out of ten, dismiss this idyllic picture as nonsensical. On this, I claim to be a good witness. I could say, if I may borrow the charming title of Marie Belloc Lowndes's enchanting book: *I, too, have lived in Arcadia.* For me, conditions, in youth, were wholly favourable. My father and my mother were, individually, both good and gifted, while their companionship was the most nearly perfect I have ever known. I was one of a happy band of brothers and sisters, variously endowed and mutually warmly attached. We liked one another. We had good times together. Although my parents were by no means rich, we had enough; there was room in our house to have grand games of hide-and-seek, and also room to be alone, when one wanted that. The house overflowed with books, pictures, music, conversation, and the constant coming and going of friends of all sorts and all ages. Schooldays in town were diversified by long holidays in the country, where we walked and climbed, played tennis and cricket, swam and sailed. Somebody was always singing: everybody was always talking. If I could, with the mind and outlook I now have, dwell in those surroundings and in that company still, I should count myself fortunate, indeed. But if I had, in order to return to them, to pay the price of reviving the mind and outlook I then carried about with me, I should refuse the opportunity.

What was wrong? I could not, then, have seen, but I do now see, and I do not think my case was in this, peculiar. I had everything to make me happy then, but I was not happy, and the cause was within myself. Obstinately, then, I was the centre of my own universe, and judging, fatuously, the entire affair in terms of what it gave or might be expected to give me, I made myself wretched. Ill at ease within myself, I was morbidly sensitive. The trouble was simple enough and common enough: a self-enclosed and self-centred consciousness acted, continuously, as a stiff, impenetrable and most uncomfortable barrier to understanding the world I lived in and of which I was a part. I was haunted by a sense that, somehow, I did not fit. Minor disappointments and trifling, and generally imagined, slights, then assumed gigantic proportions. I can recall tiny incidents from that time which caused me a degree of pain—purely selfish pain—such as has seldom, in quite that lacerating and poisoned form, visited me since, on far greater occasion. I suppose that, somewhere deep within my unconscious mind, the knowledge brooded that all this misery, this sense of being out-at-elbows with the circumambient atmosphere, was my own fault. This, however, only served to give discomfort a peculiar taint; made it, somehow, obscurely shameful.

If this seems a false or exaggerated picture, turn to the autobiographers and to the novelists for their portrait of youth. With faithful accuracy—not in expressed statement, but in implied presentation—you will find youth delineated there as dominated by a sense, on the part of the subject, of not being at home in the universe. The fault is, often, attributed rather to the universe than to the percipient, and this is true to nature ; so one feels the contrast, when one is young. Maladjustment rules the scene: the young man or young woman, whether with pride or, less often, with shame, is conscious of being an alien in a hostile environment. The world is not what he or she had expected ; it proves, on first real contact, so unlike previous dreams that anger and resentment, contempt for companions in it, inclination to smash the scheme entire, take possession. The whole confused orchestration of experience is dominated by a horrid unresolved and largely unresolvable discord.

In fiction, where this theme recurs and has yielded a series of most notable and essentially truthful portraits, one often finds that although the discord between the self and the not-self, which constitutes the major underlying theme, is recorded with penetrating particularity, its underlying explanation is slurred, or not perceived, even by the writer. His concern, after all, is to give a sympathetic and recognizable picture of the sufferings of his hero and heroine ; to set them before us as they are. So, their outlook is delineated, and with brilliance ; seldom however is it probed. The case of the reader however can be different. Studying the portrait of another, and recognizing in it traits that belong to himself, he knows, from within, that what is wrong is not the world—bad and difficult as that may seem to him—but the attitude of the subject to it : his absorption in himself, his demands on it for himself. In effect, the self blocks any vision of the not-self. If, armed with this recognition, he looks back over his own childhood and youth, stripping off the veils with which an unconscious piety has shrouded them, he will discern the explanation of the deep malaise he then carried about with him and comprehend what gave edge to pangs he often prefers, now, to forget.

In my own case, I find, when I look back, that the shadow of myself, from which I did not, then, know how to escape, was cast over the whole of an otherwise lovely landscape. That is why, although I had everything, then, to make me content and keep me eager, I was not content. That I did not understand what was wrong made it worse. Now, I can see that the cause was an egocentrism from which I had not then learned how to free myself.

Growing up has its drawbacks. I know, and do not want to underrate them. Yet none of them can be weighed against the release that comes when one breaks out of self-enclosure. Curiously enough, this phenomenon is today more generally recognized for what it is when it is stated in national than in individual terms. The danger to itself and other of the egocentric nation, angrily claiming self-sufficiency and a "place in the sun": unable to achieve adult recognition of the fact that it can only grow in proportion as it accepts a place within a whole which is more than the sum of its parts—this is plain to all. And yet we go on acclaiming the individuals who will not grow up as though they were accomplishing a natural miracle, and sympathize with their moans about the passage of the years over their heads, although these moans import no more than that the moaners are suffering from self-arrested development.

Release is, in any event, largely independent of external circumstance. I grew up in a world that looked safe and held great prospects for its inhabitants ; in a period when it was the common belief of intelligent persons that progress was an almost automatically operating rule, while its worst enemy, war, was something that could be counted out. The whole of this optimistic apparatus was smashed in 1914. It has never been possible to rebuild it on its old easy basis. After a second and far more terrible war, we inhabit a world from which the very idea of security is banished. Political interest and concern were active in my home and I have never ceased to be a highly political animal ; the horrors of 1914–18, the shame and anguish of Munich, the appalling experiences of the Nazi threat to life and its values—these things have not passed me by ; the pain of them is deeply etched in my consciousness. And yet I had rather be myself, as I am now, than revert to the self I carried about with me when I was young.

Don't let me idealize, however. I am not claiming that, except in one significant respect, I have changed as much as I could wish. Far is it from my mind to assume an achieved self-mastery or an established steady philosophy which make me immune to shocks. There is one respect in which I have learned : one change which has been accomplished. It is significant and even important, because it is capable of being described and passed on. But it is limited and simple and I do not want to exaggerate it. Let me, therefore, before I attempt to set it out, admit, with painful candour, that there are aspects of youth that I do regret and that acutely. I am not here thinking mainly of the fact that the face is lined, the feet and eyes easily tired, and the mind sets itself, unwillingly and with a stubborn resistance that requires effort to overcome, to new tasks. These things one accepts, obviously ; they are the common lot ; most of one's close friends endure them, too, with such cheerfulness as they can muster.

Harder far is it to cope with the doubt that vexes intermittently, in weaker moments, whether life—i.e. the fact of having been for x years in the world—has done what it might, if I had co-operated better in its teachings. Then, looking at faults and failings which the years have taught me to conceal but not to cure, I recognize that I have not learned to be the person that in girlhood, I imagined myself becoming. When, over the gap, I look back on that girl, I see in her very much the same shortcomings, the same errors, follies, and failures of sense and temper that continue to vex me. I hoped, then, that when I grew up, I might be like my father or my mother. I am not, alas, like them ; I am like "myself when young." It is a pity. A catalogue would be boring ; I will only mention that an inclination to hurry, in thought and action, to glance at papers without fully mastering them, to dash at obstacles, without fully measuring them, to rely on intuitions instead of going through the careful process of rational judgment, remain. *Festina lente* is a motto I admire, but do not practise. And so on.

I mention this, in the interest of honesty. It is a pity. But, there it is, and one learns to make terms with and not worry back over it. Moments of dismal self-inspection are, nowadays, moments only. The subject is, after all, one of which one has had time to get tired. One knows it, backwards. One knows that neither self-reproach nor good resolutions are going, at this date, to help much. One is, what one is. The map, for better or worse, is familiar; its main outlines are not now going to change. Why waste time on being sorry that certain features are as they are? Once, disappointments had an edge of surprise that made one beat about to find some cause for them, outside oneself. Not so now ; when things go wrong one is ready to recognize that it is probably not the fault of somebody else or of the universe, which therefore requires smashing, but one's own. One lays the blame in the right quarter.

Here is the crux of the matter. One lesson one can learn which, if laid to heart, removes from adult existence the unintelligible weight that rests upon youth. It can be summed up in a single sentence : Get out of your own light. Cease measuring up existence in terms of what it gives, and does not give, you. Cease reducing its range and scope to the cramping gauge of yourself. Man may be the measure of all things, but Me very decidedly is not. Me is the wrong end of the telescope. Turn it round; look out, instead of in, and the baffled sense of imprisonment will be transformed into wonder. You will gradually begin to take in a scene for whose apprehension no span of years can be long enough, and of companions on your journey through time and space in whom, as rarely in yourself, you can see the good which, mixed in with evil in every human creature, can yet translate and redeem it. Part of the pain of youth lies in its pervasive sense of separateness: of isolation. That pain in its turn drives from self-enclosing blinkers which block the light. To the question that haunts the young: "What is the point of my being here?" there is only Meredith's "dusty answer" so long as the operative word is "my."

So soon, on the other hand, as one gets out of one's own light enough to perceive companions and recognizes them as the essential feature of the landscape, the whole thing shifts into focus. And, unless one is extraordinarily unfortunate in circumstances or in native composition, this recognition happens, as one grows up. It is the great compensation. Loneliness loses its sharpest sting when the apprehension dawns that the suffering it causes is not unique, a doom spoken upon one because of some failure or failing in onself, but a sensation common as breathing, infinitely mitigable by sympathy, almost wholly remitted when the mind and feelings are cast, imaginatively, into the experiences of somebody else. Swift on the heels of the discovery of this deep human similarity comes the thrill of finding it partnered by a fascinating and endless diversity. You know—or think you know—all about yourself; no life is long enough to enable you to know all about other people. With yourself you may well be bored: it is a book you have read too often; not with them, unless you are tone deaf and colour blind.

The best gift that could be asked of the Fairy Godmother is, plainly, an inclination to like one's companions on the common journey. For those who possess that, the business of growing up without vain regret is easy. To democracy, the natural creed for a grown-up world, and, at the same time, the indispensable condition for bringing such a world into existence, they take, like ducks to water. Adventure, absorbing and stimulating, opens up before them ; they know what the point is, and why they are here. The point, quite patently, is something that can be realized only by action with and through others, and is, throughout, for them as well as by them. Appreciation of their illimitable variety and gradual comprehension of what makes it—here is matter of inexhaustible interest ; to the excitement of the emerging pattern there is no limit.

An inclination to like people is a gift. If not born with the silver spoon of spontaneous friendliness in mouth, you must for your own sake far more than for that of the companions of your pilgrimage, cultivate the curiosity that leads, at worst, to tolerance, at best, to sympathy. In so far as you know yourself, you know your own shortcomings, and will not therefore expect others to give you, individually, what, individually, you do not give them. Very likely, however, despite hardly acquired self-acquaintance, you start off with the notion that you are going to find, somewhere in the world, one person who will make up to you for all the failings you find in, and the disappointment you cause to, yourself ; someone who will complete you and finally end your sense of isolation by giving you that comprehending companionship which, where realized, is the highest happiness known to man. Very likely, however, you will *not* find that person, or he or she will not find you. Why should you, being the imperfect thing you are? The human endowment that can yield perfect mutual companionship is as rare as any other genius. But if you miss the one, the many remain : friendship, with its lovely varying facets, is an affair rather of giving than of taking. If you are ready to begin by giving and don't wait to be given, and refuse to let your interest dull or dry up, friends will not fail you—unless you demand of them a faultlessness you cannot offer in your turn.

Interest here is a safer initial guide than liking, yet, liking is apt to follow, where interest is sufficiently acute and genuinely disinterested. Here, in fact, comes one of the many intriguing paradoxes of human intercourse. The quick and casual eye discerns faults in others more readily than merits in them ; it is easy, too easy, to be "clever" at the expense of your acquaintance and even of your friends ; easy, too easy, to apply to other people a standard very much more severe than any which you expect them to apply to you. Characterization through defects is at once swifter and more effective than characterization through qualities. Every novelist knows, and most readers, while they are reading, realize that it takes more imaginative insight, as well as more professional skill, to give life-likeness to the "good" character than to the "bad." At the same time, readers know that the ultimate test of the artist is the extent to which he is capable of creating persons who achieve verisimilitude in that, in this like our friends, they excite affection and rouse sympathetic concern, no matter what their faults may be. It is, for any writer with adequate skill, a comparatively light matter to portray the shadow side of men or women ; far more is asked of him if he is to show, shining through the mingle of qualities which belong to a real personality, the glow of recognizable actuality. Yet it is when, and only when, this feat is accomplished that we salute the master who reflects the world as it is and people as they are. Not dissimilar is it with our personal approach to our fellows. To the careless eye, the eye of limited interest and quick impatience, they appear a dull, featureless assemblage, differentiated only when their foibles are pulled out. If so, the incurious eye punishes its owner by condemning him to ennui and isolation.

If liking be a gift, interest is a faculty that grows by what it feeds on and can be stimulated and perfected by training. This, in its turn, simply means practice—practice in the habit of looking out, rather than in, and in the inclination to be fully wherever you are and not, in spirit, somewhere else. The two go together ; the self-absorbed are, always, somewhere else : hence a continuing sense of maladjustment. The password to release is simple—the concentration of attention. Inattention carries ennui in its train ; concentrated attention is its prophylactic. If fully aware of the people around you, the people with whom you are working and living, it will be a strange chance if you do not find some of them more than interesting. If you give your entire energy to doing and understanding whatever may be your job, the effort to master it, to do it as well as it can be done, will generate interest in it, no matter what it is. People sometimes groan that life is dull for everybody except the artist. In a sense they are right; what however they leave out is that the *kind* of happiness known by the artist is available to anyone who will fully open eyes and ears to the panorama of which he is part, and go through the discipline necessary to master and control the instrument of his attention. Then, carried out of himself, he will know in degree the satisfaction of the artist, concentrated with entire devotion on something other than himself, for which his self is but the necessary trained instrument. Devotion is the essential. There are, of course, in real life as well as in fiction and on the stage, artists who are primarily individualists, and block their own light on the grand excuse that they are in themselves their instruments of vision. But not the individualism but the absorption, the concentrated attention, makes the artists, in the valid sense of a much abused word, a romantic figure.

All very well, someone may say at this point; we can't all be artists. Can't we? Perhaps not, if the word be used in its limited, technical sense. Even here, however, education directed with enough imagination would, I believe, disclose in everyone some line or other of strictly artistic response. Nothing for instance has happened in my period more exhilarating than the disclosure, through a newer type of schooling, of musical faculty and enjoyment in the children of a nation long satisfied to put itself down as unmusical. Something of the same kind is going on, too, in the field of visual appreciation. This apart—and the possibilities, here, are boundless—there remains, open to all of us, the more humble but still sufficiently exciting task of getting whatever happens to be our job done as well as possible. Anything done half-heartedly is dull: anything done with total devotion yields interest and a zest that is akin to the zest of the artist. Typing, jam making, bricklaying, dusting, accounting—anywhere, everywhere, "The readiness is all": attention is all. And what is true of more or less mechanical jobs is far more true of those that bring us into relation with our fellows. To get a group of persons to work as a group, each putting his best into the pool and all enjoying a slow achievement such as none could accomplish singly—there is no game in the world that holds such sustained and various excitement.

Implicit, I admit, in what I have written is the assumption that what one is after is a special kind of adventure—the adventure of understanding the universe in which one sojourns and one's fellows on the journey through it. By that I stand. The egotists who, triple armed in complete self-confidence, never know the pangs of maladjustment or the disappointment inherent in the process of growing up, I do not envy. In so far as they escape the pangs of awakening consciousness, they may be lucky, but they are blind. Sight brings its penalties, of course ; but understanding, however imperfect, is what gives ultimate and lasting zest to the entire process of experience. It may be expensive to be, as Henry James put it, "Finely aware and richly responsible ;" certainly, you pay for what you get ; but what you get is something that keeps you going, and keeps the whole thing, including your trifling part in it, worth while. I am not thinking of the fact, although it is a fact, that the egotist, sooner or later, crashes on his own egotism: then, finding himself in an isolation unknown to the man who has always been aware of his dependence on, and concern in the fate of, the others, he stares out into an unfamiliar universe of desolating and irredeemable bleakness. I am thinking rather of the essential emptiness of the period of his apparent success. He is then, as later, an ignoramus, cut off from understanding : living, in so far as he can be said to live at all, on a sub-human plane. His working assumption has been, inevitably, that there is no light. He is, in fact, a savage.

For those, on the other hand, in whom the sense of the others who make the world for them has once dawned, Swinburne's words may well hold:

> Enough of light is this for one life's span
> That all men born are mortal, but not man.

Here is the life-spring of the democratic creed ; the dynamic of Socialism, which is, in its turn, the complete expression of democracy. One does not have, in order to be a democratic Socialist, to entertain a romantic view of human nature ; all one needs is a constant and unfaltering recollection of the mingle of good and evil that make up the human norm, including oneself. Holding firmly to that fact of direct experience, one can again echo Henry James, whose insight into the human creature was as straight as it was subtle, and repeat his profound and searching dictum; "After all, the great thing is to give. It's what plays one least false." The egotist is, by a mysterious but inescapable law, compelled to think meanly of his fellows and, therefore, to deny the existence of light. The eye turned consistently inwards tends to despair of human nature. The eye turned outwards, like the heart attuned to care about the fate of its companions, not only finds that this direction "plays you least false :" it achieves, at the same time, a positive reassurance. Connecting the human landscape with the quiet of the sky, it becomes, stage by slow stage, aware of an often hidden but nevertheless steadily interpenetrating light. Then one can say with Rilke that, whatever the shape of one's individual place in the scheme, and even if it be one mainly dedicated to distress, one knows that the whole, the glorious tapestry, has a design, which one sees and accepts.

Wordsworth knew all about this design, this interpenetrative light, that one may block, and in youth does block, but can learn to see and to walk by. I have been constantly aware, as I have been writing, of the likelihood that he may be quoted against me, above all when I have ventured to express relief and gratitude for the fact that I am no longer young. Did he not proclaim that:

> Heaven lies about us in our infancy ;
> Shades of the prison house begin to close
> Upon the growing boy

and sigh that the Youth "must travel daily farther from the East"? He did. But, being a poet, he used words with an exact and not a casual sense of their meaning. He knew the distinction between the innocence of childhood and the ignorance of youth. Although he does not stay, since it was no part of his business to do so, to analyse the nature of the "prison house" in which the young immure themselves, he knew all about it, and about the windows that may be opened from it. At the close of his *Intimations*, he indicates both its essential shape and structure, and the way of escape:

> Thanks to the human heart by which we live,
> Thanks to its tenderness, its joys, and fears

another race can be run : other palms can be won. In the glorious *Lines Written Above Tintern Abbey*, he carries the demonstration a stage further. There he is concerned to delineate how the passing of youth, with its "glad, animal movements" and their rapturous realization of nature, instead of carrying with it loss has, in fact, brought infinite gain ; "other gifts have followed ; for such loss, I would believe, Abundant recompense." He has, in fact, learned not only to hear "the still, sad music of humanity," but to be aware of :

> A presence that disturbs me with the joy
> Of elevated thoughts ; a sense sublime
> Of something far more deeply interfused,
> Whose dwelling is the light of setting suns,
> And the round motion, and the living air,
> And the blue sky, and in the mind of man. . ."

Of man—not of Me. One can, and does, see it in Man when, and only when, one has ceased to be primarily concerned to see it in Me. Me is the great block, the block to authentic vision, the distorter of values. Me has got, as they say in my native Scotland, to be "sorted," nay, "sided." That done, one can begin to see.

SIR MILES THOMAS

Born in 1897, and after a short experience as an engineering pupil, enlisted in the ranks in the First World War. Was commissioned to the R.F.C. and awarded the D.F.C. after services in Africa, the Middle East and Russia. Joined Lord Nuffield's organization in 1924 and was Vice-Chairman from 1940 to 1947, when he devoted himself to Empire industrial and aerial developments.

I WAS a lonely child. Father died when I was a year old; I have no recollection of him at all. My mother, who had come from the Derbyshire dales to the Welsh marches when she married, had not met a very wide circle of people when she became a widow. After babyhood, I was left very much to my own resources. My first image of my mother is of a very busy woman, bustling about with rent books and ledgers; talking to plumbers, odd-job men, and a whole tribe of be-smocked and aproned carpenters and the like who used to invest the house in the morning. On her energetic shoulders devolved the burden of seeing that our heritage of "property"—mostly middle-class cottages, semi-detached houses and the like—was kept in good repair and yielding a steady income.

For this task she showed an aptitude that, in later years, I realized was of a very high order for a girl taken from the entirely dissimilar environment of mixed farming. It must have been a far cry from the almost self-contained economy of a Victorian agricultural scene, with its social activities linked directly to seasonal events—harvest homes, shooting parties, hunts, livestock shows and such like—to the hard bargaining monotony of keeping tenants satisfied with repair work without over-spending out of rents that had to be adjusted shrewdly as occasion demanded.

Apart from a vague succession of village girls who shepherded me to the local school (they were all called Janet, it seemed to me), the other person I best remember is a dear old lady who lived with us and ran the house. She was deaf—not stone deaf, but hard of hearing—and I think her insistence that I "spoke up" and enunciated clearly has had a lasting effect on my vocal habits. Nothing is worse than a person who shouts or addresses his fellow men as though they were a public meeting. Equally, one of the greatest lessons that life has taught me is the immense importance of the uttered word.

By a man's speech—the ability that distinguishes the human from the animal—one gets an immediate summation of so many factors in his character that it is surprising more people do not trouble to cultivate not only what they say but how they say it.

Living, as we did, on the northern borders of Wales, near Wrexham, our local dialect was a mixture of the rhythmic cadences of the Welsh-speaking peoples and the unaccented English of Cheshire. It may be wishful thinking, but when, in later years, I was told that in that particular district the purest intonation was to be found, I firmly believed it.

My whole childhood was unencumbered by any strong family influences. I had no brothers or sisters and no relatives nearer than Derbyshire ; so I had plenty of time—now and then perhaps too much time—to think. Maybe I became introspective ; but certainly I developed a habit, that has never left me, of being quite content with my own company. And as soon as I could read I devoured books voraciously.

Father had had a bent for applied mechanics, although his business was one of merchandizing and real estate. But the lively interests of the beginning of the twentieth century had attracted him, and he had collected a few shelf-fuls of books that explained how the steam engine worked, the principles of electricity, hydraulics and the like. Those books, with their diagrammatic sketches and explanatory legends ("The piston 'A' is connected to the crank 'B,'" etc.) fascinated me, and I know that my soul cried out in revolt when, one day, I heard mother say to some friends that she hoped I would be either a doctor or a clergyman.

My own idea was that I should be an engineer: it always has been, and still is, my great disappointment that circumstances in the past forty years have conspired to prevent me from being a better engineer. In its various high aspects, there is, to my mind, no more noble profession.

I always wanted to make things work, either with my own hands or through the mental processes that we broadly call administration. And that brings me to two most valuable lessons of life. One is the importance of encouraging young people to use their hands, to gain manipulative dexterity and a sympathetic touch. Your die-hard huntin', shootin' and fishin' fraternity will scoff maybe when I say that just as there is virtue in a rider who, through his reins, can convey to his horse the precise message of direction he desires, so there is equal value in hands that can feel through a spanner when a nut is fully tight, when the metal is sprung without being stretched beyond its elastic limit. Sense of touch is one of the fundamental means of human expression.

The other point is that children should be allowed to choose their own professions. Young folk of today are very intelligent and discriminating well before they get into their 'teens. My daughter decided, before she was twelve, that she wanted to be a doctor. There is no seafaring tradition in either my wife's family or mine, but our boy announced one day when he was eleven years old that he wanted to go into the Navy. We applauded their choices at once.

They have both worked hard to achieve their objectives—harder than they could have been expected to work at any vocation chosen for them.

I believe that self-inspired decisions or even wishes in young people—and, indeed, in older people—should be given scope and encouragement. It makes for self-reliance and develops individual initiative. Let people do what they like doing. The sparks of interest and initiative are good kindling for warmth of effort.

Equally, my experience has been that it is disappointing or, at least, unprofitable, to expect young people to show a steady straight-line development of character. Many a lad who is the apple of his father's eye at twelve years old becomes an acute source of worry and foreboding as he passes through the awkward seventeen to eighteen phase.

I, myself, was fortunate. The First World War began soon after I left school. I had a few months as a premium pupil at Bellis and Morcom's engineering works in Birmingham, but soon decided to join up. It wasn't that I was particularly inspired by high ideals of saving civilization or avenging Belgian atrocities. It was simply that everyone else of my age and circle was joining up—all the fellows who were nice to know, anyway—and so I enlisted, as a private, in the Motor Machine Gun Corps.

I say that was fortunate for me because I again came under disciplinary control. When I left the sheltered precincts of public school, I, not unnaturally, took too much advantage of the newly found freedom. I believe most boys do the same. To my way of thinking, that time of freshly tasted independence is a critical period in the lives of most young men.

Up to that moment one has been maintained out of family funds. Few parents discuss in detail their financial standings with their children. They do their best—often at great sacrifice—to preserve them from any inferiority complex while at school. The youngster gets the idea that where some money has come from, more can be found.

And the human animal, being lazy and greedy and fond of fashionable pleasure, is apt to dip too heavily into the family coffer instead of getting down to the task of earning a good living.

I believe that some of the most unfortunate young men are those who have been left an income just big enough to dull the keen edge of personal endeavour. Too great a feeling of security, of having a snug little haven to shirk into if the storm on the road ahead seems too boisterous, is no spur to progress.

Naturally, it is part of a man's endeavour to build an estate that will keep his widow in comfort and the standard of living to which she has been accustomed during his life-time ; and to permit her, if need be, to carry out the full educational and life-launching responsibilities due to their children. Conversely, I cannot see that inherited wealth should enable offspring to live lives of ease, non-productive and dissipated. I'm no Socialist, but it seems to me fundamental that the extent to which anyone enjoys the good things of this life should depend on the contribution that they themselves make to the common pool. A child is entitled to receive the education and launching appropriate to the social strata in which he or she has been born. In Lancashire they used to say that families went from clogs to clogs in three generations. Surely that trite comment is a justifiable criticism of the policy of letting rich men's sons run foot-loose.

I have never had the opportunity of enjoying it myself, but have always held the theory that, instead of a boy going straight to the university from school, and then on to a business or professional career, he could, with advantage, go from school into an office or factory for a year or two, and thereafter go to the university. In that way, I hold, he would be far better equipped to absorb benefit from university life.

Living near Oxford for a number of years has provided opportunity for noticing the entirely different ways in which advantage is taken or not taken of the self-reliant type of life that is encouraged at the university. Most of the youths who come up nowadays realize that they must equip themselves for earning a living. Pressure of national economics determines that. But here and there are boys who seem to prefer to specialize in what they call enjoying themselves.

In any event, a lad who has seen something of business from the inside, realizes how much, even in the most technical spheres, success in life depends on knowing how to handle men, rather than to operate machines. A boy with this background is so much better equipped because he knows what he wants to learn. He is a seeker after applied knowledge, rather than a receptacle that is hurriedly filled to the brim with facts, figures and phrases during the last few weeks of term so that he can spill them out again in the examination hall.

I believe that the policy of conscription, to which this country is now committed, will have a very beneficial effect on the general standard of our manhood. For one thing, the years of army life should have a lasting effect on the average physique, and to my mind there is no doubt that what one gets out of life depends very considerably upon one's bodily health.

When we are young the power of self-analysis is, quite naturally, not very strongly developed. Therefore we do not consciously associate our mood with our health. Only when one reaches years of greater maturity, does one realize the truth of the would-be humorous saying that "Life depends on the liver." For assuredly, if we are physically out of sorts, our mental processes lack the clarity and certainly the creative ability that they possess when the whole system is toned up by normal good health.

Perhaps the young man's first excursion into the realms of inter-relationship between the thought processes and the functions of the body are experienced in the dentist's chair—the wild dreams that surge through the mind, induced by the anæsthetic and sharpened by the shock of nervous disruption. Or, in milder form, the turgid nightmares that follow an upset digestion due to a heavy late meal.

The human system being what it is—self-adjusting within wide limits—there is a tendency for too little care to be given to the health of young people by themselves. In quite natural abhorence of being thought soft or unmanly, boys and young men will deliberately overstrain their physical endurance. This does not matter so much, I have found, on the field of sport, as Nature sets a definite limit to muscular activity.

It is in more social accomplishments that the unduly competitive spirit is harmful. Whatever idealists may say, there is no arguing the fact that—again because we are animals—we are all automatically competitive. Whether we exhibit that competition by running races, by mental inventiveness, or by personal adornment, it is the natural tendency of every worth-while human to make faster progress than his fellow.

The thin veneer of civilization doesn't hide the law of the jungle—a fact very evident today. While a great deal of lip-service is being paid to the necessities for peace, the material provisions for warlike activity—even if only under the guise of preventive measures—are being made all over the world.

The social aspect of this competitive spirit exhibits itself quite healthily in the young if it spurs them to greater mental endeavour or the cultivation of more charming mannerisms that make them more pleasant people. But its harmful effects can become apparent when they exhibit themselves in forms of harder drinking, heavier smoking and more rakish achievements than the next man.

The young male is peculiarly prone, I have found, to stimulations of this kind. At college or at the club it is generally considered a worthy thing to be a fellow who holds his drink well—the equivalent of the old three-bottle man. It is not until later in life that one sees the cumulative havoc played on the human system by excess of this kind during youth and middle age, and realizes how fierce can be the delayed action of excessively hard living on even the best physique.

And physically, of course, we are not all built the same. One man's drink may be another man's downfall, and a lesson that life has taught me is that everyone must make his own measures in these matters. I am as keen on good living as the next man, but I hold that one of the social encumbrances of our present age is the "treating" habit that makes it necessary for every member of a party to "stand a round" of drinks, whenever a casual gathering of acquaintances get together. Today there is an economic curb on this fashion : stringency brings some reward, at least.

I stress this matter because life in the Services and in business has impressed upon me fully the importance of maintaining at as high a standard as possible one's physical fitness. Up to the age of twenty-five, one is apt to take one's body for granted, assuming that because it has never been troublesome, it will recover quickly from being overtaxed ; and that it doesn't object to irregularities in the way of meals, sleep and muscular rest. By forty, one has realized these things are important, and by fifty one realizes the human machine has a rhythm that must be maintained, and that the important thing is regularity of habits.

Look at all our great men, and what do you find? Not giants of stature, not men of great physical strength, but men who know how to preserve the efficient functioning of their bodies. In this matter mental training plays almost as important a part as do exercise and sleep.

There has grown up during the past decade a considerable interest in psycho-analysis. Much study has been devoted to the effect of the mental state on the physical system. It is usually done under external guidance, but I believe that, without becoming unduly introspective, one can, with a little thought, exercise the predominant factors of psycho-analysis for oneself.

Here again, quiet—if not solitude—is a great help. Some people have got themselves into the frame of mind that they cannot bear to be alone. I believe that, without being a recluse, one can usefully spend a great deal of time in contemplation, and with a little practice can learn to do it at all kinds of odd moments. The difficulty is to prevent an active mind from running away on its own, as it were, and getting into the realms of day-dreaming. It is rather like a motor-car engine racing away in neutral without doing any work. The more controlled thinking that one does in solitude, the easier it becomes, and there are many ways of stimulating the process, such as walking alone, or better still, by sitting quietly in the presence of someone near and dear to you.

That companionship must always be violently vocal is something that I have never been able to understand. To me, the sublimation of the highest form of friendship is the ability to sit in silence, happy in the knowledge that one is probably thinking the same unspoken thought as one's companion.

My wife and I usually take turns when driving on a long journey, and we have frequently covered twenty or thirty miles without speaking. Many is the time that when we do start conversing again we automatically pick up the same topic—we had been thinking along exactly parallel lines—about the same place and the same people and same interests.

Maybe there is some form of telepathy in the process. The spheres in which the mind operates are really, as yet, unplumbed regions. In my experience, however, it is more profitable to spend time in creative thought or contemplation, than to fritter it away in arid periods of redundant gossip.

My advice, then, to the man entering any business or profession is for him to pay particular attention to his own bodily fitness. Too frequently have I come across people who have said that, as long as they get to the office at the appointed hour, what they do in their own time is their own and no one else's business.

I would beg strongly to differ from that point of view. The difference between the executive staff worker and the man on the factory floor is sometimes said to be that, whereas the staff man is expected to think about his business at all hours of the day and to mould his life round his occupation, the line worker can stop thinking about his job as soon as the whistle blows and he is an entirely free agent until he starts again at the factory the next morning.

I submit that the apprentice or improver who takes that point of view is apt to miss something. The young man who turns up to work in a physical condition below par by reason of his social exuberance is not likely to find promotion come his way or his earning capacity increase as rapidly as the fellow who looks after himself.

In the same way I regard it as important that people choose for themselves a congenial occupation. One of the great freedoms of this life should be the freedom to work gainfully at a task that pleases one. Life has taught me that unless a man is happy in his working hours, he will never be happy at all. A major disservice that has been dealt to humanity in recent years is the spreading of the impression that modern industry is a soulless, character-destroying job because of the rapidity of the processes involved.

People who expound views of that kind have not seen the inside workings of a modern, efficient factory. The conveyers or belt assembly systems were not put in by production engineers to depress the standard of intelligence of the operators. They are merely methods of getting work from one place to another while saving the operator from unnecessarily expending energy on moving his own body from place to place, or, alternatively, using his own strength to move the job to within his area of operation.

A man working on a moving assembly line can exhibit just as much craftsmanship and skill in doing his job well as can artisans in other spheres. Whether one does a few operations frequently or a whole series of operations at less frequent intervals is largely a matter of training and aptitude. There is no less dignity in one than in the other.

And here, I think, there is another lesson for the young man coming into business. It is that there are just as many gentlemen working at the bench as there are sitting in board rooms. When I was in uniform in the First World War I traversed the ranks from private to major. In the industrial sphere I have been fortunate to have had experience at all levels : from a grimy-fingered pupil who was paid six shillings a week for turning valve guides on an engine lathe, through machine shop and offices to the responsible position of sitting with very experienced administrators.

I have found that the British workman is fundamentally the "salt of the earth." He is very fair-minded, he is kind, he is basically honest, and he is amazingly well-read. At times he is a little emotional and he is subject to the impact of oratory. That our industrial system today has exhibited certain tendencies to be dislocated and ragged in its attempts at resettlement after the wartime upheaval is, I think, due to the fact that, in the main, management is woefully inarticulate.

I have, I think, sufficiently indicated my dislike of the garrulous man. Equally, life has taught me that we are living in a period when the ability of self-expression is an increasingly important factor in the art of leadership.

One of the most useful analyses that can be made at the present time is the relationship between advertising, publicity, industrial management and plain personal ballyhoo.

I strongly commend the young man coming into business to give thought to these matters so that he can differentiate between the good effects that accrue from kindly and honest utterances of an acknowledged leader, and the catch-penny mouthings of a sawdust Cæsar.

It is in matters of this kind that I admittedly find myself still confused, to some extent, today. Whether a man be engaged in a business or a profession, the impact of modern politics, either local or national, is bound, sooner or later, to be felt on his disposition. The more responsibility one assumes, and the wider one's circle of activities, the nearer one approaches the cloudy region wherein the political weather is formed, and from whence comes alternately sunshine and rain.

At some period or other one has to make up one's mind to what extent one will or will not become associated with such activities. It seems to me that a good rule to follow is the principle of doing whatever one does with gusto or leaving it alone ; that one should either embark on politics as a career or keep it at arm's length.

But, here again, my limited experience indicates that the main attribute necessary in public life is first-class physique, supporting mental equipment that can think fast and formulate coherent phrases on the spur of the moment.

In these days there seem to be two ways of making progress up the mountainside of life from the dour valleys below to the sun-swept upland. One is to plod doggedly up the zigzag paths of hard endeavour, gathering experience at every turn and emerging at the top, maybe a little breathless and inarticulate, but well versed and tempered by the ardours of the way.

The other method is to be rocketed brilliantly by oratorical frenzy straight to the summit. From that vantage point can be shouted vicarious advice to the toilers on the road below, and even offers made of guidance to those quite near the summit.

That, it seems to me, is something of a parallel to what happens today. Business executives who have earned the right to assume great responsibility by reason of their experience, find that political processes have suddenly put into positions of power men whose progress has short-circuited the normal methods. These people proceed to teach the business man his business, and, what is more, they do so with sincerity and good faith which are founded on the belief that their broad and very flexible outlook enables them to treat matters more fundamentally than can the trade executive who has spent his whole life studying the problems of his own business or industry.

In this respect, life has taught me the value of tolerance. One must see the other fellow's point of view and realize that, shallow as is the shelf of mob-oratory, the public, in normal times, have a disconcerting habit of being right in the long run and their selection of opinion is usually backed by some useful foundation.

In matters of this kind, one must learn to value an optimism born of sound faith. Successful men accomplish tasks and overcome difficulties which to the unbelieving seem insuperable. They do this because of their conviction that right must triumph. Moreover, a person who has faith in his conviction and continues to direct his efforts towards a given target will frequently find his efforts crowned with success if only because of their consistency.

It is far better to struggle over a stony road in the right direction, than to meander on smooth, winding paths.

I have known men in business who made a success of their undertakings simply because of their strength of character. They were not brilliant, but they were dogged. They chose one objective at a time and never veered from striving to reach it until they had attained their goal.

Their contribution to the welfare of the community and, incidentally, to their own well-being, is far greater than the dilettante vacillation of the man who lets his mind run riot, attracted one day by this bright idea, only to flutter to some other superficially shining project before the first is reached.

The first type of man is apt to be called lucky by his friends and acquaintances. The second kind calls himself unlucky.

Much as I believe that there is no such thing as pure luck, I do concede that it plays a minor part in the affairs of all of us. Its incidence is so capricious that it is difficult to find any logical basis for assuming that predestination is a supportable creed. Equally, I believe that the effect of fate can be minimized, with care. Or, to put the same thing in another way, good luck can be cultivated by intelligent recognition of an opportunity when it presents itself; but it must be backed up by an unflagging determination to work harder than the next man to make use of whatever opportunity comes along.

It is in that sincerity of effort, coupled with a deep religious conviction that our time on earth is intended to be spent in making a useful contribution to the progress of humanity, that lies the key to happiness. Religion to me is the faith that there are greater forces than those we yet understand in our daily lives. Our mere presence on this earth, our progress towards a better civilization, are parts of a pattern, of which we cannot see the full design.

Our minds are finite. Look at a star and realize that it is so many light-years away, and the mind reels at the idea of such distance. But look alongside that star into the blue ether, and the mind completely refuses to conceive the infinitive space.

I bow humbly and reverently to the realization that the well-being of one's fellow creatures, the ultimate happiness of the community, and all that is implied therein, is the truly worth while objective.

And in the attainment of that goal, the focal point is the family and the home.

For life has taught me that the whole pulsating drama of this modern age, with its swift travel to colourful scenes, exciting situations and complex undertakings, has, as its culmination, the happiness and respect of one's wife, family and friends.

L. P. JACKS

Born at Nottingham in 1860. Became assistant minister to Dr. Stopford Brooke in 1887 and was later appointed minister of the Unitarian Churches at Liverpool and Birmingham. Professor of Philosophy at Manchester College, Oxford, from 1903 amd Principal from 1915 until 1931. Editor of the Hibbert Journal from 1902 to 1947.

WHAT I have learnt from life may be summarized as all that I know, believe in, hope for and aim at, or more briefly, all that I am. For eighty-seven years I have had no other master, attended no other school than this, the most Ancient and Public of all the Foundations, and worn no other school-tie. I am still in attendance, but awaiting discharge at the leaving-age appointed for me, not without hope that I may be admitted thereafter into some continuation school carried on in less turbulent surroundings by the same Headmaster; for I perceive that my education is far from finished. To be sure, I have learnt much from books, sat at the feet of great teachers, been to college, drunk many a life-giving draught from the wisdom of the mighty dead, and many more from the wisdom of teachers who have no language and yet are the most eloquent of all; the stars above me, the graves beneath; meadows painted with delight in spring, icicles hanging by the wall in winter; murmuring streams, oak-splitting thunderbolts; dark chasms, sunlit heights ; weary toil, welcome rest ; the light in living eyes, a smile on the face of the dead and all the silent ministries of Nature. But all that had its source in life and was mediated by life in its passage from my teachers to me ; all was under the same Headmaster, and all was life-giving in the effects.

I think the Five Senses are Five Gateways of the Holy Ghost ; my Master has certainly made large use of them in his dealings with me. At my age one often "sits and thinks," or, perhaps more profitably, "just sits," like the old man in *Punch*, but with the Five Senses all awake. While thus engaged, musing, as it were in "some high lonely tower," and listening through one of the senses to the ghostly concert of the owls hooting to one another in the forest at midnight, I find myself wondering whether the arguings of philosophers in their symposia about the nature of Reality are a phenomenon of the same order as the hootings, and of like ghostly significance in the ear of the Eternal. As there is a way of *seeing* Reality *sub specie æternitatis*, much prized by philosophers, why not a *hearing* of it in the same way, and a tasting,[1] aye, and a smelling of it, too, which possibly the owls possess?

I remember an occasion when a gathering of philosophers was discussing the problem of "Appearance and Reality," then lately stirred up anew by Bradley's famous book, and the argument was going very briskly when somebody present suddenly interrupted it with the following question: "This discussion that is going on now, the problem before us, the arguments on both sides, you who are arguing and I who am listening in bewilderment—is it all Appearance or is it Reality? Do my ears deceive me? For God's sake tell me whether I am dreaming or awake." Not one of the philosophers made answer; they were as men stricken dumb with indignation and, after some angry looks at the interrupter, who had the reputation of being a nuisance, the president called for the next speaker. Well, the Five Senses for me every day and in all weathers! If they are liars there is no truth, except, of course, that everything is a lie, including the statement that it is so—a rather awkward conclusion. Such is the sort of philosophy I have learnt from life, if I am not too presumptuous in giving it so exalted a name.

I cannot claim to remember all I have been taught—I wish I did—nor that what I remember is correctly remembered, nor that what I have learnt has been effectively learnt. Between what the teacher teaches and what the learner learns from it there is often a great difference, which may be for better or for worse.

[1] "O taste and see that the Lord is good." *Psalm* 34, 8.

That there have been these differences in my own case I am sure, but whether for better or worse I know not. And of much that I have been taught, and shall here record, I am bound to say (as who in like case would not have to say?) *video meliora proboque deteriora sequor*, which is almost equivalent to saying I have not learnt it at all, or at least not effectively. God mend us all!

I have lived so long and learnt, in consequence, so many lessons from life, that indefatigable teacher, that were I to write it all down the record would run into volumes. And I am learning still; aye, and unlearning, too; for I have never learnt a new lesson save at the cost, often painful, of unlearning an old one. The tale of the lessons I have had to unlearn would fill as many volumes as the other. But learning and unlearning are perhaps two names for the same operation and the tale of this the tale of that.

In what follows I shall confine myself to a few only of the lessons which, *so far*, I have not had to unlearn. If I write with the authority of age, it is also with the knowledge that such authority has sunk to a low ebb in the eyes of the present generation. It is all the authority I have.

Every lesson here recorded informs the reader of another lesson, unrecorded, which I have *not* learnt. I might, indeed, adopt the method of recording the lessons I have not learnt and leaving the reader to infer from them the lessons I have learnt, but this would be too roundabout, and would justly expose me to the charge of shirking my task. I ask the reader's pardon if hereafter I fall into it unawares, as I easily may, since it is the line of least resistance and much in the fashion.

I am far from claiming that all the lessons recorded are to my credit, or such as to enhance me in the esteem of my fellow men. Whenever they are not so, the cause will lie not in my Master, whom I regard as infallible, but in the learner who, as so often happens, has got his lesson amiss and perverted it in the learning. The truth is that, like Mr. Bernard Shaw, I find it very hard to distinguish between life and God, and am half tempted to entitle my record "What I have learnt from God." To pursue this further would involve me in a cloud of metaphysics, which I am unwilling to do, at least at the outset.

The greater part of what I have learnt is not for publication. I must make a selection, and will begin with a lesson I have learnt about myself, and this, too, will be only a *morceau choisi*.

So now to business.

ABOUT MYSELF

My religion is the interpretation, fallible no doubt, which life has enabled me to make of the manifold experience furnished by itself. It rests upon the conviction that God is Life and Life is God and that, most assuredly there is no other God but This. I live in Him. So, reader, do you, and just as fully when you deny His existence as when you affirm it. My doubts and denials, which are many, are as integral to my religion as my beliefs and affirmations. To every belief that I hold a doubt corresponds and, to every affirmation, a denial ; each is necessary to the other, and both are from God. Every article in my creed has a note of interrogation at the end of it, and it is God who has put it there. He is the Everlasting Interrogator—one among His infinite attributes and perhaps the most wonderful. The first articulate words spoken by God to man—so the Bible tells us—took the form of a question, "Adam, where art thou?" To the last man perishing on an ice-bound planet, when the laws of thermodynamics have done their uttermost, as to the first man in the Garden of Eden, this same question will come—"Where art thou?" And the answer, if truly given, will be, "I am *in God*." Between the last man, perishing on an ice-bound planet, and any man now living, you or I, when he stands on the brink of eternity, where is the difference? I know none that is essential. Death has equal dominion over all of us.

Among the many lessons I have learnt about myself I give the first place to the revelation—I count it no less—of the depth and extent of my ignorance. This lesson overarches all the others. "Vanity of vanities," said the Preacher, "all is vanity." But he found it no vanity to put that statement on record. 'Tis the same with my ignorance. I am not ignorant of *that*. There is nothing I can claim to know with greater certainty. Let the scientific Pharisee make what boasts he will; but God be merciful to me an ignoramus!

I have learnt also, if only as an inference from my own case, but an inference continually confirmed by observation, experiment and the Baconian method in general, that all men are in a similar condition, not excepting the arch-priests of science, the profoundest philosophers and the most impeccable of the saints. While there are many whose ignorance is less than mine, there are many more whose ignorance is greater, but all of them, the less ignorant than I and the more, are ignorant to a degree which can only be described as abysmal. We are all in the same boat, or in the same caravan, making our way, across "deserts of vast eternity," to the same destination. In the grave there is no knowledge.

This revelation of my ignorance, graciously vouchsafed to me by the all-illuminating Light, is naturally a revelation of my fallibility. Grounded though my beliefs may be on the little knowledge I have, they might well turn out to be erroneous were my knowledge to become even a trifle greater. Increasing knowledge has forced me to abandon so many beliefs which I once thought unquestionable that I am little inclined to be pontifical in proclaiming those I now hold. Even in recording what I have learnt, as I am now doing, there is always the possibility that I may not have learnt the lesson aright, or, having learnt it aright, may be recording it wrongly. There is, however, one exception. Just as the Preacher's assertion that all is vanity is exempt from the vanity asserted, so the knowledge of my ignorance and fallibility is itself infallible knowledge; on that I am dogmatic to the uttermost and pontifical as any infallible Pope. This exception is of the utmost importance and for the following reason.

To be ignorant, and consequently fallible, is one thing; to *know* that you are ignorant and fallible, as I do, is a different thing. How different! To be ignorant is to be in the dark; to know that you are ignorant is to be in the light. Knowing my ignorance, as I hope the reader knows his, I count myself among the *illuminati* and a son of God. It is my share in the Godhead, my inheritance of the divine nature; a point at which

God and I are veritably one. For God is Light, and therefore invisible. As we do not see the light, but only illuminated objects, so we do not see God, but only a God-illuminated world and our God-illuminated selves. Without His Light we should see nothing and know nothing ; nay, we should *be* nothing. For He is Life as well as Light,and the one in being the other. Have you come to the conclusion that there is no God? Without God you could never have come to that conclusion, nor to any other. You have found it by virtue of the fiery Logos which gives the Light that lighteneth every man born into the world and every object in the world from the greatest to the most minute. Along with the theist, you, the atheist, are among God's witnesses, and, before God, I know not which of you bears the more cogent testimony to His existence—perhaps you. For I am bound to admit that you have a strong case ; but, the stronger your case, the stronger your witness to God. Save as God-illuminated and God-penetrated neither theist nor atheist would have a word to say on either side. He is proved by being disproved, being Himself a Living Paradox, as you and I, made in His image, also are in our measures : Paradox calling unto Paradox, the human to the divine, whenever we worship in spirit and in truth. He is the Great Absurdity, you and I being Little Absurdities of the same order—though perhaps I should speak only of myself. On theist and atheist He makes His sun to shine and His rain to fall with no difference, nor can I find the slightest indication anywhere that the theists are His favourites. Hard sayings, but true. Yes : to be ignorant is one thing : to know that you are ignorant is another. We become significant in knowing our insignificance. And this whether we sit on a Papal Chair in Rome or stand on a soap-box in Hyde Park.

What are you and I when measured against the awful immensities and eternities of the universe? What is the Pope? What is the orator on the soap-box? Mere nothings and equal in being so. Pride surely is the deadliest of the sins, or at least the silliest of the absurdities. And what pride so inflated and silly as that which prompts us to deem ourselves, or our race, the summit of creation and the darling of the Creator? But you and I may *know* the folly of that pride, if not the wickedness of it, which Lucifer, whose fall it occasioned, did not know, the science of theology being then unborn, and God's existence, in consequence, a fact beyond question. Let us, then, be of good cheer. In knowing that we are nothing we become something, and something, believe me, than which the whole universe is not greater nor more august. *Sursum corda!*

ABOUT GOD

The truth about God, as my Master has taught me to see it, seems to lie at a point midway between the atheist who declares that God does not exist and the pantheist who declares that nothing exists but God. In this, as in all other great matters, and many small ones, life has instilled into me a profound respect for the Aristotelian doctrine of the Mean and never failed to chastise me for my frequent lapses from moderation. It has been said that our worst vices are virtues in excess, from which it would seem to follow, though I am not quite sure that it does, that our best virtues are vices in defect. At all events life has left me convinced that in theology, as in morals, truth lies about the mean between two extremes. From a religious point of view too much theology is worse than no theology at all. Theology when carried to excess is the death of religion. It is like the Elixir of Immortality which, if you take an overdose of it, kills you on the spot. All the sects are based on extremist theologies of one kind or another ; were they to practise moderation the differences between them would vanish and there would be only one religion in the world.

That God exists, though not to the extremity asserted by the pantheist, I find impossible to deny. "Of all points of faith," said J. H. Newman, "the being of God is encompassed with most difficulty, and yet borne in upon our minds with most power." Life has "borne it in" upon me with power that I am wholly unable to resist and equally unable to account for.

There would be little point in saying that I believe that God exists unless I make clear what I mean by "God" and by "existence." I will only say, though I might say much more, that I apprehend the existence of God as the constant pressure upon me, and upon the whole creation, of a Power that makes for Excellence. I say for Excellence, and not only for the particular form of Excellence known as "righteousness," but in endless variety. For example, as I sit writing this essay I am conscious, beyond all gainsaying, of a pressure upon me, urgent but not coercive, to make it as good an essay as I can, to tell the truth in it and to tell it in the best way. If the essay turns out a bad one, as it well may, that will be because I have failed to respond to the pressure which is urging me to make it a good one, the pressure of the Power that makes for Excellence. That Power, which permeates the universe, is God. His existence is *dynamic*. I never escape from Him, nor, reader do you, atheist or theist as you may happen to be. Though you take the wings of the morning and fly to the uttermost parts of the sea, the Power that makes for Excellence will be after you, will envelope you in its embrace and press dynamically upon every motion of your mind or body. Were its pressure to cease for a moment you, too, would instantly cease to be.

Life has not taught me to explain God. But neither has it taught me to explain myself. My own existence, though a fairly certain fact, remains for me an unfathomable mystery deep as the existence of God. To be sure I know well enough that there cannot be a One without a Many ; that is an elementary truth of metaphysics; but metaphysics do not explain *how* many are needed to constitute the One ; the proposition would be equally true if there were only three human souls in the world instead of two thousand million ; and throws not a ray of light on the question before me, the question, namely, why one of the two thousand million should be the particular individual who bears my name and whom I know as myself. Granted that the existing two thousand million is the exact "many" needed to constitute the One, or the exact total of human souls required by God to carry out His purpose (though I do not see how it can be proved), that, surely, is no reason why L. P. Jacks should be one of them. Another man, bearing another name, would have filled the place and completed the quota as well as I, or better. Why *me*? There is no answer. I can think of many reasons why I should *not* exist, and others perhaps might think of more, but not of one which necessitates my existence either for God's purposes or for man's. Yet here, to my amazement, I am, a manifest absurdity in the universe. No man, says Leslie Stephen, can give a convincing proof that the world would not be better off if he were hanged by the neck five minutes hence, and, certainly, if every man were hanged whose absence from the world is judged by some other man to be better for the world than his presence, not many of us would escape the gallows. Once more, we are all in the same boat, a crew of absurdities, two thousand million strong. By the grace of God we are what we are, where we are, when we are, who we are and as many as we are. Even if I could prove, which I cannot, that my existence up to the present moment has been necessary for the maintenance of the universe, that would not justify my existence a moment longer, and would be no answer to those who think it high time I took myself off, as doubtless some do, seeing that I am now very old and ripe for the undertaker, but still occupying lodgings and consuming victuals needed by younger men in an overcrowded and hungry world, a liability, in short, rather than an asset. Life has not taught me the answer to that riddle.

I have learnt from life that my own existence is intermingled with God's, but in a manner so baffling that all my efforts to disentangle the two come to nought. The line of demarcation between them, the line where immanence ends and transcendence begins, I cannot draw. It seems to be ever on the move, now here, now there. In nothing am I more acutely aware of my fallibility.

I used to think, following a convention well established among the pious, that all the hits (or counted such by me) were God's doing, and all the misses (called sins by some and, more charitably, mistakes by others) were due to me. I think so no longer. I now see that some of the shots I counted hits and were so counted by the markers (fallible men, those markers!) were really misses and some of the misses were really hits. It may well be that a Divinity was directing the misses or, as Shakespeare says, shaping their "ends." I am strongly inclined to think so, but cannot prove it. On the whole it would seem that God's existence and mine are sometimes two and sometimes one, and a mystery under either condition.

I perceive that in this section I have been mixing up what I have learnt about God and what I have learnt about myself. The reason is obvious. God and man *are* mixed up and religion, of which I have next to speak, results from the mixture.

ABOUT RELIGION

My religion, such as it is (a poor thing, my masters, but mine own) has not been derived from the study of theology, of which I have studied more than is good for me, but direct from life, as I suspect that yours, reader, if you have any, has also been, whether you know it or not. In my study of the theologians, and of the philosophers, too, I am often reminded of that great scholar, from Oxford way I believe, who became so learned in the classics that he did all his thinking in Greek and Latin, but had to consult the dictionaries to find out what it meant.

As for the Psychology of Religion, I find it little more than a scientific dictionary called by another name, and make a point of forgetting it in my devotions, which otherwise it would kill. I have little use for its analysis, except as an intellectual pastime, which, however, is far from condemning it as useless. Strange things happen when lovers take to analysing their loves, of which the conversion of love into hate, and that for no reason at all, is not the most uncommon. And religion is either a love affair or nothing. Had Dante paused to analyse his love for Beatrice the *Divine Comedy* would never have been written. How often is reality sacrificed to word-play!

Some make religion an affair of the heart, others of the head, or of heart corrected by head, or of head corrected by heart. Some base it on Reason ; others on Revelation ; or on the two in conjunction. Some assign it to the emotions, or to the imagination, or to a special religious faculty, or to a unique experience. "*Words! Words!*" Such is the comment on the Psychology of Religion that life bids me utter when I consider the flowers of the field how they grow and, considering them, fall in love with their beauty. As who but a churl would not

> When daisies pied and violets blue,
> And lady-smocks all silver white,
> And cuckoo buds of yellow hue
> Do paint the meadows with delight?

This love affair, like others in the same category, is an affair of the *whole* man, who is something other than any of the faculties named above and far greater than their added totality. Are you religious? Then it is as a whole man that you are so, in the indivisible unity of mind and body, with all that these include to the faintest motion of your spirit and the last drop of your blood ; ditto if you are irreligious, though I think you will find it hard to be irreligious with the whole of you. To encounter God is to tremble *through and through*, as Dante trembled when he met Beatrice on the street, and as all men do when they fall in love. I beg you, if you have not already done it, to read a great book—*Man the Unknown*, by Alexis Carrel. There you will get a glimpse of what the Whole Man really is, of what *you* really are. You are a marvellous being, fearfully and wonderfully made. All the miracles recorded in history or legend are as nothing in comparison with the miracle that keeps you alive from moment to moment. When I meditate on these things in the night watches, as I often do, I am overwhelmed with astonishment at the bare fact that I am alive and can find no fitting words to utter my praises of the Power that made me so and keeps me so, has kept me so from the time I was in my mother's womb till now, and will keep me so to the end and perhaps beyond it, making the end into a new beginning. "Bless the Lord, O my soul *and all that is within me* bless His Holy Name," is the best I can do. *In tuas manus, Domine, meam animam commisi.*

The religion of the whole man has a leaning to silence and an abhorrence of vociferation. The Sons of Thunder have no place in its temples and are the least fruitful of its missionaries. Get you gone, Boanerges, say I : your voice is so loud that I cannot understand a word you say. I will not say silence alone is becoming, though silence is very good for religion, and perhaps best. Songs express it better than discourses, poets better than theologians, music better than speech, and thirty-nine Psalms (the thirty-ninth and the hundred and thirty-ninth especially) better than thirty-nine Articles. Of all the music in which it finds a voice I think the "still sad music of humanity," is to me the most revealing:

> Who never ate his bread in sorrow,
> He knows you not, ye heavenly powers.

That also I have learnt from life.

ABOUT PRAYER AND PRAISE

The God whom life has taught me to worship needs no prayer of mine to induce Him to do me good. I cannot conceive Him as *waiting to be asked*, as not knowing that I need His help until reminded by somebody's prayer, or as knowing it but holding His hand till somebody begs Him to act. Surely the great God is no such churl! Did He create the universe, with me as an atom of it, but illuminated with the consciousness of it, because He had been asked? Has He kept me alive these eighty-seven years, never for an instant withdrawing His everlasting arms from beneath me, as an answer to my prayers? Does He need to be reminded that I am here, as though He were "talking, or pursuing, or on a journey, or peradventure he sleepeth and must be awaked"? Nay, nay! In whom do I live, and move and have my being? In Him. Whose the vitality of the air I draw in with every breath? His. Whose the pressure of the atmosphere, fifteen pounds avoirdupois to every square inch of my body? His. Whose the firm support of the ground under my feet and the light of consciousness wherewith I am conscious of it? His. In whose light do I see what is visible, in whose sound hear what is audible, in whose strength do what is doable? In His. Who keeps my heart beating from moment to moment and the blood coursing through my veins? He who keeps the earth spinning on its axis, the fires burning in the sun and Orion on his stately march amid the constellations; He who paves the Milky Way with millions of worlds. Awful thoughts, my masters, and tremendous facts! Make it your practice, I pray you, to begin every day by meditating for a few moments on the majesty and the mercy of God. "Thou needest no prayer of ours to persuade Thee to bless us, for as the heavens are higher than the earth, so is Thy mercy beyond the striving of our thought." So let all liturgies begin.

While thus teaching me to pray little, life has also taught me to praise much, nay, without limit, the one lesson being included in the other. If I often pray the kindly Light to lead me on amid the encircling gloom, that is more by way of gratitude for the light already given than of petition for its continuance, and springs, not from doubt that light will fail me, but from confidence that it will be given, whether I ask for it or not. The Kingdom of *Laus Deo* has no boundaries.

> Were the whole realm of Nature mine
> That were an offering far too small.

There is many an experience of mine for which, taken by itself and in isolation from the organic totality, I can utter no blessing but only a curse, if I am to utter anything at all. Such is a toothache, and a thousand other aches that flesh is heir to, mine and other men's, of which the heartaches are the worst. But when I view these agonies, not in isolation from the sunset touches and the chorus-endings, but as interpenetrating these beautiful things, and by them interpenetrated, then it is that my Song of Praise for the Beautiful Whole to which they are organic breaks out with irresistible vehemence ; then it is that life reveals to me the mutual necessity of joy and grief in the weaving together of its many-coloured pattern. For that sublime and beautiful Whole, alive with the high tension of the Godhead in every woven fibre of it, I bless the Lord, and it is the whole of me, gathered up in time from all the years that I and my ancestors before me have lived, and extended through all the space to which my utmost vision can reach, a thousand light-years from the spot where I now stand, that utters the blessing. *Thank you!* In those two words my devotions come to a head. If there is any other solution to the problem of evil, then I know it not. My solution is "thank you."

To whom is my "thank you" addressed? Of course I must answer "to God," and have so answered already. I like not the name. Ignoble use has spoilt it ; its associations are misleading ; the sound of it is ugly, and therefore unfitting to its beautiful object. Used in public it needs the addition of liquid adjectives, such as "eternal" or "ever-blessed," to soften the ugly sound and save it from suggesting a moral tyrant, a remorseless inquisitor, a magnified clergyman, or a wooden idol, as it so often does.

How then shall we name the Eternal, the Ever-blessed ? I will only say, though I might say much more, that the simple word "*Thou*" conveys, not indeed all that I mean by "God," but the essence of what I am aware of in the Object to whom my devotions are addressed. Let "Thou," then, be the name. If "I am" be the name He gives Himself, "Thou" will suffice for the response of this other "I am" which is myself. Is not "I am" the innermost name of all the human children as it is the name of their Father?

These, again, are hard sayings, that is, things hard to say. In all I have learnt from life, there is nothing harder to put on record, nothing for which the written word is so imperfect a vehicle, nothing the letter is apter to kill, than the lesson which teaches me to give thanks, not indeed for everything but for the whole of which everything is an organic element. *That* is good ; *that* is the beautiful Neighbour whom life bids me love as I love myself, and short of loving whom my love of the neighbour next door will be, at best, but a half-hearted affair. No creed contains that lesson, but its echoes may be heard in many an ancient Psalm, in Greek tragedy, in the majestic verse of Dante and Shakespeare, in the work of great musicians and, perhaps best of all, in the still sad music of humanity and in the songs of poets inspired to sing it, such as Burns, Wordsworth and Keats. Taught me the the lesson has assuredly been ; but who can claim to have learnt it perfectly? Not I. Here, however, is something which came out of me long ago, one of many such, in a time of great distress. Feeble though it be, it still remains the best recording I can make :

When my soul is in heaviness and my heart is disquieted within me:
When darkness is round about my path, and all thy tempests go over my head:
Then will I betake me to the Great Congregation to hear the psalm of thy redeeméd and to cast my burden on the Lord.
Thou shalt cause me to hear of joy and gladness: the songs of the blessed shall visit me in the night:
They shall declare the might of thy spirit: they shall also make mention of thy peace:
Of love made perfect through suffering: and the rest that remaineth for the children of God.
As a cloud of witnesses they shall surround me: as ministering spirits they shall strengthen my soul.
They fought the good fight, they kept the faith: they came through great tribulation, enduring unto the end.
And now, O Lord, they rest in thy keeping: they shine as the stars for ever and ever:
That the lost may be gathered in from all nations: and thy way made known to the uttermost parts of the earth:
To such as wander in the wilderness: and to them that are afar off upon the sea.
Thou callest us into the communion of thy beloved: the glorious fellowship of the children of light:
That we may walk in the joy of thy presence: who wilt greatly refresh us with the river of thy life.
O, send out thy light and thy truth, let them lead me: let them bring me to thy holy hill and to thy dwelling place.
O, draw me from out the great waters: lead me to the rock that is higher than I.
Then shall my soul return unto her rest: I shall come to the haven where I would be.

ABOUT CHRISTIANITY

Some there are who think that we are now suffering from an overdose of science, that we have bitten off enormously more than we can chew of our scientific victual, that our knowledge of Nature's secrets has become a fatal surfeit and, remembering Nagasaki, predict an end to the human race as the consequence of our excess. Can we in like manner advance too far in the knowledge of God? Can we have an overdose of that? Of pretended knowledge, yes ; of that the smallest dose is too much, and there is plenty of it to be had. Of hearsay knowledge, too, such as we impart in theological colleges, the dose may easily be overdone. But of real knowledge, No. Of that the dose is strictly limited by God Himself. To that He has set bounds that we may not pass. We can know of Him no more than He permits us to know, which is very little of His full Reality, but all our frailty can bear and all that is good for us. In this, as in all else, "He knoweth our frame, He remembereth that we are dust." There is much talk of "man's increasing knowledge of God." I count it vain talk, and greatly doubt whether man's knowledge of God has advanced or ever will advance beyond the point reached by the writer of the hundred-and-third Psalm. "Verily Thou art a God that hidest Thyself," and well for us that it is so. Think (if you can) of all the energy pent up in all the atoms composing the material universe. What would happen if all that, now marvellously and mercifully held under restraint, were suddenly set free? Well, something like it would happen were God to reveal His full Reality. None could see Him and live.

Well for us, I say, that He is a *Deus Absconditus*, that clouds of thick darkness veil the full shining of that Light from the eyes that it would blind, from the vision that it would quench. Life has taught me to be thankful for that. *Laus Deo*, once more. Were either God or the atom to go all out, the whole universe would be volatilized, which perhaps has happened before, and not once but many times, for Eternity is large. Perhaps the two Explosives are the same, differing only in their manner of exploding ; and the soul of a man another of the same order. Who will release the energy pent up in the soul of a single man? Were the soul to be "split" I would not like to be standing by.

If the definition of a Christian be that of a warm-hearted and open-handed gentleman, a good Samaritan and a good neighbour, beloved by all decent folk and feared only by scoundrels ; thinking evil of no man, long-suffering towards fools ; a fair dealer, a loyal friend, a welcome companion and a sound sportsman ; free from envy, greed and censoriousness ; a man of charity, compassion, gratitude and kindly humour ; ideal in his aims, businesslike in his methods ; fond of children, flowers and all beautiful things ; considerate to servants, chivalrous to women, kind to animals, courteous to all men ; penitent in the House of God, humble in the presence of the Sphinx, but a terrible fellow when Apollyon has to be dealt with ; brave in danger, patient in sickness, cheerful in misfortune, radiant in gloom, temperate in prosperity, resolute in adversity, calm in the face of death—such a fine-tempered and gallant gentleman, Christianity's best product, of whom the opposite is a cad, life has ever urged me to become; such I fain would be, nay, in my poor way, have striven to be, but, alas, am far from being. In that sense, and to that modest extent, my Master has made me as good a Christian as anybody else who has followed that gleam, though not as good as those who have succeeded better than I, which, thank God, so many have done, of whom I hope you, reader, are one. Were the earth peopled with such, the Kingdom of God would have come, always provided they had their counterparts in the female denomination; otherwise, not. For Sigurd is no good without Brynhild; as Ruskin said, "the soul's armour is never well set to the heart unless a woman's hand has braced it." Would that men everywhere would forsake their stupid worship of the Political Idol with its ritual of mischief-making, and concentrate on the breeding, multiplication and nurture of such Christians!

But if you define a Christian, as history (never to be flouted) requires you should, to be a believer in one or other of the Church creeds, Catholic or Protestant, in the creed of Pope Pius, Thirty-nine Articles, Westminster Confession, or what other you will, then I am no Christian, have no desire to be, and am prepared to go to my God, as soon I must, on those terms. My Master has led me beyond the pale, outside of which, according to a great tradition, there is *nulla salus*, and there He bids me stand today and to stand undaunted. When, some thirteen years ago,

I was involved in trouble for lifting up my voice from the pulpit of an Anglican Cathedral and proved by a Bishop, in a well-reasoned speech before the Convocation of York, to be no Christian (though not necessarily a bad man) I accepted the verdict, with sorrow indeed, but without complaint and, I must add, without the least desire to turn myself into the Christian I was declared not to be.

But God forbid that I say a word in disparagement of the historic creeds. They represent an immense, prolonged and heroic travail of the human spirit focused on the things that matter most, equal in concentration and intensity to the toil of science which, in our day, has resulted in the splitting of the atom, but expended in the better cause of finding deliverance from the burden of life and the dominion of death, to which the progress of science, *in the total*, has contributed nothing at all, but greatly increased the burden,[1] and enhanced the triumph of the "last enemy" by providing him with a richer spoil. I doubt if our age is doing anything to the glory of God comparable to that great achievement of the creed-makers. That I cannot accept their formulations is of little import. Neither can I worship the gods to whom great temples were built in Egypt and Greece ; nor, reader, can you. But let not that abate our reverence for the builders and the awe in our souls as we gaze on the majestic ruin of their work ; let it not blind us to the fact that their work was wrought to the glory of the Most High, though perchance they knew it not. The gods for whom those altars smoked are dead for ever, and our chanted creeds now fall on many an unbelieving ear; but may it not prove to be that the ages which built the temples and the later age which built the creeds will be judged in the final audit to have been better employed than the age which split the atom and went in fear of being hoist by its own petard?

In all the Credos named above I recognize the striving towards

[1]Inventions which ease the burden in detail (e.g. the telephone) have the effect, by accumulation, of increasing the total burden to be borne, so that men may become worn out in the use of labour-saving devices. And many do.

a tremendous Reality, faintly glimpsed in all of them, but articulated in none, that *mysterium tremendum,* whose light, like the orce in the atom, would instantly slay us all, were it not hidden behind a veil and mercifully held in restraint. Nor can any man, or any company, convocation or council of men, give expression to it, and least of all can I, though every moment of my existence proclaims it a Reality beyond gainsaying or question, for which, however, understatement is the more fitting ; best apprehended when, giving it no name, as of one who carries an identity card, we address it simply as Thou ; real to our apprehension when so addressed, but then tremendously real. For such address to the Godhead the Creeds substitute an account of it, a *compte rendu,* which inevitably becomes an overstatement and misses the mark by shooting beyond it. I find more truth in worship than in Creeds, in reverence than in theology. In three-fold reverence for what is beneath us, around and above; beneath, the teeming earth and the haunted cemeteries of the buried generations; around, the marvel of incessant creation and the amazing multitude of the creatures, each one fearfully and wonderfully made; above, the Abode of Light, home of the fiery Logos and the burning Seraphim, embracing the universe as with the arms of a lover, and binding it together in love—in such worship, all men may yet unite, but in theology never! Beyond the circles of the organized Churches with their many creeds is the circle which embraces them all, aye, and much more than they, whose centre is everywhere and circumference nowhere, wherein there is no temple—the Holy Catholic Church of those who worship in Spirit and in Truth, the Beloved Community, the Great Congregation, the Beautiful Whole. Life has made me, I dare not say a member of that Church, but a candidate for membership. Verily there is *nulla salus* outside it! *Sit mea anima cum illa in saecula saeculorum.* Amen.

If we take the Christianity of the first believers, up to the end, say, of the first century, as the norm of what Christianity is, I greatly doubt if there is any Church now in existence which can truly claim to be a Christian Church. The nearest approaches to the original form, if form it may be called, are to be found, I think, in the Society of Friends and, at the opposite pole, in the

Church of Rome ; in the former, as "a union of those who love for the sake of those who suffer," or Kingdom of God ; in the latter, as retaining most of the mystery element, an immensely potent element, which came in, not indeed at the very beginning, but soon afterwards. The "mystery" (1 Cor. ii, 7 ; xv, 51) preceded the growth of the "familiar story" in the Synoptic Gospels, a story by no means familiar to St. Paul, the great apostle of the mystery, except as regards the Passion and Resurrection of the Christ, though this, indeed, is the *terminus ad quem* of all the Gospels, the clue to their purpose and the heart of the mystery itself.

But in spite of these approaches (and there are others less near) there remains a great difference, if not an unbridgeable gulf, between our Christianity, of whatever complexion, and that of the first believers at the dawning of the faith—and what a bright morning that was, and how difficult for us to recapture the radiance of it! Verily that "radiant morn has passed away" and our Christianity has become like an old man groping among the shadowy recollections of his childhood :

> Whither has fled the visionary gleam?
> Where is it now, the glory and the dream ?

Reduced to plain terms and briefly stated the difference comes to this ; that, whereas theirs was the Christianity out of which the New Testament came, ours is a Christianity which comes out of the New Testament. Let the fact be deeply pondered that Christianity was a living religion, firmly planted over wide and populous regions from Edessa in the East to Rome in the West long before the New Testament as we know it came into existence, long before there was any authorized Christian Scripture to which appeal could be made as the Rule of Faith.

At that stage, and it was one of astonishing vitality, never surpassed in Christian history, Christianity *had no literature of its own*, no Divine Revelation within the cover of a book or a roll of papyrus, nothing wherewith to propagate its Gospel and overcome its adversaries save the force and fire of the faith within it and of the *ipse dixit* by which the faith proclaimed itself. Between our book-mediated Christianity and the Christianity which produced the books that mediate it, the difference is surely immense, and requires to be emphasized.

Only those who know by personal experience what faith is will understand how the first successes of the new religion were achieved or even how they were possible. Today they would be impossible for the simple reason that the type of Christianity which produced them no longer exists. Nor does the material exist that would respond to its propaganda and accept its message. The propagandists would immediately be challenged to produce evidence for their bold assertions that Christ was risen, his kingdom at hand and immortality to be had almost for the asking; and, failing to produce it to the satisfaction of critical science, would soon be criticized into silence. No such ordeal awaited the first missionaries of the Gospel. The fuel was ready to take fire. Once started it became a conflagration.

To be sure, these Christians had the Old Testament behind them and made abundant use of it in their controversies with the Jews, for whom it had authority, St. Paul quoting it twenty-nine times in the course of the Epistle to the Romans, and without a single reference to the Gospel teaching. But this was Jewish literature, not Christian, and was of no use for the major task of converting the pagan world.

Imagine, then, what would be the prospects of a Christian missionary in our day who should set out to convert the world to the Gospel of Christ with only the Old Testament at his back or in his pocket. Those were the almost incredible conditions under which Barnabas, Paul and many another devoted missionary whose name has perished undertook their task and achieved a measure of success at which we, in very different times, can only gaze with astonishment.

Many years have passed since my Master first drew my attention to this difference and taught me to meditate on its significance. The sequent lessons to which my meditations led me are too many to be recorded here, and I must leave them aside along with innumerable others. Suffice it to say that their general tendency is to confirm the good Bishop's proof that such as I are not Christians. But who is?

ABOUT MY DUTY

It has become the fashion in these days of hearsay and booksay Christianity to regard a man as no better than he ought to be if he answer the question "am I my brother's keeper?" otherwise than with a ringing affirmative. Well, life has moulded me into precisely such a villain. I answer the question with a ringing "No!" Reader, I hail you as my brother. But I am not your keeper and will not allow you to become mine, no, not even if you stand in the Apostolic Succession. To be sure, if you find me lying by the roadside, wounded, helpless, and robbed of my money by prowling bandits, or by that arch-robber, the State, you may then proceed to "keep" me until I am safely deposited at an inn, with the landlord's bill paid in advance to the time when I am a man again ; and if the parts are reversed I will do as much by you; *and more also*. After I have seen my ill-used brother comfortably to bed, procured a doctor and a nurse, etc., etc., I will sharpen my good sword on the inn grindstone, remount my horse, return to the scene of the outrage, track the robbers to their den (which may be in Whitehall), and there I will fall upon them like a thunderbolt and teach the scoundrels a lesson that will make the story of what *they* have learnt from life a tale well worth the telling. After which the road from Jerusalem to Jericho will be safe for poor travellers, whether Samaritan or Jew, aye, and for priests, Levites and the clergy of all denominations; and it will be written in my epitaph "he was his brother's keeper with a vengeance."

All this I have learnt from my Master to regard as my duty, *mine* but not necessarily yours or any other man's, which, heaven assisting, I will do as aforesaid and, having done, will straightway repair to the Tribunal and there I will confidently submit my conduct of the affair to the judgment of good Christian men who, whatever they may say in their official capacity, will approve what I did in their hearts and, whatever texts they may cite against me, will wish they had done it themselves, and at worst let me off with a caution—thanks to the Gothic element in their Christianity, that syncretist religion, which some think as important as the Greek element and hardly less important than the Hebrew. Reader, I trust the Gothic element is active in you, who are now my judge, as well as the Hebrew and the Greek : the three are powerful in combination. And should you ever chance to be again going down from Jerusalem to Jericho, think, I pray you, not unkindly of your erring brother, who refused to be your keeper, but made the road safe for your journey.

Yes: I still refuse. Once we are men again, you or I, and the incident closed, no more "keeping" on either side, if you please! In God's name, it shall not be! I absolve you, my brother, from responsibility for promoting my happiness and I decline responsibility for promoting yours. Let every man promote his own happiness, though I think he could be better employed, and count that pursuit a foolish adventure at best. That you and I have reciprocal duties I do not deny, but "keeping" each other is not one of them.

Whenever the temptation arises to play the part of keeper to your brother, as it frequently will under the influence of the bad examples abounding in these days, make sure, I beseech you, that you have your brother's consent to the arrangement before embarking on your "keeping" operations. Look at the matter from his point of view and consider how you would react if the positions were reversed. Otherwise, believe me, there will be trouble for both of you. What poisonous quarrels have arisen in private life from neglecting the precaution to make sure that your notion of good agrees with that of the brother to whom you propose to *do* good, and, further (mark this!) that even if your notion and his agree, he is yet willing to have the good done him by *you*. And consider what happens on the great scale when one nation says to another "Brother-nation, I am your appointed keeper. I have a mandate to keep you. Go to then, I will keep you according to my excellent democratic notions of how a nation should be kept, teaching you democracy and making you as excellent a democratic nation as myself. For I am old, wise, experienced and strong, while you are young, foolish, inexperienced and weak. Go to, then, and consent to be kept by me." How does "brother-nation" answer to that? Again I say—*circumspice*. Life has taught me to be observant of these things. Reader, I trust you are not inobservant of the same.

Among our reciprocal duties none stands higher in my esteem than the duty *to leave each other alone*, but always provided it be coupled with the correlative duty of conscientious and loving attention to one's own business. There is a poisonous doctrine abroad, daring to call itself Christian, and now erected into a principle of State policy, which encourages the maximum degree of interference in other people's affairs. This wicked doctrine, sometimes called "altruism," life has taught me to abhor, and to regard that man only as a true altruist who confines his interference with others to the minimum necessary, while otherwise devoting himself to the clothing of his own business with all the excellence it admits of. I am all for *laissez faire* and *laissez passer*, but in their true and original meanings of "let every man get on with his job" and "let the goods he produces circulate freely according to the principle of Free Trade"—the summary of all altruism worthy of the name either public or private. And note this. Of the two doctrines, the maximum and the minimum, the latter is immeasurably the harder to practise. To go for the maximum of interference is to take the line of least resistance, the line of self-conceit, in which all the meaner elements of human nature, of which the censorious element is the meanest, come into action and become habits, until we end by confirming the maxim that our worst vices are virtues in excess. Hypocrisy lies that way. Alas for the crimes committed in the name of Benevolence ; there seems to be no end to them! In the early days of my schooling I was inattentive to this lesson and it was only after many chastisements, both corporal and spiritual, that my good Master at last drove it home. Be more teachable, O ye young men, than I have been! It will be good for you.

ABOUT THE RIGHTS OF MAN

Briefly, that he has none! No right to life, since no man has the right to be born into the world, and consequently no right to liberty, nor to the pursuit of happiness, nor to anything else within the compass of life. Life, liberty, and power to pursue happiness are gifts bestowed upon him for no merit of his, and his abuse of them has been so shameful that, were he to get his deserts, he would be instantly deprived of all three. He is utterly dependent upon God for every moment of his existence. To the mercy of God he owes it that he is still alive, free and able to indulge in the folly of pursuing a happiness which never is but always to be.

But, note well, that while a man has no right to these things, no other man has the right to deprive him of them. Nor has that monster, the State. "Him," said the fathers of democracy, "him, whether his name be George the Third or his title Mr. President, we will suffer no longer to ride in his juggernaut car over the lives, liberties and happiness of poor men. A hook shall be put in the nose of that Leviathan and a bit in his mouth, and let him become a tame and useful beast.". Is not this what the American Constitution is driving at?

A truce, then, to all this botheration about the Rights of Man and to the companion botheration about happiness! Your Charter of Human Rights has no basis in reality, and the wise man shall say "fudge!" when he reads it. Give him rather a Charter of Duties, but tell him not that the Assertion of Rights is one of them.

As to the Conquest of Happiness, about which Bertrand Russell has written a book, I, for one, will not engage in it, unless it be in the conquest of the supreme happiness which consists in learning to do without it: all the other conquests are Pyrrhic victories. Does not history prove and your own experience attest that the assertion of rights is the perpetration of wrongs and the pursuit of happiness the attainment of misery? I have read a story—Anatole France, I think, was the author of it—about a philosopher who devoted his life to discovering the secret of happiness. At last he discovered it, only to find that his own happiness vanished completely and for ever the instant the secret was out, and rapidly sank into his grave. He had eaten of the fruit of the Tree of Knowledge. "To be perfectly happy is a terrible thing." *Nessun maggior dolore*. Do you not perceive that Death has dominion over it all?

> Our natures do pursue,
> Like rats that ravin down their proper bane,
> A thirsty evil ; and when we drink we die.[1]

CONCLUSION

"Above all the travail of humanity, in the midst of which we are living, let every follower of the gleam proclaim on high the divine principle of love, of devoted love, to the end that a religion may arise, crown of Christianity and of every other religion, all taken up into one and concentrated on the perfecting of humanity in the life of the spirit, that is, in communion with God."[2]

Such is the *terminus ad quem*, the port of arrival where my weary ship, star-guided over the great waters, drops her anchor in firm holding at the long last. A fair hinterland lies beyond. Arise, ye pioneers, and get to work! Again I say, gird up your loins and get to work!

I began by recording something of what life has taught me about myself and perhaps I have been doing nothing else all through. But is not that what every man does who writes a book, or a part of one? Is not the *Republic* a book about Plato; the *Divine Comedy* a book about Dante ; *Hamlet* a book about Shakespeare ; *Back to Methuselah* a book about Mr. Bernard Shaw ; nay, even *Colenso's Arithmetic*, from which I learned to add, multiply and divide, a book about Colenso?

Standing on the brink after eighty-seven years at school, and looking out on the "deserts of vast eternity" that lie before me, I hear the voice of my good Master bidding me take courage, and assuring me that the conclusions to which He has brought me are but the starting points of new revelations which shall better them all. From my heart I thank Him for the lessons He has given me and for the great times He and I have had together; for the long wrestle I had with Him by the Brook Jabbok, which,

[1] Shakespeare, *Measure for Measure*.

[2] Alfred Loisy, *Les Origines du Nouveau Testament* (page 34).

made a man of me, and for the ladder He showed me at Bethel with the angels going up and down in their ceaseless ministries between earth and heaven. A magnanimous Master I have ever found Him, and not least in His chastisements for my frequent inattention and stupidity, which I thought rather cruel at the time they fell upon me, but now know to have been kind, for without them I should have been utterly lost. For the chastisements also I thank Him. For all the nonsense I have talked about Him—I, too, have been a theologian—I would pray His forgiveness ; but there is a smile on His face that tells me the prayer is unnecessary. So I will end with the following Canticle which came out of me about the same time as the other I have quoted, but is still the best summing up I can give of all I have learnt from life, both of what is here recorded and of innumerable other lessons that are not for publication.

My heart shall indite a good matter : I will bless the Lord who giveth me light :

I will say to the sorrowful, Be comforted : and to them that wait for the morning, Be glad of heart :

For the glory of the Lord is risen upon the earth : the day breaketh and the shadows flee away.

Lo, the Master calleth his servants : be ready to meet him, O my soul :

Who forgiveth all thy sins : who healeth all thine infirmities :

Who openeth thy way into the kingdom of heaven : who maketh thee heir of eternal life.

O Lord our God, lift up the light of thy countenance upon us : renew thy promise as in the days of old.

In thy light we shall see light : and thou wilt lead us to thy holy hill :

And dwell with us and be our God : and the days of our lamentation shall be ended :

And all tribes shall be gathered together : and thy spirit poured out upon all flesh :

The old men shall dream dreams : and the young men shall see visions.

Then shall the earth clothe her in beautiful raiment : she shall shine as the daughter of the Great King :

The houses of mourning shall be full of light : and the rod of the oppressor shall be broken for ever :

And man shall rejoice in the work of his hands : and the habitations of darkness shall be no more.

Be glad, O ye nations, and shout for joy : be strong and of a good courage, ye servants of the Lord :

For the living God is our helper : he that sitteth above the heavens shall bring it to pass.

Glory to him that hath his throne in the heavens : and his kingdom in the heart of his servants.

His kingdom is an everlasting kingdom : of his dominion there shall be no end.

BERNARD DARWIN

Born in 1876, and educated at Eton and Cambridge. Captained the Cambridge golf team in 1897 and has played for England on many occasions. Is golf correspondent to "The Times" and "Country Life," and is the author of many books, in the subjects of which golf and Dickens figure prominently.

BY COMPARISON with those of my distinguished fellows my contribution must, I fear, be trivial and almost frivolous. They represent the world of great and solemn things, and I, as far as this book is concerned, represent only the world of games. I have very small claims to do so save in this, that games or rather one game has shaped my career, which must inevitably have been a very different one without it.

"O Sairey, Sairey," said Mrs. Harris to Mrs. Gamp, "little do we know wot lays afore us." I do not suppose that it ever occurred to a beloved uncle of mine in the early eighties that he was profoundly affecting the life of a then very small nephew. And yet if he had belonged to any other regiment in the British Army that nephew's life might have lain in quite other and, as I make bold to think, less agreeable channels. It chanced that he was in the King's ; therefore he was quartered near Liverpool ; therefore he went to Formby to learn a strange new game called golf ; therefore when he went home to Wales on leave he borrowed some flower-pots for the holes and laid out a course at Aberdovey ; therefore I took passionately to golf when I was about eight years old. If I had not begun then I might never have begun at all, or at any rate I might not have learned to play, as I did, moderately well. If I had not played moderately well nobody would have wanted me to write about it, and if I had not written about it I should probably not have written about anything else. Q.E.D. It is clear that, as far as my obscure history is concerned, those flower-pots were liquid lead and wedges in the hands of fate.

A game having played so large a part in my life the least I can do is to stick up for it and I mean to do so. Golf bears the reproach of being "an old man's game" and it certainly has the advantage that it can be played with pleasure and even with success for longer perhaps than any other; but that point may be overemphasized. Once a man is a game-player, or for that matter an oarsman or an athlete, he remains so in spirit and in sympathy though he may long have ceased to take an active part. Rowing is a pursuit which most men must give up when they are still in the prime of their youth and yet it produces an enduring enthusiasm and an intimate world of its own. If one goes to Henley, as I have occasionally done with an eminent friend, feeling a little strange and shy at that esoteric festival and in such illustrious company, nothing is more striking, nothing, I think, more moving, than the sight of many comparative elderly gentlemen decked out in the gay plumage of their youth. The blazer of dark or light blue may have grown a little constricted or may even have had to be replaced ; the cap (having, like the Grand Panjandrum, a little round button on top) may seem, judged by modern standards, to perch insecurely on the very crown of the head ; but both proclaim *Et Militavi* and between those who have fought gloriously on the river there is an eternal bond and a fellowship second to none. As an inveterate dry-bob I make them my respectful compliments. Some of them may remain comparatively active by teaching the young idea from the towpath, but whether they do or not, they are for ever oarsmen though they never again sit in a boat.

So it is at Lord's or Twickenham or St. Andrews or at any other place where there meet together the votaries of a particular game. To each place belongs a particular fellowship, with its own "shop" and its own memories ; but they are all merged in a greater one, which speaks or at any rate understands the same language and has the same feeling for games, never wholly to be acquired by one who has not played. A common background or environment early in life makes for a very particular and a very comfortable bond. Those who become friends later and are then separated by circumstances, may feel strange when they meet again, and as if it was hard to pick up the threads; but to come across after long years one who was at school with us is, by comparison, to begin again naturally and easily where we left off. The common background of a game has, I think, much the same beneficent effect and indeed perhaps what I am trying to say is no more than this—but it is a great deal—that games provide a very good way of making friends.

I do not propose to write at large *De Amicitia*. I take as axiomatic that it is good and pleasant to have plenty of friends. But there is this to be said about the friendships made through games, that they bring together people in very different walks of life and having otherwise very different interests. In the ordinary way a man is apt to have the majority of his friends among those of his own business or profession. That is natural and right, but it may make for rather too confined and parochial a circle. A game is like a club, another, to my mind, very pleasant institution; it forms a link between those of varied pursuits who might not otherwise know each other. Game-players have a bad reputation for talking shop, which is to the uninitiated incomprehensible and intolerably dull; but they are not perhaps quite as black as they are painted ; they do have lucid intervals. Because men meet at Lord's or St. Andrews it does not follow they talk of nothing but cricket or golf. Through the original bond of a game we may make friends with those who can tell us all manner of exciting things about a life far removed from our common playground, which might have been a closed book to us. Some lines of J. K. Stephen's come into my head and may help me out.

> Some have travelled and some have fought :
> And some have written, and some are bitten
> With strange new faiths : desist
> From tracking them ; broker or priest or prince,
> They are all in the old School List.

There are many friends whom we do not track into their other occupations ; we may hardly know what they are ; but we have that common meeting place, that environment we all love ; we are always glad to see each other again there ; it has made and it keeps us friends.

There is one point on which I would particularly insist, namely that if we keep up with our game, even though we have ceased to play it seriously or at all, we ought to be assured of a number of younger friends. This must be good for us in keeping us younger ourselves and it is certainly most reviving to the spirits. It well becomes me to say so because I feel as if I had been exceptionally lucky. I have not missed a university golf match since I first took to writing about the game and that has brought me the pleasure of knowing many generations of undergraduates and of knowing some of them very well. The Oxford and Cambridge Golfing Society was founded the year after I went down from Cambridge which means that I have now been a member for some fifty years. That has meant many happy hours on tours or at our annual meeting at Rye spent in the company of those, who, as the years go on, grow collectively ever younger than myself, but do not seem to be so. In youth it gave us a great glow of pleasure when someone of an elder generation suggested that we dropped the respectful "Mr." or even called him by his Christian name. When we are old the glow produced by the converse process is at least equally heart-warming. I have always tried gently to discourage young gentlemen from "mistering" me, and they have responded with the most cheering kindness.

It may be said that: "Superfluous lags the vet'ran on the stage" of games as of other things and doubtless there is the danger. He may become a ridiculous and a tiresome figure. Perhaps he is so regarded, for what other people think of us is often mercifully hidden. Yet I have a faint hope that he is not, if he can behave with circumspection. He must not, I venture to suggest, too resolutely refuse to grow up, but must try to learn his place. He must know when to join in the fun and when softly to vanish away, for the too juvenile old gentleman is beyond all question a bore. He must not want to manage his juniors, but must let them manage their own concerns. He must not put his oar in unless he is asked, and then with great discretion. And he must, as far as he possibly can, avoid the undue praising of time past.

The inclination is, I am well aware, almost overwhelming, especially so in the matter of games. If I tell my juniors that some favourite book of the past is far superior to those of the present, they can do more than assume I am talking nonsense, they can convince themselves of the fact by reading the book. If, on the other hand, I tell them that no one really knows what golf can be unless he saw, let us say, John Ball or Harry Vardon, and that some modern champion is not worthy to black such heroes' boots, they can think I am talking nonsense, as I almost unquestionably am, but they cannot prove it. I have in my armoury the most irritating of weapons; I saw these great men and they never did. Doubtless this is an admirable argument, but doubtless also it is one that we had much better keep to ourselves. Youth is sometimes goaded to quote statistics, to say, for instance, that some modern batsman has made more runs than an illustrious predecessor. Alas! that will serve it but ill, for crabbed age can retort with the far superior bowling and that on worn wickets which the elder champions had to face. That fact of first-hand knowledge gives an advantage that is all too ruthlessly used. Age suffered from it years ago from a still older generation, and now that its own turn has come it will not lightly let it go.

Games are singularly provocative of hero worship and it is in the nature of things that the worshipper must be younger than the hero. Once we are of the same age as some god-like creature and can speak to him not looking upward but almost on terms of equality as man to man, something of the divine quality goes out of him ; he is still great but he is almost human. I find it impossible to believe that youth now looks at the heroes of today with quite the same wide-eyed, unquestioning reverence with which I used to gaze on the great Willie Fernie, as I followed him, an infinitely respectful little boy, round the links of Felixstowe. My brain realizes that it probably does, but my heart refuses assent. The fact is that comparisons between heroes of different epochs are always futile and almost always exasperating. True when several contemporaries meet together with nobody by, they may, if they please, indulge themselves and say in effect (with Mr. Macey the old parish clerk in *Silas Marner*) : "There's no voices like what there used to be, and there's nobody remembers what we remembers, if it isn't the old crows." But if there enter to them one of another generation they had better relapse into a conscience-stricken silence.

This is a counsel of perfection. Few can follow it and I am sure I don't, but I try. Some people do not even try, but seem always to be angry when they write about the present. "A time when golf was really golf, and such modern rubbish as hammer-headed drivers, handicap trophies, and endless other doubtless 'improvements' was happily unknown." So wrote an old Scottish gentleman and when I was an undergraduate it used to make me rather angry. Today I still remember it as an example of what to avoid, if possible.

There is one side of game-playing friendships, not I hope too sordid but, let us say, eminently practical, which deserves a word. They are in many cases extremely useful. It is easy to think of a first job, a first brief, or some other such start in life that has come to its recipient from his fame on fields of play. But it is worth remembering that it is only a beginning ; man cannot live by games alone and the start must be followed up. If it is not, the helping hand is likely to be soon withdrawn. On the other hand, if it is, the beginner acquires much additional merit with the world for turning his back on temptation and sticking to work. It may be possible but it is certainly not easy to strike a middle path.

I can think of one distinguished game-player (not a golfer I may add) who, having for some years done nothing in particular, thought he would try the City. His friends rallied round him and on his first day there came an agreeable little spate of commissions. It seemed an ideal life ; he felt like Mr. Mantalini "on Tom Tiddler's ground picking up the demnition gold and silver." He arrived on the second day to find, strange to say, that the flood of orders had run dry. "The City seems very quiet today," he remarked, and after the third day he cast the dust of it off his feet for ever. The incidents of my story may have been a little compressed for effect, but in its essence I believe it to be true. Whatever the career, games can often afford a helpful push at the beginning but after that the player has got to be like a cabman, always ready on the rank.

It is perhaps both too priggish and too obvious to say that it is a mistake to do nothing but play games, and in any case there will in the future be very few able to do so even if they want to. Nevertheless, I will say it because it is what I should so dearly have liked to do myself at one time of my life, and so have reason to bless the fact that I was not able to. To many the very notion must sound abhorrent, but I still think that for some little while it would have been extremely agreeable, and for those who are really distinguished in games the desire must often have been horribly urgent. Yet those who yield to it come too often to rather a sad pass. Once their greatness has begun to decline, they seem too often to fall to those unsatisfactory occupations, faintly suggestive of Mr. Micawber, of selling something on commission. Wine and motor cars in particular suggest themselves. If they do not live overtly on their friends, they must have little sinecures invented for them. They are apt to be known pityingly as "Poor old so-and-so." A certain glory still hangs round them and we in this country are very faithful and forgiving to our old heroes of play, but it is a miserable, heart-breaking end.

Everybody who wants to point the moral can probably think of some who have made this fatal mistake and likewise of those who have avoided it. In the one case it would be cruel and in the other impertinent to give examples from among those now living. But perhaps it is permissible to give one name from the past. Alfred Lyttelton always seems to me a shining example. Perhaps nobody is ever such a swell again as one who is a swell at school, and at Eton Alfred Lyttelton must have been by far the greatest swell that ever lived ; incomparably good at all games, high in the school, having a charm that made everyone his willing slave. At Cambridge he repeated and added to these triumphs in a larger world. When he came down he must have had innumerable friends who would have done anything to serve him and make life easy for him. He resolutely turned his back on games, save strictly in their legitimate place, worked hard at the Bar, and as everyone knows, rose to distinction both in his profession and in public life.

It may be said that here is nothing more to praise than in any other creditable and successful career, and that he who puts away childish things and turns firmly to work is simply a reasonable man with a sense of proportion. I confess I do not think so. "Fame is a glorious thing though it lasts but for a day" and the really famous player of games breathes a very heady incense. Because he is entirely wise to make a sacrifice it is a sacrifice none the less, not merely of the crowd's adulation, which is by comparison a mean thing, but of many happy hours and much pleasant company. He has to be to some extent a new boy again, to come down from the top of one ladder to the foot of another. He may be merely sensible, but he has shown more sense than a good many people would show if they were in his shoes, and I for one always feel a great respect for him. To think about nothing but games is to be a lamentable Peter Pan, and is in the end a soul-destroying mistake ; but I think it is wrong to underestimate the temptation.

I mentioned just now the merits of a sense of proportion. They are doubtless great in all the affairs of life and not least in the matter of games which ought to be kept in their proper place. I only wish I could have possessed them myself but I know very well that I never did. I always minded too much, which often made me very disagreeable to play with and made me unhappy myself. Having got that egotistical confession off my chest I may discourse more generally. "I could fight pretty well," said a very great golfer to me once, "if I could see the humour of it." That was a wise speech, the more so as it came from one who realized that he had not always been able to live up to his precept.

I think William James the philosopher has somewhere praised the sovereign remedy of "Don't care." I venture, so far at any rate as games are concerned, to substitute "mind" for "care." Not caring is admirable in retrospect ; when it is all over it is doubtless a mistake to be kept awake by the thought of a missed catch ; but games played without caring at the time are not worth the playing. We must want to win for ourselves or our side, and the preliminary "May the best man win" is, if genuine, a wretched, anæmic sentiment. If not, it is but an insincere flourish and deceives nobody. To be a good loser is a great and shining virtue, but it comes into being only when the match is lost and not before.

We in this country have often been accused by other nations of being hypocrites ; we cannot in the least understand why, and the accusation appears wholly unjust. Yet in games I think we are sometimes a little hypocritical in that we pretend to care—or mind—much less than we do. It may not be wholly our fault, for we seem to have been brought up to it in all sorts of ways. At school we regarded as a hero the boy who could dash off his copy of verses in no time and do them pretty well; not the one who toiled at them and did them better. We are always disposed to think too much of him who could do all sorts of wonderful things if only he would try. Preparation is something of which we have never thought very highly, wherefore many people, with a speech hanging over them, persuade themselves that they will be all right when it comes to the point. It is a fallacy which has produced many excruciating hours for the wretched listeners and has made our after-dinner oratory something of a byword.

This is apt to be our point of view in games. We reserve our greatest admiration for the "natural" player ; his conqueror, who has worked at the game, we damn with exceedingly faint praise and the epithet "made" or "artificial." I am not arguing the point of how far it is right to make a toil of a pleasure; I am only gently protesting that if a man does work hard to master the technique of a game, he need not pretend that he doesn't. It would never suit our national temperament to become slaves of a professional coach as do the young college athletes in America; nobody wants us to do so and he would be disappointed if he did. But we need not be such humbugs as we often are in professing not to care when we are really straining every nerve and sinew for victory. It really is such palpable humbug ; but I think we are growing rather more honest than we used to be.

These mild and random reflections must now come to an end. "We cannot refrain," wrote with a full heart a Scotsman of ninety years ago, "We cannot refrain for the life of us from closing our remarks on golfing with some expression of our intense attachment to it. . . . Golf, thou art a gentle sprite; we owe thee much."

I feel that I must say the same, for my debt is a large one in point of good times and good friends. Let me not appear complacent; but it is no use regretting that one was not born an entirely different sort of person. The other day the members of the Brains Trust were asked what they would do if they could start life again, and while most of them seemed reasonably satisfied as they were, one of them wished that he could have been a gardener. That went home to me because I wish that I had learnt to have more interests and do more things, and one of them is gardening. I am profoundly ignorant of it and not in the least worthy to be the owner of my own garden. That is a great mistake and another was not to learn to be a fisherman in the days when the River Dovey ran almost at my door. I might surely have spared a few days from the links. Both gardening and fishing would have been such pleasant, pensive things to do and incidentally to write about. It would have been wiser to store up more resources.

However, I am not going to repine and particularly at the moment at which I chance to be writing. In a short time, if all is well, I shall once again be going down with a team, though only in a non-playing capacity, to play againtt Cambridge, a team of old friends of various ages, against some who will, I hope, become new ones. To be able to do so, despite the long gap of the war years is certainly a cause for gratitude and I am very grateful. If it had not been for those Aberdovey flower-pots I should not be going to do it. There must be regrets and reservations but after all there is something to be said for making your work out of your fun. To spend a good part of your life doing the thing you happen to like best, in pleasant places and in pleasant company, seems to me not unenviable. I am afraid I would do it all over again.

VICTOR, 2nd EARL OF LYTTON

Born at Simla in 1876, the son of a former Viceroy of India, and best known for his connection with Indian affairs (Under-Secretary of State for India 1920–22; Governor of Bengal 1922–27). Also prominently connected with the work of the League of Nations[1].

WHEN ONE has reached the allotted span of threescore years and ten, one ought, I suppose, to be able to summarize what one has learnt from life; and if one's life has been full and varied, one ought to have learnt a good deal. But when one attempts to record the lessons of life, it is difficult to know where to begin and in what order to set them down. Some that were the hardest to learn may not have been the most important, and others may have been learnt so easily as not to be recognized as lessons at all. How also can one distinguish between the normal development of qualities and ideas with which one started in life and others which were generated by actual experience? The inventory is not an easy one to make; but I will try and set down such things as my memory can supply me with.

I was born into a family richly endowed with worldly possessions and into a generation which still enjoyed the complete security of a hundred years' peace. The Napoleonic wars with France ended before my father was born, and all my own children were born before the wars with Germany began. The security of my home life was shattered while I was still at school, and the security of our national life before I was past middle life. My father was Viceroy of India at the time of my birth. He was British Ambassador in Paris when he died. I was then fifteen years old, and up to that

[1]The Editor and Publishers learned with sorrow of the death of Lord Lytton as this volume went to press.

age had known only the sheltered existence of a large comfortable home with plenty of servants and the highest social position. Immediately after my father's death we lost all our money through the speculations of a friend in whom my father had trusted and who had betrayed the trust. Our scale of living had to be reduced. Our family home was let: we moved into a small house, and all expenditure was reduced to a minimum.

This experience provided my first lesson in life, and what I learnt from it was that money was not essential either to happiness or to human dignity. Our poverty did not involve any social ostracism. My mother, whom I had known only as a social queen, either as Vicereine in India, as hostess at Knebworth, or as Ambassadress in Paris, accepted the complete change in her standard of living without a word of complaint or the slightest loss of dignity; and her example made a deep and lasting impression upon my mind and character. It enabled me to understand the truth of a saying she used often to repeat to us : "Lose money, lose little ; lose honour, lose much ; lose heart, lose all." When Queen Victoria made her one of her ladies-in-waiting, the contrast of her periodic attendance at court, when she would wear her jewels and drive in a royal carriage, did not make more difficult her complete acceptance of the modest standard of living which economy necessitated when she was at home, for she accepted and filled this office not as a social distinction, but as an opportunity for service; and we learnt from her that all forms of service can be both honourable and satisfying.

As I am speaking of my mother, I may say that the greatest thing I learnt from her—the thing which has most contributed to my peace of mind in life—was the acceptance of the inevitable and the rigid exclusion of that form of self-torture which comes from regret. So long as alternatives are possible and issues are in the balance, the anxiety of doubt cannot be avoided, but as soon as the die is cast, a decision taken, or an event occurs which nothing can alter, I have taught myself to banish all thoughts of what might have been, all doubts as to whether the decision was right or wrong, all regrets for what is irrevocable. I can say that this is one of the things I have learned from life, for I was not born with this capacity, but acquired it by rigid self-discipline. It is a habit of mind which I recommend all young people to try and acquire while they are young, for it cannot be acquired later.

A variation of this mental attitude is contained in a phrase which George Wyndham used often to repeat, in the days when I was his private secretary in Ireland. "Remember always," he would say, "that everything counts and nothing matters." By this he meant that no effort must be spared, no least thing left undone to win a game or to attain the object on which one has set one's heart, but if one fails—it doesn't matter, and must not cause one to lose heart. That always struck me as wise counsel for ambitious youth.

To return to my childhood days, another thing that I learned early was that where there is innate sincerity class is no barrier to mutual respect. The hero of my childhood was not my father, but his valet. My playmates were the children of my village. I would go bird's-nesting with the son of our coachman, and play cricket with boys from the village school or the little Londoners in a cottage home for waifs and strays. The point is not that I made friends with them, but that they had no difficulty in making friends with me. Those were days when children were taught good manners, both at home and at school. The boys would touch their hats, and the girls would curtsey to my parents, and their parents called me "My Lord," but our friendship and intimacy were complete and sincere, a far more comfortable relationship than exists today, when the assertion of equality has only led to bad manners and class-consciousness. All my life I have had friends in all classes and have learnt from them that sincerity is the best ingredient of friendship.

Having been born towards the close of the nineteenth century and now approaching the middle of the twentieth, I am able from personal experience to compare them in this matter of sincerity. I am struck by a great increase of this quality in all social matters, and an equally marked decrease of it in the political field, especially in all international relations. I attribute both developments largely to the wars of the last thirty years. War, like death, is a terrible reality. It is a ruthless sifter of truth and sham. In times of war men and women are judged by what they are, and not by what they pretend to be. Humbug and pretence cannot long survive in the atmosphere of war, and only that which is true and sincere commands respect.

The nineteenth century was a period of prolonged peace and great intellectual activity, but being an age of romance, it was largely one of make-believe. The Romantic Revival, which began with Scott, was a revolt against the formality of eighteenth-century style, but the departure from conventions and the breaking down of previously accepted rules which followed in literature, art and music, were accompanied by great artificiality in dress, behaviour, and habits of thought. Truth counted for nothing; everywhere was make-believe. Brick houses were covered with stucco to look like castles; ruins were built to give an air of romance to the countryside; clothes were designed to conceal as far as possible the shape of the human form; loose conduct was overlaid with strict morals or lofty sentiments; poverty concealed by a false show of wealth. In almost everything the counterfeit passed for the truth.

Although much of this elaborate artificiality had been discarded before the end of the century, traces of it lingered on until 1914, when for the first time in its history the country became involved in a war which affected the whole population and not merely its professional soldiers and sailors. The social revolution brought about by those war years marked a complete change from all nineteenth-century habits, customs, dress and behaviour. In the fierce testing fire of that war-experience, only what was natural and genuine could survive; and the process then started was completed during the even more totalitarian war conditions of 1939–45. These two wars effected social changes in this country as complete and far-reaching as those brought about in France by the French Revolution at the end of the eighteenth century, and greater than any which could have come about in a hundred years by a normal process of development.

But whereas the effect of these wars on private life was to introduce a greater measure of sincerity and less artificial habits and behaviour, in public life their effect has been the exact opposite.

It has been said that truth is the first casualty in war. Military authorities regard truth as a dangerous crime. In order to deceive the enemy, it must be suppressed, and may be perverted. Governments that have practised deception for many years as a military necessity become skilled in the process, and continue the habit long after the necessity has disappeared. As most of the nations of the world have either been engaged in actual warfare, or have been obsessed by the fears and suspicions which are the fruits of war, for the last thirty years, scarcely a vestige of truth or sincerity now remains in their relations with one another or in the language of their diplomatic communications. Words today in the sphere of international politics have lost all meaning, since they bear not the slightest relation to the facts or the intentions which they profess to describe. Examples of the divergence between profession and performance, or of the use of words in a sense completely at variance with their generally accepted meaning could be selected almost any day from the newspapers in which the speeches of political leaders or the reports of international conferences are recorded. A single example, however, stands out so prominently as to be within the memory of everyone.

On August 12, 1941, the President of the United States and the Prime Minister of Great Britain met each other on the high seas, and issued a joint declaration which came to be known as the Atlantic Charter. This famous declaration was subsequently accepted by thirty-five other nations which were at the time of their acceptance allied belligerents against the Axis Powers. It was presumably intended to be a statement of their war aims, and was generally regarded as such. Although couched in vague terms, it defined the general principles which these countries pledged themselves to follow, if ultimate victory should give them the power to dictate the terms of peace.

The Atlantic Charter began with the following two clauses:—

1. Their countries seek no aggrandizement, territorial or other.
2. They desire to see no territorial changes that do not accord with the freely expressed wishes of the peoples concerned.

These principles, thus defined, clearly applied not only to any ultimate settlement between the Allies themselves, but also to the enemy countries against which they were then fighting. The only possible interpretation to be put upon the words is that the signatories of the Charter pledged themselves, in the event of victory, not only to respect the integrity of each other's territory, but not to make enforced annexations of the territory of their enemies. "They seek no territorial aggrandizement" can only mean "They will not increase their own territories by adding to them territory taken from other countries." "No territorial changes that do not accord with the freely expressed wishes of the peoples concerned" can only mean "people shall not be transferred from one country to another without their consent." At the time the declaration was made no one doubted that the words used had these meanings, and the object of the declaration was presumably to weaken the will-to-war of their enemies by assuring them that their surrender would not involve the annexation of their territory. Unless this were the object, there was no point in making the declaration at the time it was made.

Now compare the profession of the Atlantic Charter with the performance of its signatories, when the unconditional surrender of their enemies was finally secured. Their performance is to be judged not only by annexations or territorial changes already made without any regard to the wishes of the populations involved, but by the proposals for further territorial changes that were later discussed at the Peace Conference in Paris, and already agreed upon by the countries whose statesmen were the original authors of the Atlantic Charter. By such common consent has this great declaration of high altruistic purposes been consigned to oblivion that it is not even referred to by those who have suffered by its disregard.

As to the misuse of words, "democracy" is perhaps the one most commonly employed without the slightest regard to its real meaning, and "democratic," "freedom-loving" and "peace-loving," or "fascist," "reactionary" and "imperialist" are epithets used as carelessly as those selected by a schoolboy from his *Gradus* when writing Latin verses—the first three being interchangeable for those of whom I approve and the second three for those of whom I disapprove.

In national politics the tendency has been much the same. Here, too, Truth is a displaced person, seeking a home and finding none. Party window-dressing to captivate the electorate would be deemed fraudulent in the prospectus of a business company. The language of politicians, whether when praising their own party or criticizing that of their opponents, has little more relation to fact than that of international diplomacy. The action of government, whether when praising their own party or criticizing that of their opponents, has little more relation to fact than that of international diplomacy. The actions of government departments are as grotesque and cumbersome as the Victorian crinoline. Looking back at the end of a long life, I can say that in my experience, whilst in all personal relations, in society and in business honesty, sincerity, straightforwardness and truth are the qualities expected and largely met with, in politics romance is still as fashionable as in the last century.

I have had many other experiences. I have travelled round the world and lost a day somewhere in the Pacific Ocean. I have visited many countries and seen beauty in many forms—dawn in high mountains, the phosphorescent sea under a tropical moon, fireflies dancing in Italian fields, the incomparable serenity of an Arctic night, the pink glory of a flock of flamingos rising from a blue lake in Indian sunlight, the song of birds, the dazzling purity of sunlit snowfields, and the loveliest buildings that human hands have erected. From all these I have learned that it is not only in our infancy that heaven lies about us. The gates of heaven are open all round us for those who have the eyes to see through them. Such services as I have been able to render have been lavishly recompensed by high honours and decorations; but one of my most cherished memories is the honour paid me one day by a little girl in the Whitechapel Road, who put her hand in mine and said, "Please, sir, will you pass me across the road?"

As we travel through life we learn many things from personal experiences, from intercourse with our fellow men, from travel, from books, but on the whole we find, I think, only what we look for; and at the end the truth is we are not so much that we are what life has made us, as that our life has been for us what we have made it. It is one of the kind provisions of nature that our memory is more retentive of pleasant then of unpleasant experiences. We remember always the few fine days we have enjoyed; the countless cold wet ones are soon forgotten. So it is the beauty rather than the ugliness of life that lingers in my memory, the kindness and generosity of friends rather than the hatred and cruelty which also abound.

While I was still at school I became acquainted with a lovely Greek sentence in a play of Sophocles, where Antigone says, "I was not born to share men's hatred, but their love," and all my life these words have defined my attitude to the causes and movements which I have espoused. In religion, in politics, in social reforms, I have shared the sympathies and been repelled by the antipathies of every cause, and thus I have never been able to become a wholehearted partisan. I eschew labels, because I have found that in the great religious and political struggles of history, and in those of my own lifetime, the adherents of all creeds and all parties, while they condemn the cruelties and hatreds of others, are themselves cruel and vindictive to their enemies. To me cruelty is revolting, whether it is practised by Catholics or Protestants, by the Inquisition or by Atheists, by Jews or anti-Semites, by Nazis, Fascists or Communists, by aristocrats or Socialists. Every cause which aims at the relief of human suffering, the removal of injustices, or the increase of human happiness has had my sympathy and support. Every act of spoliation, or persecution, or cruelty, or injustice, has my condemnation, even though practised by friends or done in the name of justice or retribution. I can see some good in all political parties, all good in none. For the same reason I am impatient of sweeping generalizations about other countries. I neither share the prevalent British dislike of all foreigners, nor the hatred of particular countries because we have been at war with them. I suffered many insults and much rudeness from Germans in my young days; I have plenty of cause to dislike them, but I owe my life to one German doctor. I made many friends when I was in Japan; that friendship does not exonerate their countrymen from blame for the cruelty they practised in the war, but it prevents me from branding all Japanese as uncivilized savages. In my young days it was a crime to be a pro-Boer, yet every Englishman today would be proud to shake the hand of Field Marshal Smuts. At the beginning of the last century an English general declared that he could not sleep in his bed at night so long as one Frenchman remained alive ; yet no Englishman today regards France as a potential enemy, no Frenchman has reason to fear England. Before the present century closes our fears of Germany or Russia may be equally out of date.

One last word I may add for the benefit of the younger generation. It is customary to believe that progress is a law of nature, and that the world goes on getting better and better. My life has taught me that this is not so. Experience emphatically disproves this comfortable belief. We have seen in recent years cruelty, brutality and persecution which at the beginning of my life no one would have imagined possible, deeds which surpass in their horror the worst crimes of the Middle Ages. Yet those who perpetrated them believed that they were justifiable, such is the hypnotizing quality of blind partisanship. No, if the world is to progress we must take a great deal of trouble and be ceaselessly vigilant. Otherwise the world will easily deteriorate, and the advance of science only increases the danger. Greater knowledge has but added refinements to cruelty, and science has now placed in men's hands such power of destruction that unless means can be found to end war, the next war will end the world.

LORD ASHFIELD

Born in 1874 at Derby, and educated in America where he became a general manager of various electric railways. In 1907 was appointed General Manager of London's Underground electric railways and from 1916 to 1919 was President of the Board of Trade. Chairman of the London Passenger Transport Board 1933–47, and now a member of the British Transport Commission.

I OFTEN WONDER whether the rising generation of today fully realize the extraordinary and even revolutionary age in which they are living. The changes that have taken place since the latter part of the last century, when my active working life began, have indeed been revolutionary. To those whose experience in life has been confined to the last twenty years, our present age may seem by no means extraordinary. Perhaps only those who have lived and worked over the past fifty years, and more especially those in positions of responsibility, can appreciate to the full the amazing transformation of social life that has taken place as a result, in the main, of scientific and technical advances.

The social historian of the future will, I think, regard the period in which we are living as remarkable for two things. In the first place, there has been the rapid and ever-growing acceleration in the rate of progress of scientific research and technical development, and the accompanying rise in the standards of material comfort, not merely of the privileged few but of all classes. This rise in the general standard of living during the past fifty years is obvious and significant, but the wider diffusion of the good things of material existence could not have been achieved except by a marked growth in the national income, and this in turn could come about only as a result of technical advance. Progress in science and technology was rapid enough before the Second World War, and it is a matter for some reflection that the needs of war should, as in the First World War, once again have given a fillip to research, and telescoped into a few years what before the war would have been regarded as the work of a decade or more.

I now come to what I would describe as the second major social phenomenon of our time, to which perhaps too little constructive thought has been devoted in this country. The ever-rising standards of amenity and comfort, which we have come to regard almost as a birthright, could not have fructified if there had not been a parallel evolution in industrial organization. I refer to the emergence of the large corporation, whether public or private, which to an increasing degree has come to dominate the scene, not only here and in the United States, but also, I gather, in collectivist Russia.

It is curious how the large undertaking—in the past necessarily under private ownership—has so frequently been regarded as a sort of evil emanation of "Big Business" and, so it has been contended, of necessity socially undesirable. Yet it requires no profound economic analysis to realize that the rising standard of living for all is dependent on mass production, and that the technique of mass production involves large plants and large-scale organization—in other words, the large corporation. Who owns it, whether private enterprise or the State, is immaterial from the point of view of its fundamental social purpose, namely, the production on a large scale of goods at a price within the reach of the mass of consumers. And the same applies to services, including such natural monopolies as power, water and transport.

It is obvious that large undertakings of any kind present major problems of organization. It would be idle to pretend that a complete solution to these problems has been found, whether here or in the United States, where much thinking and study have been directed to analysing the conditions under which the large productive units such as General Motors, to name only one great enterprise, can survive. One cannot deny that questions of administrative structure are of the first importance : the chain by which authority is devolved, the limits of devolved authority, the degree of specialization of function, the test of efficiency, the problem of ensuring the succession—to mention some of the questions that need to be discussed and determined—are all matters of the greatest significance. Yet, important as the machinery of administration may be, it must never be forgotten that such machinery exists merely to enable human beings to co-operate for the achievement of a given purpose and that, in the last analysis, it is the human factor that, in administration of whatever kind, determines success.

The large corporation, whether public or private, has come to stay. It is not so much an integral part as the condition of the survival of our present social and industrial order. The retention and improvement of the standard of living already attained, and the wider diffusion of that standard are alike dependent on the success with which these great bodies are administered. Those whose duty it is to direct their affairs at a high level—and I am thinking not only of chairmen and members of boards, but also of the senior officials—have a very heavy responsibility. The successful discharge of this responsibility is not determined solely by the form of organization, though a fundamentally wrong form of organization may go far to frustrate the efforts of all. Nevertheless, our Anglo-Saxon way is the evolution of administrative structure by trial and error, rather than by the method of *a priori* analysis. As a people we are always inclined to apply the simple practical test, "Does it work?", rather than to inquire, "Does it conform to strict logical analysis?", an approach which seems to be favoured by other peoples. The former method of approach may not suit the logician, but somehow or other it suits the Anglo-Saxon. At any rate it gives, I suggest, fuller scope for personality and originality and, ultimately, for the human factor. It is to the problems of human qualities and human relations that the attention of ambitious young men and women, whom it is to be assumed have had a satisfactory basic education, can most profitably be directed. What, then, are the qualities needed by those who are destined to take the lead in the large corporations, whether public boards of the pattern of the London Passenger Transport Barod or the new National Coal Board, or the great private undertakings which are household names both here and abroad?

When everything has been done in an effort to select and train the right men to carry on the affairs of an undertaking after the present administrators have retired from the scene, there can still be no certainty that the problem of the succession has been solved. Men who show every promise and seem to have, within reason, qualities which fit them for leadership are frequently found in the upshot to be lacking in certain vital respects. There may be, for example, personality without fundamental character, or without background obtained by patient study and reflection and from observation of men. And there is the case of the man of profound learning, unilluminated, however, by personality or sagacity or knowledge of men and the springs of conduct. There is every shade of personality between such extremes. What qualities, then, should we seek in those who may be called upon to administer these great enterprises?

It is evident that "character" is a fundamental but not always decisive quality. Learning, too, is valuable, though by no means essential. But there is one faculty that is indispensable in the great, as in the smaller, affairs of life, and that is the quality of decision. No organization, great or small, can survive unless everybody in it knows that, both in matters of policy and daily administration, they can get clear binding decisions without fumbling and procrastination. In matters of policy, there must be in the minds of all concerned the knowledge that once the issue has been thoroughly discussed from every angle, and everybody who is entitled to be heard has given his opinion, a decision will be taken which can safely be acted upon in the sure knowledge that there will be no vacillation, and that those who have to carry it out, however difficult and unpleasant it may be, will be supported through thick and thin in the execution of the policy that has been decided upon. This may all sound very elementary, but in my experience it goes to the root of successful management. Without this quality of decision nobody can safely be entrusted with the oversight of the affairs of any undertaking, and least of all of these great corporations which employ, under present-day conditions, perhaps hundreds of thousands of men and women and the actions of which are capable of influencing for good or ill the comfort, well-being and prosperity of the community as a whole.

I have hinted that decision is not enough ; it must also be speedy. The reflective and, it may be, more scholarly types of men, do not always sufficiently appreciate that any decision based on sound judgment is better than no decision at all. It is true that a decision may not always be the best one but, such is the complexity of human affairs, we can never be confident that we are fully acquainted with all the relevant facts. It so often happens in real life that the decision taken on the basis of an incomplete knowledge of the facts turns out right in the end. Very often, too, there is more than one solution to a given problem. It must never be forgotten also that in the affairs of life the decision may itself influence the psychological environment, and may well render proper and workable an imperfect and even "wrong" judgment, perforce arrived at in the absence of a full knowledge of all the considerations involved.

There is no magic formula by which the superficially simple quality of making up one's mind can be instilled, but the mere possession of this indefinable quality is not enough for its successful exercise, which depends on other factors upon which it is impossible to lay too much emphasis. Many second-rate minds are under the delusion that little more is involved in making a decision than the mere exercise of overriding authority. But a decision has to be carried into effect and this will never be efficiently done unless the decision seems to those who have to execute it to be essentially a reasonable one. It should be obvious that, if decisions are to be fully effective, the co-operation of those who have to carry them out must be enlisted. A decision does not turn only on a knowledge of the material facts but also on judgment of the reactions and outlook of the people who may have to act upon the decision as well as of those who, as "consumers" in the widest sense, may be affected by it. In other words, the quality of capacity of making decisions must be tempered by common sense or that more intuitive variation of common sense, usually described as "horse sense," or its more refined version known as sagacity, perhaps the most valuable all-round quality that those in charge of affairs can possess.

I must leave it to the professional psychologists to tell us whether sagacity, like brains, is something with which one is born and not an acquired quality ; whichever it is, I am at any rate confident that it can be developed by various means within the reach of most of us. Thus, those who aspire to high places must enlarge their experience by having many contacts, acquaintances and friends outside the immediate activity with which they are normally concerned. They must cultivate a wide range of interests and be prepared to gather knowledge from the experience of others in all walks of life. When all is said and done, the basic principles of administration are the same, whether it is the oversight of a government department, a great railway or a major industrial enterprise. It all goes back to the judicious selection of the essential facts from a wide assembly of information relevant in varying degree to the matter in hand, and to its ultimate interpretation in terms of human values. How other people react and behave in similar circumstances must always afford fruitful guidance in dealing with one's own problems. The recluse and the pure scholar, however gifted, have little place in the higher levels of administration.

But making friends and being a good "mixer" are no substitutes for wide reading, which is indispensable for anybody who may, in the fullness of time, be called upon to exercise great responsibilities. I sometimes hear people say that they are too busy to find time for reading. This is a serious self-criticism for, in my experience, men who have made their mark are almost invariably omnivorous readers, though, admittedly, reading should be reasonably selective. Of all types of literature perhaps that which affords most guidance to the would-be administrator is biography. I think a study of biographies, not only of the great personalities of history like Augustus, Marlborough, and Abraham Lincoln—to quote just a few examples—but also of the lesser personalities, will serve to enforce in vivid fashion the importance of the quality of sagacity and more than that, the need for both tolerance and patience, which in its most developed form is the art of timing, almost a sixth sense, without which no administrator can be successful. One may have made up one's mind about the right course to be pursued but the moment may not be right for putting the decision into effect. Examples in the realm of warfare will occur to everybody. What so often distinguishes the successful from the unsuccessful general is the sense of when to strike. Military analogies are not always a safe and sure guide in civil affairs, but there can be no question that the successful administrator is invariably marked by a sense of the proper moment when to take action.

I have been dealing so far with what may be termed the psychological aspects of administration, which, as I have endeavoured to convey, transcend any questions of the structure of the administrative machine. However perfectly functions may be adjusted between the various parts of an organization, however carefully the chain of responsibility may be contrived, the organization can only be effective if those who control it have the faculty of giving sagacious decisions at the psychological moment.

A few words must be said about the essential nature of administrative decisions. Large questions of policy commonly involve the integration—if the use of this fashionable but much overworked word may be permitted—of a variety of factors, commercial, financial, technical and, nowadays, frequently political. It is the business of the appropriate sections of the organization to produce information and advice bearing upon the various aspects of the problem under review, so that those with whom the final decision rests may be properly informed in making their judgments. The complexity and changing character of the world in which we live necessitate consideration of a wide variety of facts and opinions before any conclusion can be reached. It is the art of the administrator to distinguish the relevant from the irrelevant, for in actual practice it will nearly always be found that the ultimate decision turns on one or two essential features of the problem under consideration. This capacity of being able to "see the wood," as distinct from the "trees" which constitute it, is the crucial quality of the administrator, which differentiates him from the typical technical adviser whose job, by its very nature, is not to take the broad, integrating view, so much as to give technically correct advice upon the purely, it may be, engineering or scientific aspects of the matter. It would be an over-simplification, however, to represent an administrative decision as fundamentally little more than an exercise in skilled judgment in relation to selected facts. As I have already said, one can rarely, if ever, know all the facts and their possible implications, and it is here that there is scope for the precious gift of imagination which inspires all great leadership. This is indeed an innate quality which is hardly susceptible of cultivation. The administrator endowed with imagination has the invaluable faculty of seeing the familiar from new angles, which is the condition of all innovation.

The need for imagination in administration cannot be over-emphasized. One of the major problems of large-scale administration is the fundamental incompatibility of two opposing forces. On the one hand, there must be an established routine if the efforts of large numbers of persons are to be directed towards the achievement of some common purpose ; on the other hand, progress implies innovation and the disturbance and, it may be, the complete supersession of an established routine, perhaps to the temporary discomfort of many who have become habituated to it. The danger in every large organization is ossification, which expresses itself in a dislike, and sometimes even hatred, of the introduction of disturbing innovations. The inertia of the great organization must always tend to be in the direction of avoidance of change, and the inhibition of the novel and unfamiliar. Imagination is therefore essential to the healthy survival of any large institution ; without it there can only be decay, owing to an increasing lack of adaptation to the ever-changing social and economic environment which, in private enterprise, culminates in the simple process of bankruptcy, but in public enterprise in lower efficiency and lower standards of living and welfare for the community as a whole.

So far I have been talking about those qualities that mark the successful administrator in the sphere of decision, particularly in relation to matters of policy, but no large enterprise of any kind can be conducted without negotiations which involve dealing with one's fellow men, as representatives, for example, of other undertakings, trade unions and government departments. The process of negotiation is often visualized as a sort of battle between opposing interests, and this may not infrequently be an apt description of what takes place on such occasions. But the true purpose of negotiation is a settlement which is not only mutually acceptable, but one which will endure because of its inherent fairness to both points of view. Much can be said about the art of negotiation, but there are a few simple principles which all my experience tells me should guide those who may have the heavy task of representing organizations in their external relations with other bodies. It is fundamental that there should be mutual trust and good faith, if worth-while settlements are to be reached, which both parties will respect and scrupulously adhere to. It never pays to take a trick by "cleverness"; for you generally have to go on living with those with whom you negotiate, and a man who has once been tricked is unlikely to forgive his opponent, and will be looking out on a future occasion for some way of getting his own back. In negotiations, again, there must never be any private or mental reservations about what is intended in any agreement that has been reached, or about the interpretation to be placed on particular phrases or words in which an agreement is embodied. There can be no confidence between negotiators, if either party says one thing but means another, or, as sometimes happens, seeks to import into an understanding something which can perhaps be read into what was agreed, but which it is known full well was never mentioned or intended by either side during the negotiations. Such tactics are the death knell of that mutual trust between negotiators without which no satisfactory and conclusive adjustment of opposing interests or points of view can ever be effected.

It is characteristic of all large organizations, whether public or private, that there should be a great deal of high-grade work on paper. When a decision has been taken upon an important issue or, it may be, an agreement has been reached with an outside body, such as a trade union or a government department, what has been settled must be recorded in black and white in clear and unambiguous terms. In the preparatory stages, too, leading up to a decision or an agreement, it is generally necessary for written statements to be prepared, setting out the essentials of the matter in hand, and appraising the various considerations to which regard must be paid in order to reach a conclusion. The proportion of even educated people capable of producing a good draft is disappointingly small. It is not a matter of fine writing, but of clarity and conciseness of expression, and reasonable skill in the use of words. The majority of us can, with some effort, master this indispensable art, at any rate sufficiently for such purposes as I have indicated. There is one good way of doing this. I have already referred to the habit of wide reading as having particular value in extending our knowledge of men and affairs. The careful study of works by writers whose style is acknowledged, coupled with constant practice in writing, will usually help one to acquire at least a measure of competence. There is the parallel but distinctive quality of being able, not merely to write clearly, but to speak clearly, for nobody can get very far these days without being called upon, sooner or later, to address meetings of one kind or another, whether inside or outside his organization. In the field of what I may term external relations, involving contact with government departments, trade unions and other organizations, capacity to speak clearly and convincingly is practically indispensable. I am not, of course, referring to oratory, but merely to a capacity, by word of mouth, to convey in simple fashion to other people what one means. Lucidity of thought is, in a sense, a prerequisite to clarity in writing and in speech, but the development of facility in writing and speaking will be found of itself to promote lucidity of thought.

I hope that nothing I have said will be thought to prescribe standards of ability and conduct in higher administration which, in the aggregate, may seem to be the attributes of the superman. Geniuses are few and far between, and they usually lack a large proportion of the more homely qualities to which I have referred. The world's work has in reality got to be carried out, in the main, by ordinary, common-sense folk who do their best, stimulated perhaps to higher levels of achievement by leadership and a sense of social duty. Those in positions of responsibility must not be visualized as people set apart from the common run of humanity, but rather as those upon whom the burden of leadership has been placed and who, as fallible human beings, are doing their best to do their duty. Like other people, they have their moments of weakness, of doubt and indecision. You have only to read biographies to discover how true this is. You will also discover how such personal qualities as those I have described have enabled men in positions of authority to face up to and often overcome their personal difficulties. The importance of the ordinary individual is often insufficiently appreciated by "clever" people. Yet every organization, in the discharge of its functions, must depend very largely on the efforts of average human beings, even in the highest places. It is here that the vitalizing force of leadership comes into play. All experience indicates that the future success or failure of the large corporation will depend ultimately on the quality of the leadership, including the creation, not only of a sense of unity, but also of a common social purpose amongst staff of all ranks.

It will, I hope, be evident that, in the long run, it is the personal qualities that count—power of decision, common sense and sagacity, judgment, imagination, fair dealing—and to these I would add, freedom from self-importance. There can be dignity without conceit. And there is yet one further human quality with which all other qualities should be suffused, and that is a sense of humour, coupled with a tolerance for the imperfections of human nature and a general willingness to give and take. How often can a sense of humour help in the conduct of difficult negotiations, when tempers are frayed and nerves are on edge. How important it is to preserve a just balance when dealing with human beings at all levels of responsibility, and make sympathetic allowance for their shortcomings, unless they are due to obvious negligence.

Finally, I need hardly say that I am not pretending to offer some general formula or code of guidance that is universally applicable, nor do I intend to imply that the only worth-while thing in life is the oversight of the affairs of great corporations.

If my remarks appear to overemphasize the problems of higher administration, that is simply because my experience in life has been in that particular direction. One can repay one's debt to the community in many other ways, for a balanced society is the product of the efforts of all in every walk of life. Let us never forget the ordinary person, whose patience and competent discharge of his daily task, when all is said and done, are fundamental to progress and who, after all, constitutes, in the main, society itself. Those who feel an urge to make their contribution to the common welfare must be willing to work hard, must be keenly interested in their environment and in their fellow men, and, above all, must be imbued with a sense of duty and a consciousness of social purpose in all they undertake.

FRANK O. SALISBURY

Born in 1874. Studied art at Heatherley's and the Royal Academy Schools and, later, on the Continent. Exhibited first picture at the Royal Academy in 1899 and has specialized in the painting of portraits of world-famous personalities and of contemporary scenes of great historic importance to Britain and the British Empire.

WHEN THE Court was out of town the keeper of the Royal apartments showed me over Buckingham Palace, and as we passed from one room to another I noticed that although he had a bunch of keys he used only one separate special key, and finally I asked him to let me see this wonder key that opened all the doors large or small. Placing it in my hand, he said: "That is the master key that opens all the doors in the palace; the only duplicate is in the possession of His Majesty the King."

Immediately there flashed across my mind the thought that every man is the proud possessor of a Master Key, not to the doors of a palace but to the House of Life itself. Built on a strange and complicated plan, this House is full of winding stairways and narrow passages leading to closed doors. Only with the magic key in his hand can the leaseholder, for the House of Life is no freehold, fling wide the doors that bar his progress and make his way to the light and warmth of the upper rooms. A marvellous key, indeed, and at the same time a talisman since, wisely used, it will bring into being new halls of achievement, gleaming shrines of renown, in which the human spirit can find rest and renewal.

This Master Key was mercifully placed in the hand of our first parent by the Almighty Himself when He pronounced what must have seemed the dread sentence: "In the sweat of thy face shalt thou eat bread." And it has proved to be, throughout all the ages of mankind, one of the most precious and beneficent gifts of God. It is the Key of Industry. We may also with profit remember the story of a wise father, as his sons set out into the world, placing in their hands three keys which he himself had tested and proved of unrivalled efficiency.

The first, a golden key forged in imperishable metal—The Love of God.

The second, a key of heraldic significance and beauty—The Love of King and Country.

The third, a key of magic metal—The Love of Work.

The doorstep to the temple of wisdom is the knowledge of our own ignorance. Whatever our early schooling may have been the university of experience is the decisive test. Self-education is most valuable ; untiring energy and concentration is a great character builder. When we leave home and take up responsibilities in the wider world of endeavour we find in whatever walk of life we may choose, that to succeed we must apply the knowledge we have gained to the task of life.

I was working away at my canvas painting a portrait of a city business man who, after watching me quietly at my work, said : "You have to apply yourself to your work in the same way as I have to do in the city." Yes, there are extraordinary parallels, but some have work they like and others make a success of work they dislike—theirs will be the greater reward. We only get out of life what we put into it. The law of the universe is against something for nothing. To accept what has not been earned is to degrade character, and sooner or later corruption and degeneracy set in. Humanity must be obedient to the law of creation which ordains that there be a balance of justice and reward.

The glory of achievement shall be the rearguard of the industrious man, but the spectres of greed, envy, and malice shall haunt the steps of the slothful.

President Harding made this great observation : "Let no one beguile you with dreams of idleness. Work is the supreme blessing of mankind. Without it life would be an intolerable existence."

Confronting us is the constant challenge: are we content to take the line of least resistance, the easy way, to move on the lower plane of life, or boldly facing the world are we determined to solve the problems—preparing for the worst and hoping for the best? Man is often at his noblest when life tugs at him with almost unbearable tension; it may be the dawn of success unless the heart fails. A great cotton merchant told me that if he managed to solve his business problems successfully three times out of five he had conquered.

A man who had achieved a wonderful work under very difficult circumstances was asked the secret of his success. He said: "I work as though everything depended on me; and pray as though everything depended on God."

When I was painting a picture of St. Galahad fighting the Seven Deadly Sins with sword drawn and uplifted, courageously facing his deadly ominous opponents, I felt I wanted some words to fit the subject, and at that moment the telephone bell rang. When I took up the receiver I recognized the voice of a college professor who started his conversation by saying: "Last night I took for my subject with the men, 'The immediate availability of the divine resources." I replied: "How wonderful! Repeat those words, for they are the very words I was needing at this moment."

As a student early in my career I learnt a very fine lesson which I did not fully appreciate or understand at the time. My elder brother wrote to Lord Leighton, President of the Royal Academy, to ask his advice about my going to Florence to study art during the winter months, and although my brother was personally unknown to him a reply by return of post was received in his own handwriting.

The importance of dealing with your daily correspondence immediately after breakfast before starting work cannot be overrated. Deal with every problem at once, so that your mind is absolutely free to concentrate on the important tasks of the day.

This is a principle to be carried into every walk of life. It denotes an orderly mind and is the harbinger of success. Have a place for everything. I even arrange my colours in my paint box so that I can put my hand on any colour instantly and almost as if in the dark. Sometimes in a hurry I throw a tube back in the box which means much time is lost in searching for it. The successful business man files all his letters. In a shipowner's office I noticed his desk was clear of all stray papers. Order prevailed everywhere. Order promotes the formation of good habits, and the more we turn over to habit, the more shall we be free to exercise the higher faculties.

The natural world is the realm of order, and we too can make life a noble rhythmic process. This principle applies also to punctuality. Great men are always to the minute. The most perfect models of punctuality that I have known were King George V and Mr. J. Pierpont Morgan. One day the King's private secretary telephoned me saying His Majesty would sit for me on Saturday week and arrive at my house at 12 o'clock. The day came, and, having received no confirmation of the appointment at 11.30 a.m., I thought I would telephone and make sure everything was in order, but refrained from doing so. A few minutes before the appointed time, however, I went to the front door and as the clock was striking twelve the royal car entered the drive—punctual to the minute. Mr. Pierpont Morgan frequently pulled out his watch to show me that he was on the tick of the appointed hour.

One day Mr. George Baker of America telephoned me to know what time I should be in my studio as he wished to call and see me. I told him I should be there at nine o'clock. But that morning on my way to the studio I had to call and see a sitter and was delayed because I had called too early. The result was that I arrived at the studio twenty minutes late. Imagine my surprise when on arrival I was told that Mr. Baker had been waiting twenty minutes. I felt very ashamed, and in making my apologies I said : "Punctuality is the politeness of princes." He, however, a dear and great man, began to apologize for being early, and I did not wish to clear myself by turning the tables on him.

We mere humans should take example from the clock-like precision of Nature. So orderly is the rule of Nature that scientists can calculate to a fraction of a second the arrival of a certain planet in a certain position in the heavens.

We must live up to the great reputation of Big Ben, who throughout the years has marked the seconds and minutes with undeviating exactitude.

We cannot overrate the importance of training our outlook on life. We may be over critical or suffer from a prejudiced outlook and thereby lose the true fullness of life. If we view a work of art for its defects we may easily miss its beauty. A great artist was looking at a picture in a gallery with great enjoyment and drawing attention to its good qualities when an art critic standing by said : "But you have said nothing about its defects." "No," replied the artist, "I get the most out of life in looking for the best."

A beautiful garden had been constructed with terraces, arches of roses, winding grass paths and crazy paving, and a friend asked to be shown over it. After going round it with his conductor his only comment on leaving was : "Do you mind if I tell you that there is a cobblestone loose in the pavement?"

At the outset of my career a friend of my father counselled me never to look a second time on an ugly sight, but to turn away, and if a mind and vision is thus automatically trained it only registers and remembers the beautiful and thus life's garment of beauty rustles infinitely around.

There is so much in this war-wrecked world from which we should wisely turn away—wrongs, nuisances, and follies that unfortunately we can do little or nothing effectively to correct, but which stab us with pain whenever we catch a glimpse of them. One of the vital questions I ask myself is, which is the greater tragedy—having eyes and seeing not, or having eyes that look only for the unpleasant and the ugly?

The modern art council in promoting the exhibition of modernist art with all its debased incompetence, is not fostering the right outlook, and if that is the best they can set before the public today they are just encouraging a taste for the morbid and sordid.

We also have to consider how we look at and sum up the attributes of personal character as well as the features of the natural material world. I had a dear friend who with a beautiful childlike virtue trusted and believed in everybody, and sometimes he was greatly imposed upon and disappointed. But he never altered his habit, and one day when he was challenged for his seemingly stupid trustfulness he said : "I always trust until I have very definite proof for distrust." I must say that by his radiant spirit he certainly got the best out of life. So I have learned to take a generous outlook in regard to personal relationship. It is worth while responding to the childlike instinct. We may have many rude awakenings, but there is no doubt such an attitude has many compensations, for it has a far-reaching helpful influence on the person trusted. Cultivate a wise outlook not allowing your penetrative judgment to be unwisely deluded.

I was walking one day across a common with a dear old bishop who was sitting to me, and coming towards us was a doubtful-looking beggar who came up to us to beg for alms. I felt very sceptical about him and was confident that whatever we gave him would be spent at the next public house, but the bishop put his hand in his pocket and gave liberally. He would not risk letting a deserving man pass by and suffer.

It is a dull life if we restrict our expressions of pleasure, restraining ourselves in case we appear to be acting in bad form. Spontaneous expression is guilty of being curbed because of a self-centred feeling of importance, sometimes from a feeling of diffidence. We wonder whether praising this particular achievement is in line with popular fashion, or whether we shall be thought less of for our expressions. But there is a danger that we impede progress by taking everything for granted and as a matter of course. Therefore take risks but do not flatter ; that is dishonest. Be not sparing in your expressions of appreciation when any work in any walk of endeavour has given you real pleasure. Remember that "All great things are wrought in the atmosphere of appreciation." We seldom realize that in giving praise when it is due we also stimulate our receptive qualities. It is also important to keep an open appreciative outlook upon the work of our contemporaries, enjoying their achievements even if they overshadow our own. It is harmful to genius and character if we allow ourselves to be discouraged or jealous of another's achievement. Enjoy to the full all work sincerely conceived or beautifully wrought. Wisely calculate how you stand, and learn where you can be receptive and appreciative.

Thus the mind grows and the spirit sets the guiding compass that leads to higher heights of expanding vision. Whether we narrowly confine our vision looking inward, making self the centre, or whether we cultivate the habit of looking outward with a wide vision purely selfless is a matter of fundamental importance to every one of us. I was very interested when reading recently that Swedenborg sets forth the principle that selfishness pertains to the devil and hell, and selflessness to God and Heaven.

Experience has often proved that as soon as a new enterprise or adventure is undertaken unexpected difficulties arise. Endeavour so often leads down dark passages, but it is the uncertain that gives zest to life. If all were clear we should not understand the meaning of romance or the satisfaction of conquest. Thus I have discovered for myself that when a task assumes an almost unconquerable proportion it is unwise to worry. Do your best, and having done that put it aside and clear it out of your mind. Forget all about it, sleep over it, and you will be surprised how in the morning you will approach the subject with a clear vision and know immediately what is wrong. In moments of relaxation light will come. It sometimes seems as if some unseen Master had bent over your shoulder and whispered into your ear, and you instinctively know the right thing to do.

Intuition is only given to him who has done his best and undergone long preparation, said Pasteur. It is a greater power than reason ; it is the whispering of subconscious thought, subtle, elusive, and such promptings must be quickly followed up. Work proceeds the flash of inspiration, and it is only thus we unlock the treasure-chest that lies hidden in the depths of our being.

In my student days I sacrificed a game of tennis because I looked into the sky and saw a beautiful sunset. I secured my paint box and ran to the hilltop for the vantage point. When I arrived there nothing but a black cloud remained, but having come so far I said : "That black cloud I am going to paint." So in went the black cloud, when suddenly to my surprise as the sun met the horizon it burst through the cloud and shot wonderful golden and red rays transforming the cloud into marvellous beauty. In a flash with a brush full of gold and red colour I slashed the rays in, and I learnt the great lesson—to work for the inspiration, not wait for it.

It is wise to take a philosophical view of life and not be incapacitated by seeming failure, to cast off disappointment like an old garment, confident that in the end things can and will come right however difficult. If we do our best we have every right to be sure that all things work together for good.

Great adventures, great creations, great discoveries have usually been nurtured in hardship, pondered over in sorrow, and established with difficulty. Most of us make the mistake of praying for the removal of our difficulties, forgetting that nothing is worth having if it comes too easily, and it is these struggles in the fields of accomplishment that make for character.

Life has its complexities. We must not imagine a difficulty to be real when it is not. Judge calmly without prejudice, because half our troubles never arise. We so often stain today's blue sky with tomorrow's clouds. When motoring the sky in the distance often looks dark and ominous and we are awestruck and fearful. Yet as we approach the cloud passes harmlessly over our heads, bringing to mind William Cowper's noble lines : "The clouds ye so much dread are big with mercy, and shall break in blessings on your head."

In life there is the problem of closed doors, doors which we seem to have no key to open—in other words disappointment. If our lives are properly organized and proceeding in harmony with destiny those closed doors may be a blessing in disguise, and we may be thankful we possess no key to open them. A ship-owner once said to me that no doors had been slammed in his face except those for which in after years he had had to thank destiny.

And how often even in the blitz what seemed to be a terrible catastrophe proved to be a blessing in disguise. A friend's fine business house in King Street, St. James's, was wiped out, but in a short time he was in a finer place, and the disaster proved to be the best thing that could have happened for him, blitzed and blessed.

On returning from America I was shocked and staggered to find the beautiful trees near my garden cut down and a sixty foot red brick building erected which spoilt my studio light so that I had to leave. But it proved to be the most fortunate move of my life, although at the time it appeared a terrible disaster.

Few walks in life give one such an opportunity of close personal touch with an individual as that of an artist. My work as a portrait painter has brought me into intimate touch with men and women in all walks of life and world-wide spheres, not only in the Empire but in Europe. It has been my privilege to spend many quiet hours with successful men of great achievement, and naturally their friends wanted a portrait to perpetuate their memories in recognition of the services they had rendered to their day and generation.

In the work of translating form and feature to canvas the artist discovers those rare qualities that lie beneath the surface, and he does or should endeavour to enter the soul and try to reveal and perpetuate it in the portrait.

I have thereby been privileged to discover and learn the secret of achievement. It is not easy to sum up in a few words, but this I can say: that spiritual ideals have been the inspiration of thought and power, and the secret of success. Some have openly revealed it, while in others the truth was enshrouded and somewhat hidden under the natural cloak of reserve. Happily, however, I discovered the secret in their attitude and outlook on life. I shall never forget a very rich experience I had when painting the portrait of a successful Boston business man in my studio in New York who, dressed in his hunting suit, looked a real sporting man of the world. In the quiet hours we had together talking of current events and trying to settle the destiny of nations, our minds moved on to spiritual levels and just a stray word seemed to give us a mystic key, and looking up "Behold a door stood open in Heaven" and we had an experience, that seemed to outstrip the limitation of time and the material world, which took us high into the Watch Tower of life.

By the spiritual ideals I mean that these men, great in their services to humanity and having risen from obscurity to world-wide fame, were not dependent upon their own strength. All their activities were linked up with their faith in the Divine Power, the Word that was made flesh and dwelt among us.

Analogies and parallels that exist in life around help us to appreciate this thought. All growth is co-operative with the cosmic forces of creative energy. The gardener only gets out of the garden what he puts into it by way of work and energy, and in the sphere of human enterprise and personal experience one reaps only what one sows. Sooner or later comes the reward. The world may scorn and be unkind through envy and jealousy, but in his own heart the worker is consoled and encouraged. Co-operation with the natural and universal law does not necessarily clear away all difficulties, but by trying to obey these laws a key is forged that opens the door of the armoury of God where the warrior is armed, fortified, and braced for any encounter. Then difficulties vanish, and as the stalwart warrior moves forward devils fear and fly.

When man struggles and fights on, breasting discouragement, it is marvellous how, when enemies try to overthrow his work, by some mysterious way incidents of encouragement occur as an offset to cheer him on his way. The psalmist evidently had such a parallel experience as this in his mind when he said: "Thou prepareth a table before me in the presence of my enemies and my cup runneth over."

Thus we of the simpler walks of life can with the Magic Key enter the high Watch Tower of the house of life, and with the glorious men of achievement look out upon life's enchanting and ever-widening vistas and distant horizons with confidence, courage, and hope.

ADMIRAL OF THE FLEET, LORD CHATFIELD

Born in 1873, the son of an Admiral. Entered H.M.S. "Britannia" in 1886. Was Flag-Captain to Beatty in battles of Heligoland, Dogger Bank and Jutland, and became Fourth Sea Lord in 1919. Commanded 3rd Light Cruiser Squadron, 1923–25; Third Sea Lord, 1925–28; C.-in-C. Atlantic Fleet, 1929; C.-in-C. Mediterranean Fleet, 1930–32; First Sea Lord and Chief of Naval Staff, 1933–38; Minister for Co-ordination of Defence 1939–40 with a seat in the Cabinet.

IT IS not easy to recall what life has taught one, or when those lessons began ; but it is certain that however old one may be, there are still lessons to be learnt. The lessons will vary in type according to certain periods in life, which one may broadly designate childhood, youth and maturity. I think of the mind in childhood as empty space, virgin soil or nearly so; for even in infancy the mind has born in it a divine spark, as well as instincts and hereditary traits. But compared with the millions of thoughts that will crowd into it, the mind in childhood is almost empty. So I think of the early impressions, as planting themselves deep in the most inner substance of the mind ; there they will ever stay, part of the basis of one's character. Millions of other impressions will superimpose themselves outside them, keeping them firmly in place, always there to influence you for good or evil. The early impressions are therefore the most enduring ones ; those which come later in life will not have the same foothold, while in old age, they will, so to speak, only be able to cling to the circumference of the mind and will easily be forgotten, blown away by a breath of air. How vital then is it, that the early impressions are good seed, well planted.

Who forgets his early school experiences? I can see vividly in my mind today, a schoolroom and a blackboard in a small private school in South Wales, where I was being educated to pass into the Navy. On that blackboard, the young master wrote two well-known sayings:

> What is worth doing at all is worth doing well.
> Whatsoever your hand findeth to do, do it with all thy might.

I know now that those sayings took deep root in my mind, that they influenced me on countless occasions in a strenuous life, and are still there.

Entering the Navy so young and going to sea when only fourteen, my life was early of an adventurous nature. The sea life gripped my mind; I had, as the most insignificant member of a ship's company in a large sailing corvette, to struggle to emerge, however slightly, above the mass of humanity by which I was surrounded. My very insignificance among the 250 officers and men was, in itself, a lesson. I was to learn that it was not for myself I was to think, so much as for the ship. I had my small task in every duty on deck or aloft; however simple it might be, the task was mine. If I failed in my task, something however small went wrong, and I suffered for it physically and mentally, like the last man in in cricket who makes a "duck."

These early lessons in sea life sank deep into my mind; I was one of a team, to think not of myself, but of my ship and shipmates, and not to let them down. None too easy at first, it became gradually a natural and pleasing principle. Those around me possessed the same spirit, however good or bad they might be in other ways; trained to get the utmost out of themselves; to fit themselves to perform, to the utmost of their ability, the duty in the ship for which they were most adapted.

And I learned also in those young days, something equally great in importance—to get on with one's fellow men, and to be even tempered; because ill-temper in a community does not pay and often leads to ruin. The basis of all such qualities is unselfishness and self-sacrifice, both terribly difficult things to acquire. They were easier to acquire at sea, because one had as an inspiration, the safety of the ship and her efficiency, as well as the team spirit the ship herself enforces on her crew.

Let not the reader think I wish to imply that all these lessons became part of *my* early character—far from it—but the lessons were somehow planted in my inner mind. It was as if they said to me, "these thoughts you cannot engrain, thus early, in your personality, but we shall always be in your mind, normally forgotten ; nevertheless, each time you make use of us we shall grow stronger and sink deeper into your character. One day we may become part of it, but for the present we shall be at hand, ready for you to turn to in a difficult moment."

There was another side of these early lessons. One began to judge one's fellow men, and to choose one's friends from those who acquired them in the same manner as oneself. That is normal in life. Similar personalities do not always blend, but similar characters do so.

Now, the spirit in a ship, as I have briefly related above, is the basis of normal discipline ; a discipline which is never irksome, unless it is abused by those in authority. Discipline in a ship is more vital than in any other calling, for unless an order is obeyed without a moment's hesitation, an accident may occur, or even a ship be lost. It is, in consequence, the easiest quality for a seaman to absorb, for its need is self-evident to the most stubborn will. It makes it easier to turn out of one's hammock, or bunk, in the middle of the night when so ordered, though your inclination is all the other way ! It is a far easier quality to acquire than self-discipline, but it may help that also. To discipline one's thoughts and actions in ordinary life, even though it is to your vital interest to do so, is much harder, for you can so easily twist your mind to deceive yourself into believing that some unpleasant task is really too much to expect of you. As a mischievous wit once suggested, "It is better to earn a slight reprimand, than to perform an unpleasant duty." Moreover, if you do not allow your sense of self-discipline to act, you only harm yourself, and it can appear but a minor loyalty in life. It is so often true to say that the harder choice of action is the correct one.

The sailor, arrived at years of discretion, his character and personality roughly hewn, full of ambition and hope, begins a more definite stage: that of both obeying his superiors and learning to command others. His acts of command will have to be applied in two ways—first to enforce his authority ; to teach those under him to obey him with keenness ; to make them an efficient team and, if he can, make them more efficient than any other team in a ship or fleet. Secondly, to look after those he leads, as the head of any community must do. If he is to succeed he must have himself been "through the mill," understand the minds of those he commands, know what is wanted, the extent to which his ship's company can reasonably be stretched, without reaching (except in emergency) the elastic limit.

This will also be a matter of *judgment*, another important quality which can only be gradually acquired : which needs trials and errors to bring it to function. It is a quality which grows with one's years, and is of ever interesting value as one rises in the world to greater responsibilities.

If you are to get the utmost out of those you command, you must possess their confidence and, at least, must not be disliked by them. I have told in my autobiography how, as a young commander, I was appointed to a ship in a poor state of efficiency. I had first to plan how to get the ship efficient; then to endeavour to inspire the ship's company and tell them how I intended to achieve the plan: to make them realize that I could succeed only with their help and with team spirit, that I would reorganize them, that each man would have his task, and that by pulling together we could make the ship proud of herself and no longer a disgrace. Soon they gained confidence in me and in themselves, and the ship became an entirely different vessel. I also gained confidence in myself.

Self-confidence is an essential quality at sea ; but it must be a confidence justified by the ability to analyse in one's mind the pros and cons—to give full weight to essentials and to discard the lesser factors. Self-confidence goes hand in hand with good judgment : you can have one without the other, but you will not then rise so high in life. Your aim, then, must be to have confidence in your own judgment. If you are early to gain self-confidence you must seize the opportunities life offers you. Most young people hesitate if offered a difficult task: to accept it needs *courage*.

Courage itself, as we all know, has varying forms. It is more often connected with the lack of fear in danger or of fear of death, or the readiness to face the risk of it. But it has many lesser forms. It requires courage to take on some difficult duty, which if you fail in it, will lower your good repute ; yet if you are to gain self-confidence the one thing you must not do is to refuse. To accept the duty and fail to do as well as was expected of you, is better than to shrink from it. You will at any rate gain experience and improve your judgment ; so will you face your next task with improved self-confidence.

The necessity for boldly seizing every opportunity to gain experience was early impressed on my mind. I have related elsewhere, some of those occasions when I was offered and accepted difficult tasks ; how sometimes I succeeded, and sometimes I did not. The consequences of failure are small in early life, but later in life, to fail may be penalizing to your career. One must therefore learn *the value of taking proper risks* when young and profiting by experience. If you do not venture to take risks in your youth in every side of life, you will not be able to do so when older : so you will be marked down as over-cautious, a damming limitation in a sailor.

If you are to take risks successfully you need *luck*. Luck plays a big part in life from birth to death. It is beyond your control, but the man who breaks the bank at Monte Carlo must at any rate have had the courage to try to do so and to risk his money! Luck seldom comes to those who do not deserve it. Admiral Beatty was a case in point. He had great luck early in life, but he took the tide at the flood, seized his chances and had the character, energy and ability to press on with courage to the top of the naval ladder.

The successful taking of risks, and the part luck plays in it is an important factor in life that I would dwell on for a moment.

Little can be accomplished worth doing, without taking risks. There is also an excitement in doing so. Shall I cross the road now, or wait until it is absolutely safe? How often do people ask themselves that question in a thousand forms. There was no battle Nelson won in which he did not take risks; risks that to an ordinary mind would seem unjustifiable. Both at the Nile and Trafalgar, he exposed part of the British Fleet to severe punishment in order to gain a tactical position which would be annihilating to his foe. He trusted to the skill of his captains, the courage and ability of his men, and to their confidence in his experienced judgment. What a lesson his deeds have been to all who have followed in his footsteps and held similar responsibilities.

In neither of these two classic examples was luck a contributory factor. Yet we know how good luck can retrieve incorrect judgment in taking a risk—"saved by the skin of his teeth!" Some call it fate or destiny. You are considered to be one of the lucky ones if you succeed ; unlucky if you fail. That may be true or may not be. If you believe too much in your fate, you will become a fatalist. If you believe too much in your luck it will let you down perhaps at a great moment. Let us rather think of our "future," and be determined to control it ; to face life with all the talents God has planted in us. We must boldly face the rules of life. Life is a hard taskmaster. To be master of your future, you must accept life's rules ; hard, unsympathetic, unreasonable they may be. But if you strive to keep them, gradually they will respond to your will. One way to broaden the opportunities of appreciating correctly the risks in life is—*to learn from others.*

There is an immense amount to be learnt from the successes and failures of others—not only those with whom one's life runs, but from those of the past. There is seldom, if ever, a big risk to be faced, which has not been of a similar type faced by some character in history. You can learn an immense amount from the careful study, as opposed to the casual reading, of great biographies. How much can the seaman learn from past British sailors, and by imagining himself in their place, seek inspiration to follow their example, or be guided by their misfortunes. But from those of one's own time one can also learn much. The knowledge you thus gain is not comparable with that gained by practical experience, but the sum of it is considerable and a valuable addition in your own mind to what you can personally absorb. To do this, however, you must have the "determination to learn" firmly in your mind, so that you will gain the right lessons, even without thinking of it at the time. Quite apart from the stimulus you can yourself obtain from others in that way is the support you can give to others. I remember when commander-in-chief, a flag officer commanding one of the squadrons of the fleet informed me he was very disappointed with the disciplinary powers of one of his captains. An order he himself had given to the ship had only been half-heartedly performed ; did I think it would be best for him to go on board and address the ship's company? I advised him not to do so, at this stage, but to send for the captain and tell him he was expected to "command" his ship. Tell him, I said, that if he cannot get his orders obeyed instantly and willingly, I will send another captain to command the ship who will do so. With that support, a minor incident was overcome rapidly. It is essential to give full support from your own experience to those under you. One day you will arrive at an age when you no longer worry about difficulties ; they will no longer appear difficulties, for you will have confidence in your ability and rapid judgment.

One of the temptations in life to be guarded against is that of sinking into a spirit of *complacence;* "to slack off." As we climb the hill of life, it is natural to rest a moment on reaching the summit of a ridge. The temptation is to stay there, satisfied with your efforts. To advance again and tackle the next peak needs a special quality—*energy*.

Energy is one of the principal factors in a successful career, whatever walk of life you may follow ; though some professions give more scope for energy, and greater rewards to the energetic, than others. A dull and somewhat monotonous existence is perhaps enforced in office or factory. Life at sea in the Navy gives, on the contrary, full scope for energy. This partly arises from the periodical change from ship to ship, which gives new openings, new men and material to handle, new hopes, a chance to try new methods and ideas. To have brought a ship, or the part of her allotted to you, to a state of efficiency and then to rest on your oars is a legitimate aim ; but the sailor will not rest for long. A new appointment will come ; a new ship to learn, a new ship's company to train and enthuse, new weapons to master ; perhaps to serve under a new captain or admiral. Such a life is bound to test the human character to its highest and to keep it alert. In the new post, the new ship or fleet he joins, he may be unknown: so his future career will be judged, not so much by what he has done already, but by what he is going to do now. It is a test of *constancy of effort.* Let us suppose that what you have done in the past leads to a new and more responsible appointment ; now, a fiercer light is to shine on you. You will need to show a new zeal, more energy, more ability ; new adaptability to circumstances and to the exactions of those under whom you are to serve. This periodic need to arouse out of yourself a fresh energy and effort prevents that stagnation that is so harmful to character and achievement. Only by developing in himself the quality of persistent energy, can the seaman climb from peak to peak, each one more difficult, requiring finer judgment, improved self-confidence, greater adaptability, higher power of leadership, greater self-control and greater struggles with himself.

Life would be unbearably Spartan and difficult, however, if he never relaxed. The mind as well as the body needs change, and the most effective way to get it is by *physical exercise*, especially by taking up games and sport of every kind. In some such way one should usefully employ and enjoy one's moments of sport. Frequently, I have felt mentally overtired after a long day in an Admiralty office ; have gone to my club and played two or three games of squash rackets, then home to dine, all my tired feeling vanished. Sitting motionless in a chair stagnates your circulation and gives you a feeling of mental exhaustion. Stand on your head, or go for a run, and you will find you are not really tired, but ready for another spell of mental work. But apart from the value of exercise for a man leading a sedentary life, games can give you an altogether happier existence. To change your mind from mental study to sport and back again, balances your mind and your life : the difficulties become smaller, the worries disappear and the improvement of your physique improves your mental qualities—*Mens sana in corpore sano*—there is no better advice, I believe, to give to the young, than to balance your mental work with physical exercise—and not only to the young!

I have now stressed the value of certain qualities in life for those who follow an active and practical career. To be born with, or to acquire some or all of these qualities will help, but even if you possess them, they will not bring success in life automatically. You may be energetic and self-confident, but lack self-control ; have good judgment but fail to use it ; be full of ability and zeal but steer a wrong course. Something more is essential, you must have *an aim in life*, to draw the qualities out and concentrate them on a target : some fiery need in your mind which will inspire you, direct you and enable you to get the most out of yourself and your abilities. To realize this, you have only to reflect on the period we have been passing through and, indeed, still are. England has the great qualities I have mentioned. In normal times they lay dormant, you might imagine they were not there ; only in times of national trial and stress do they show themselves clearly, centralized in a struggle for preservation.

As a seaman my aim was early marked out for me. It was to follow the example of the great seamen of the past I had read about, and that of the best of the leaders of my time. Somehow I must attempt to rise to a position of authority whence I could do useful work, lead others aright, make the utmost of my talents, be they two or ten, and so accomplish something for my country. It was my distant star. But in his daily life, the young seaman is beset by many reefs, which occupy most of his thoughts and which he must safely circumnavigate. It is the next point he has to round, that his mind must concentrate on, sufficient unto the day . . . Yet the next point will, when rounded, uncover a further one on the horizon. So he must know in his mind, in his inner self, how far he intends to travel. Gathering up the experience he has gained, he will use it to pass through the more difficult waters now ahead, until he reaches the testing end of the highest achievement of which he is capable.

The reader may ask whether these experiences and ideas I have written are useful to those who do not follow the seaman's life. To those I could reply that this article is about "What life has taught *me*." Nevertheless, I would answer the question whether the sea teachings can be applied to other walks of life : I think they can. I have stressed the influence of life on the sea, and of the ships in which sailors mainly live, as it can inspire the young—the team *spirit* of the crew, and its effect on the mind in early life, of working for the ship rather than for oneself. It is the natural consequence of a common aim, a common responsibility, of getting the most out of the vessel you are part of, and of ensuring her safety and success. Having achieved it you obtain pride and happiness in the ship and in yourself. Should not that same spirit animate those in other walks of life? The "ship" is where you are, where you work, and your shipmates stand around you, those who work with you for a common purpose.

This spirit acquired early in life can dominate the mind of all, as it does that of the sailor in all the stages of life through which he passes. It will become the basis of your character. It is a spirit that has not been "invented," rather has it developed naturally through the centuries ; it is common to the seamen of all nations, at least in principle. I believe that if a young man in any other profession, would develop it in the same way and absorb it into his own life, it could not but help him to realize more fully this proper comradeship of man ; to be more temperate in his dealings with others ; to be more humble in success, less disappointed in failure; to realize more clearly that he does not stand alone and unsupported in the world.

Everyone must work for his own advancement ; but life has taught me, that to make your own advancement your exclusive aim can only lead to disappointment and regret, and a feeling of unfulfilment. It is not what position you rise to in life, but rather it is the use you make of the opportunity that the position gives that matters. It must be your ambition one day to accomplish something for your country and for others ; that must be the spirit in which you strive throughout life and that will stand by you in the endless struggle.

If during life you put all you can into it, then at its later stages you will find it will return something to you, perhaps with interest. Even should your hopes in life be unfulfilled, you will have developed inside your mind a power for good. You will have something to give to everyone who needs it, and you may be sought by those who need help.

A good ship is one in which the crew is united in a great aim—duty, efficiency and happiness—and in which the individual has developed the maximum of comradeship. Every good sailor wants to join her. So we can make England our national ship ; but only if we pull together in the right spirit with a common unselfish aim.

SIR BERTRAND WATSON

Born in 1878 at Stockton-on-Tees, and became Deputy-Coroner for the County of Durham from 1902–11. Mayor of Stockton 1915–16 and its M.P. from 1917–23. Appointed Metropolitan Police Magistrate 1928 and, after a brief break for reasons of health, was made Chief Metropolitan Magistrate in 1941.

IT HAS ceased to be the fashion to wait until about the age of seventy before writing one's autobiography. Modern youth has shown no more respect for the traditions of memoir writing than it has for most other traditions, and it may be that—to avoid a charge of being old fashioned—the editor and publishers should have invited contributions from those young enough to be the grandchildren of some of the writers here assembled. My experience in juvenile courts has taught me to treat the views of youth as seriously as those of more advanced years, and I have no doubt that had the scope of the book been extended in this way, the result would have been most instructive. Yet it seems to me that the youthful contributors would—quite unknown to them—have been under one very serious handicap, for until one reaches a certain stage of maturity it is almost impossible to distinguish between what life has taught one, and what one has merely absorbed from other people in the way of opinions and judgments. The distinction is not easy to define, but it is in my opinion supremely important and one of which I am particularly conscious as I review my sixty-eight years.

It seems to me that up to the age of about twenty-one my whole life was so influenced by three men that I then could only have written this contribution in terms of what I had learnt from them ; and even today I am not absolutely certain as to which of my opinions are not directly traceable to them. It is natural, therefore, that I should begin with a tribute to them and their influence. They were my father, G. M. Savery (my headmaster from the age of eleven until seventeen), and C. J. Archer (to whom I was articled for the next five years).

My father was a timber merchant and Justice of the Peace well known in Stockton-on-Tees, and was an excellent product of the Victorian era. By modern standards he might be judged a little stern, unbending and remote, but my memory contains nothing but infinite affection and respect for a most powerful, just and high-principled personality. It was he who undoubtedly planted within me an ideal which I have always endeavoured to live up to in my work—to be primarily interested in and guided by the highest moral principles. It is, by the way, an ideal that is not such an inconvenient companion as many might think—though it does imply or involve a certain stability and single-mindedness of purpose in life, and I realize that the rough and tumble worlds of, say, modern commerce and politics (to name only two) make it immeasurably more difficult to preserve one's moral equilibrium.

G. M. Savery, the headmaster at Harrogate College, was another powerful personality, and one to whom the term "disciplinarian" could with more justice be applied than to my father. Yet once again I was fortunate in seeing the ideal of perfect justice being lived up to most successfully. Strict though he was I never once heard a boy complain of his judgment, and all who had the privilege of passing through the college under his supervision must have gone out into the world with the conviction deeply impressed on them that if they were fair and just it would indeed be difficult for the world to speak ill of them. Savery had been president of the Oxford Union when Asquith was up at the university, and it is no little tribute to his striking personality that when I mentioned his name to Asquith somewhere about 1920 an immediate and genuine interest was shown by the great statesman in spite of the passage of years.

Moral integrity also meant much to C. J. Archer, but my debt to him was perhaps more the result of his extraordinary competence and sound judgment as a solicitor, for daily life with him for five years not only taught me my craft in a way that could not be bettered, but made me realize the spiritual value of a full day's work done to the best of one's ability. He set an example of efficiency and conscientiousness to all around him that was most infectious and, incidentally, it was he who signalled in the beginnings of my full maturity and mental independence. When my articles were signed he turned to me and said, "I hope you will never regret the serious step you have taken this day." On the lips of a lesser man the words would have been a mere formal expression, but as they fell from him I could sense to the full the deep spirit of responsibility that characterized his whole life, and I was filled with a resolve that I should not lightly depart from his standards.

Since then I have, of course, been guided by the advice of many people and on many occasions, but my judgment and opinions were somehow never again subordinated as they previously were to those three men, and I must account myself fortunate that such a trio moulded my young mind. The importance of such influences is in fact the first, and one of the most vital, of life's lessons.

I must mention Archer again because he illustrates another important lesson. As I have said, he possessed outstanding capabilities as a solicitor, and it was several times suggested to him that he should move to London where he would be able to exercise his talents to the full, and where he would undoubtedly have had a most successful career : but he chose to stay in Stockton-on-Tees. Now I realize that success should not be an end in itself, but careers that halt early in life often have a suffocating effect on the soul, and most young people have a natural desire to avoid that fate. To them I commend this advice: do not let yourself be lured by the deceptive glitter of the big cities. The best foundation for a successful career is usually made in one of the small communities where one knows, and is known by, many of the inhabitants. If you give of your best in these restricted surroundings for, say, ten or fifteen years, then by the time the mid-thirties are reached it will probably be found that the prizes of the Great

City—which once seemed so unobtainable—will be yours for the asking. The alternative plan is, of course, quite possible, but in my opinion it is not only much more hazardous and difficult, but not likely to be so reassuring and satisfying to oneself. When I reflect on my own career—Deputy-Coroner for the County of Durham at twenty-four, Stockton-on-Tees Councillor at twenty-nine, County Councillor at thirty-five, Mayor at thirty-seven, and Member of Parliament for Stockton from thirty-nine to forty-five—I believe that the steady progression has contributed greatly to my peace of mind and has given me a much more reliable sense of perspective than would otherwise have been possible. To enjoy a meteoric rise to fame, or to be launched, with few preliminaries, into the whirl of modern public life, or to find oneself in desperate competition with the city millions at an early age, is surely not conducive to the best and natural development of a man's personality.

Before I leave the biographical details of my life perhaps I should deal with one question that I have often been asked—Why did I retire from politics so early and so suddenly when my position in Stockton-on-Tees indicated a long and safe tenure as its M.P.? The fact is that though I stood as a Liberal, party politics never had much attraction for me. I was M.P. for Stockton-on-Tees because I knew the local folk and their affairs intimately and, I like to believe, because they knew from my record that they could rely on me to represent them unaffected by purely party considerations and loyalties. My supporters came from every class of people, and I was indeed the first Member for Stockton-on-Tees to be returned unopposed. Even in 1922, when unemployment at Stockton-on-Tees was heavier than at any other place, I was comfortably re-elected in a three-cornered fight. But in 1923 the Coalition broke up, and with it went any hope of the sort of political life that I enjoyed : so I left the arena to others, and have never paid a shilling to any political association since. I can view with nothing but regret the gradual intensification of political strife until today even a position on an urban district council is somehow related to a complex point of foreign policy, and candidates for public offices of all kinds are not so much well-known local personalities pledged to safeguard local interests as nominees of a group with national political associations and whose loyalties must, as a result, be somewhat divided. It may even be that the next generation will witness the intrusion of politics into British justice. How fortunate we are in that respect at present can be seen by a comparison between the conduct in our courts and in those of many foreign courts. Sitting at Bow Street as Chief Metropolitan Magistrate I dealt not only with all the cases of espionage and treason that were tried in secret during the war, but with those similarly charged in public after the cessation of hostilities. In spite of the fact that much of the evidence given must have aroused indignation in the hearts of many of the public sitting close to the prisoners, never once did I notice the slightest hint of disapproval, and the prisoners might—to a casual foreign observer—have been in the dock on a charge of misappropriating a bundle of firewood. That such an attitude on the part of the public did not indicate indifference and "softness" is proved by the fact that in every case the Court was packed and there was sufficient evidence for me to commit the prisoners for trial at the Central Criminal Court.

But though my experiences in this connection reflect nothing but credit on the public I regret to say that much of my experience as a magistrate has led me to note a very sad decline in the general moral sense, and a consequent increase of crime for which there is not the slightest excuse. I have heard it said that poverty is the prime begetter of crime : that with the removal of poverty the incentive for much lawlessness will disappear. I can categorically assert that my legal and public experience of the past fifty years points entirely to the contrary view. In my young days it was true to say that cases of petty larceny were often committed when the cause appeared to be poverty ; but the culprits were only a very small percentage of those who could have pleaded equal justification—and it must be remembered that the poverty of fifty years ago was much more real than it is today. Since then the standard of living of all the lower income groups has improved enormously, yet the indisputable fact remains that larceny and crime in general has increased substantially—and with little obvious cause. Time without number I have had housewives, young girls, youths and men with long records of excellent service, brought before me and charged with shoplifting or some petty fraud when no plea of shortage or hardship could possibly be substantiated (in actual fact the plea is rarely made). Devoted husbands, mothers and wives break down in the witness box when confronted with the inexplicable actions of their loved ones, while the culprits stand mute or offer the feeblest of excuses.

How can one explain the position save by assuming a serious collapse in moral values?—that these are cases where men and women, in all other respects normal and respectable citizens, simply see no harm in appropriating money or goods to which they feel they have some obscure right. "Why shouldn't I travel without paying my fare?—the Company won't miss my 2d. I may as well 'scrounge' some of the building materials at the corner of my road : if I don't someone else will. Mrs. Brown next door has a pair of real silk stockings, why shouldn't I?—even if I can't really afford it this week; and the big shops are making plenty of profits anyway." And so they go down the slippery slope. What is to stop them?

In my opinion the prime cause of all this is the rapid loosening of the influence of Christianity over a large section of the community. When moral values are no longer regarded as absolute then it is not difficult for people to say to themselves, "I have as much right to that as so-and-so," or, "If I had not been unlucky at dog racing the other night I could have bought those books" ; and society run on those lines is heading for disaster. Christian morality, on the other hand, puts the individual in no doubt as to the nature of his actions. He might feel that fate is dealing harshly or unreasonably with him, but he is under no illusion as to what he *ought* to do, except perhaps in dire extremity. Retribution for the failure to give him his just reward on earth must be left to more knowledegable hands than his. For who knows what is his just reward?

To me it seems deplorable that even those last few sentences of mine will seem "old-fashioned" to many readers. Still more out of date, no doubt, will seem to them my reflections on the weakening of the marriage bond. To those of us who have been granted an insight into innumerable domestic disasters and tangles one fact stands out quite clearly—that whatever the original merits of the opportunity for divorce they are fast being quite outweighed by the consequent general failure of people to attempt to master the art of living together. I say "consequent" deliberately, for it seems obvious to me that if people marry in the knowledge that a divorce can be obtained relatively easily much of the incentive to give and take in married life will be gone, and the fragile fairy-like barque of marriage is likely to be sunk by the first and most mild breeze that it meets. Nor will one or both of the partners make much attempt to resist the temptations that probably occur to most married people at some time or other. The fact is that the choice of a wife or husband is the most grave decision in a person's life, yet circumstances today are tending to invest the occasion with no more importance than the choice of a new hat. I can never give sufficient thanks to my wife who, since our marriage in 1909, has been my supreme help in every part of my private and public life ; what happens to those who have not been so fortunate in their choice is too often seen in cases brought before me, both in adult and juvenile courts. It may be argued that the surest method of satisfactorily dealing with a wretched married life is to allow the partners to begin again by divorce proceedings. Unfortunately, one of the surest ways of *causing* a wretched married life would seem to be to tell the husband and wife that the law allows them to make only a feeble and formal attempt to surmount what must—by the very nature of things—be inevitable difficulties and problems. This is a dilemma which our society is not dealing with very successfully, but the recent suggestion of Courts of Conciliation was a wise and timely move in the right direction. Easier divorce is merely another modern slope down which we can slide with every increasing momentum.

The suggested Courts of Conciliation remind me of the system of "probation" whereby a defendant who has been "overtaken in a fault" is placed on probation and receives help and advice from an experienced probation officer. This system has met with much success, and has often been the means of altering the rest of an offender's life. When I was at Lambeth I placed on probation a man, aged seventy-nine, who had spent the previous sixty years of his life mostly in prison—mainly for offences of stealing. Thanks to the co-operation of an exceptionally helpful and good-hearted probation officer, who met the probationer weekly, the old offender is now eighty-five, and for the last six years has led an honest and happy life! The one occasion when he seemed to doubt the wisdom of his new life was when I heard him reflect during a particularly nasty spell of flying bombs that it was a good deal quieter in the provincial prison that he knew so well.

At this juncture it is probably not amiss to reflect on the events of what I regard as the second half of my career (after I retired from politics and devoted myself exclusively to the administration of justice). I had been called to the Bar before retiring from politics, and practised mainly on the North Eastern Circuit. To have a working knowledge of both branches of the legal profession has been of the greatest value to me, for however excellent is the Clerk of the Court a magistrate who has been trained as a lawyer is obviously in a very favourable position for the efficient exercise of his powers. This, however, is not to discount in the slightest the value of lay magistrates. Indeed, were I asked for my opinion of the ideal Bench I would say a trained lawyer for the chairman with a layman on one side and a laywoman on the other. Unfortunately, it is not practicable today to provide a stipendiary magistrate for every Bench.

In 1928 Sir William Joynson-Hicks recommended me for appointment as a Metropolitan magistrate, and my work as such has mainly been at Lambeth, North London, Clerkenwell and Bow Street, most of those coming to the courts being of the working classes for whom I have a profound respect and liking. In 1936, however, I resigned my office after two serious heart attacks, and at the age of fifty-eight it seemed likely that public life was, for me, finished. Yet it was then that I was to learn one of the most remarkable of life's lessons. Under the direction of a wise medical adviser I took a complete rest of nine months, during which time I was able to watch the building of a house on some land I had bought on the cliffs in the beautiful little village of Studland, on the Isle of Purbeck, Dorsetshire. I also spent a few winter months in Italy, at Rapallo.

At the end of this rest I was a new man, and I gradually resumed the chairmanship of the London Police Court Mission, and joined my local Bench of magistrates at St. Pancras. In 1938 there came a vacancy on the Metropolitan Bench and I was "reinstated" to the first court where I had sat, namely, Lambeth ; and then in 1941 I was appointed to be Chief Metropolitan Magistrate, to which were added the honours of knighthood and of being made a Bencher of Gray's Inn.

In 1936 such a state of affairs would have seemed impossible, but my illness proved to be a most beneficial act of providence, and I can only offer this advice to others: that if it is at all possible, a complete voluntary relaxation from effort for several months during the early fifties should be the aim of everyone, and should a serious illness overtake one in middle-age the victim should be prepared to see in it the kindly workings of fate, rather than the reverse. As Bernard Shaw has pointed out, many famous men (including himself) are indebted to Nature for applying a timely brake in this way, though, as he added a little cynically, she overdid it a bit in such cases as Mozart! The truth is, I suppose, that most men tend to forget the advance of years and try to drive the human frame as though it still belonged to a young man. Thus, if a man does not learn this lesson in time, Nature gives him a few hints, and if he still refuses to learn then Nature applies rather stronger methods of persuasion. It is not necessary to abandon an active life very early—which may be a bad thing from many points of view—but it is necessary to slow down the tempo of one's life and to avoid sudden stresses and strains suitable only for a young person. It is also necessary to cultivate a variety of interests. My recreations have been golf, lawn tennis, riding and swimming (a combination that guaranteed me some pleasurable exercise in practically any weather), but most of my leisure hours have been spent in reading, and on the two occasions that I have been ordered to spend six weeks in bed I was deeply thankful to be able to enjoy this never failing solace.

If the advice of the last few paragraphs is heeded by middle-aged readers then this contribution will have more than justified itself, but if a few more words may be added to summarize what life has taught me, here they are: It has been my unvarying experience that people receive from their fellows broadly and generally the treatment that they have shown to others. If one shows kindness, respect and courtesy, these are the qualities which are received in return. As a Metropolitan magistrate for eighteen years I have never failed to marvel at the way in which offenders accept the penalties and often imprisonments it has been found necessary to inflict. And I have never received an unpleasant anonymous letter.

Lest those last few words should sound a little self-complacent I would like to emphasize that I consider them to be primarily a sincere tribute to the qualities of the British public, and to their respect for British justice. They are also an indirect but heartfelt tribute to the three grand personalities with whom I opened this contribution, and to whom—under God—I owe everything that is fundamental in me (though life without my wife is something I neither can nor would care to imagine).

C. C. MARTINDALE

Born in 1879 and educated at Harrow, Stonyhurst and Campion Hall, Oxford. Received into the Roman Catholic Church 1897; ordained priest 1911. Is a member of the Society of Jesus and has been on the staff of Farm Street Church since 1927. Has travelled widely abroad and is equally well known as author, journalist and broadcaster. Was in Denmark when it was overrun by the Nazis and was interned by them throughout the war.

CHRISTIANITY HAS always contained the notion of "witness," and indeed, the belief that "witnessing" is a duty. This must mitigate a man's extreme distaste for talking about himself, especially of what is most intimate to him, and perhaps he may be excused from so much as trying to mention that "most intimate," if only because he knows he could never explain it. On the other hand, when one is old, one probably becomes less sensitive to comment, though more rueful, perhaps, yet less indignant, in proportion as modern life allows one less and less of privacy. (But one is told that it is very "reactionary" so much as to want a private life—one must identify oneself with—merge one's self in—some more vast "society." Of that, later.)

Yet after all, when the period of accumulating experience is on the whole over, the period of "understanding" begins or proceeds, and this is always one of simplification, so that less and less needs to be *said.* I do not really want to *say* much more than that life has taught me (I hope) to love God and my neighbour better. True, I would not want to suggest that some sort of "abstract," Life, has taught me anything in particular. I suppose that I can dilate—not so much on *what* I have learnt as on how and when I have gradually learnt it. I suppose I must then say that I have been "schooled" by my home, by the Catholic Church, by moving around *as* a Catholic (I cannot imagine what, e.g. travel, or war, would have taught me had I *not* been a Catholic), and by what God, I wish humbly to acknowledge, has directly taught me: but that, precisely, is a "most intimate" about which I will not write, because I could not even if I would. Anyhow, it would only relate to a *method* of teaching me the "what" that I mentioned above—a better love of God and of men. One begins, no doubt, by accepting rather than learning, but also, perhaps, by disbelieving. In my home that curious mixture of piety and worldliness, so common in Victorian days, prevailed. Thus if I did anything careless, like upsetting a cup, I was given to understand that God was grieved: but if I cried, I was told that "little gentlemen never cry." I was taught to make all sorts of sacrifices for Poor Children, and indeed for Little Black Babies (connected by me with Sunday picture-books, cowrie shells, palm-trees and St. Paul, for whom I developed an active detestation), but also, was forbidden to play with all but a hand-picked few—in fact, I was once asked by some children in our square to play hide and seek, and replied—n.b., in perfect innocence: "I was sent out here to amuse myself, and not to play with *you*." Even "They" found this remark—not my abstention—rather exorbitant. Hence a divided and partly falsified state of mind grew up—you had to profess love for people you disliked: you must believe that God had given you the toys you knew had been bought: you must believe that your grandfather was a mixture of Abraham and Jove, but above all "very good": "goodness" dwindled downwards through a hierarchy of uncles, aunts and cousins. There was no reason to suppose that visitors were "good." Hence a mixture of affection and discomfort, of belief and scepticism, tending to an ultimate resentment of home and elders. But I retained an "evangelical" sense of a present God (much less, of Christ); a twist not only towards obedience but to reverence; a conviction that right differed from wrong, a lie (mental, too) being the worst of sins: a certainty that the distinction between being a gentleman, and not, was absolute and that one must *therefore* be infinitely considerate of the poor, the sick, servants, in short, the "less fortunate." My childhood bequeathed, too, to me a love for the sonorous rhythms of Old Testament and Apocalypse : the *sense* was not my affair.

My private school was happy. Did it *teach* me anything more than the sort of exterior social code that was then demanded? I can't say that *it* taught me Latin, because I simply rushed to Latin and fed on it : anyone should have seen that I ought to have done Greek, but, being destined for the diplomatic service, and French being almost a second "native" tongue to me, and since I had an almost morbid knack for mathematics (other than arithmetic which I still can't do), I was kept on the Modern Side. But my imagination was being fired by any book in French or about France (like the *Tale of Two Cities*), or by exotic books like *The Last Days of Pompeii* or Rider Haggard's *Cleopatra.* I cared nothing for the "plots"—but the atmospheres! the magic! though do not suppose that I was *only* "thrilled"! I paralysed my "people" by asking for an Egyptian Grammar for a Christmas present and could read obelisks quite well when I was eleven or so. I lived thus in mysterious worlds, which anyhow *had* been real as even French fairy worlds were not. Add to these the *Ingoldsby Legends*, which, in a way, I suppose, introduced me both to the macabre and to "papistry," to coarseness and to heraldry.

But ultimately more important were Virgil's *Eclogues* and *Georgics* : they came to life for me and gave me a golden Italy into which I could emigrate from the harsh world of my public school when I passed on there. "Harsh," for such inevitably was a public school if you couldn't conform to type, which I think I would have done, if I could, but couldn't, largely owing to devastating shyness ; public opinion, however, was intransigent—*ne quid nimis*—not even too good a French accent. Well, I soon lost *that*, but could not make imagination fade into common day. Virgil began to mean more than a mystic Italy : the *Æneid* suggested to me a Heavenly City, a Rome of which I really think Virgil at times caught glimpses and felt homesick for it. *Tendebantque manus. . . .* Hands were reaching out in a passion for whatever shore might lie invisibly beyond every Styx or Lethe. And I was soon shifted to the classical side, and oddly enough

Æschylus made me appreciate Isaiah, because (so far as I was then conscious) of a certain allied magnificence proper to these two seers, but, I now honestly think, more deeply because of the frightful problem of Doom and Guilt in the *Agamemnon*—the torment of the Chorus when Clytemnestra denied all responsibility for her husband's murder: "That thou art guiltless of this murder—who should vouch? Nay, nay! Yet indeed a Vengeance from ancestral days may have been thine Accomplice. . . ." Incipient adolescent anguish! I am fated to be irrevocably I, yet I "ought" to be so many things that I am not and can't be! Vocation *versus* Fate. Moreover, at this time all young men of taste were feeling bound to be disillusioned and to peer wistfully at the fading Christian view through a hedge of green carnations. This pose found tough antagonists, one of them being Browning. One master—*one*—was cursed with the belief that Beauty existed and that he should open our eyes to it (but this belief was derisively disallowed by healthy young barbarism, so he had a very bad time). He showed me *Rabbi Ben Ezra*, *Abt Vogler*, the *Grammarian's Funeral*, *Pictor Ignotus*; "Thoughts hardly to be packed into a narrow act. . . . All I could never be; all, men ignored in me . . ."; "A circle premature"; "Tastes sweet the water with such specks of earth?" In all this was a real but an austere joy; a washing with glacier water.

But a more formidable antagonist was "Plato-Aristotle," that is, snippets of these read in view of scholarships and lumped together as "philosophical." A yet chillier air! But crystalline, in which I caught shining ideas of "truth," "reality," quite superseding what was "English" or "un-English," what was "good enough for your grandfather and therefore for you," or "nothing remains the same and you can have no certainty." It is evident that none of this was *responsible* for my seeking to become a Catholic some time after leaving school, but all of it helped me towards that. The perception that beautiful things were both vehicle and veil of something more real and more beautiful and more lasting: the hazardous vision of a City based upon earth yet co-extensive with the world, involved in time yet everlasting—a spiritual yet not inhuman Rome: an immutable Truth rooted in God and free from circumstances nor requiring to be "up to date" nor able to be "out of date." School as such did not teach me anything about the Faith as such ; nor did books—till the very end I read no controversy : nor did persons, clerical or lay : the only two priests I met for a minute or two, I disliked ; an aged relative who was a convert I felt (priggishly) to be as silly as she was charming. I cannot say that "life" "taught" me into the Church : I am not bound to say anything about the "education" directly given, as I hold, by God. Not long after this I obtained admission into the Society of Jesus, much assisted by St. Aloysius Gonzaga, whose personality enthralled me as much as his biographies revolted me.

Jesuit training begins with two years of noviciate, during which I learnt to put more order into my sensitive and imaginative life, deriving courage to do so from spiritual considerations ; and, having so far been purely egotistic, instantly dissociating myself from anyone or anything I didn't like at least in the outside world, I had (and wished) to habituate myself to living "in community" and to prepare for much associated work which I foresaw with great repugnance. After about six months I became rather seriously ill, and was sent to finish my noviciate in Provence, at Aix. This was a gift straight from heaven. Life was, of course, austere, but spent in a world of incredible beauty and warmth and in a *traditionally* Catholic atmosphere. The very house there had belonged to the Society of Jesus from pre-suppression days : it was large, simple and noble : where I arrived as a stranger, I felt instantly at home. Moreover, I spent some months in our holiday house, up in the mountains enchanted with wild lavender, thyme, rosemary and pine needles, swimming in a sapphire fountain and climbing into fig trees where I ate, at dawn, purple fruit still dewy. In this Paradise no snake hissed.

After my noviciate, instead of doing the normal two years of classics and mathematics in the Jesuit "juniorate," I was sent to our house of philosophy where I should have spent three years (these are devoted to philosophy and science), but after two, being ill and having four years of Oxford before me, I went straight to our hall there. Well—those two years had taught me at least that to have a rigid control of one's thought was as important as having a skeleton. But at Oxford, my first reaction was that I could not possibly confront the amount and quality of the work necessary for doing decently in the schools. However, while preserving (I trust) the mental and moral skeleton to which I alluded, and without which I should have been something of a jelly-fish, able to sting but liable to melt, I woke up suddenly to History, and felt free to move around in those other cultures, other worlds, with *knowledge*, in which I had for so long dwelt "impressionistically." But, no less important, my two years of scholastic philosophy had made me very critical of the critics, more sceptical than the sceptics. True, at times a sentimental love for the pagan world needed to be brutally disciplined: at others, theory had to be humanized. A "critical humanism," so to call it, was to prove invaluable when I should study theology.

Another asset was, an invigorating relief from an inferiority complex that has always, indeed, endured; but after all, the seemingly "impossible" had been done, and not too badly. Yet whatever inclination to criticize, indeed to disbelieve, had been augmented by Oxford, I could apply first of all to my own performances. I knew that I easily committed, or overlooked, most frightful howlers, and so, readily listened to adverse criticism, though by no means always accepted it: no amount of praise could make me think I had done well what I felt to be, as usual, second rate or worse: if I genuinely thought I *had* done well, I was glad and forgot it. I could see that my taste was still developing, so that self-judgment must be tentative: but even so, I did not guess how admirably I had been vaccinated against Modernism. After Oxford, I taught classics for a year in one of our colleges, but this proved too heavy; and then two years teaching Greek and French in our "juniorate." The first of these years taught me the pleasant lesson that you can get on quite well with boys even if you are not a mighty athlete, provided you regard them as much older and wiser than yourself: most of them are an agreeable mixture of mule and mystic, can be devastatingly polite and abruptly foal-like in their antics, constantly drawing correct conclusions from quite wrong premises, clamorous and shy, finding thought an agony yet fascinated by an idea they have hatched for themselves, always able to see through you if you are fool enough to pretend you know what you don't, and often destined to be still faithful friends after the traditional "forty years." True, those first friendships were to be consolidated by close contact during the first Great War; but it was now that I might have guessed that kindly life meant indeed to surround me with a multitude of friends.

After this, I did my four years' theology, being ordained after three in August, 1911 : it has, in fact, been said that Ordination, drawing now so near, is the true rector of such houses. Speculation is not much to my taste ; but one professor, in my first year, applied the historical and critical method with much learning and humanity to the subject matter, and I liked to see how the great theological formulæ came into being ; and since all Catholic theology, and doctrine, form an organic whole, my first year enabled me to move comfortably forward, save that after my second year I became ill, was sent for the third to a French house where I found admirable professors, and met many whom I had known as novices and, by observing their development, could the better examine my own. My fourth year was spent in Dublin, but I was too ill to study seriously.

After this I coached older boys and young men in scholarship and other classes at Stonyhurst till the war broke out in 1914 and snapped life into two halves. In that "Second-Lieutenants' war" it felt as if one's friends in the next world would soon be as numerous as those in this. At first this was very bitter, as I was not able to be chaplain (I was grateful for this afterwards : you could do much more out of uniform and unpaid), especially as boys, obviously, could no more concentrate, nor, indeed, could I. But happily for me, I was sent to Oxford where I lectured on Latin to handfuls of young men, but where, under the inspiration of my rector, the late Fr. C. D. Plater, I began to go to military hospitals. Ultimately I had six such hospitals in Oxford alone and others at a distance ; also, two battalions of army cadets were quartered in colleges and an ever-shifting multitude of R.F.C. cadets, a high percentage being Catholic. A club was created for these ; vast aerodromes were developed in the neighbourhood ; I was asked, too, to visit two very large camps for German prisoners, and numbers of friends returned wounded to London hospitals. Moreover, Fr. Plater inaugurated a system of weekend "retreats" for the wounded, and for cadets. The latter I had charge of : also of the former when he was ill. For pure happiness, I have known nothing to surpass such retreats. This episode ended with the great influenza epidemic during which I was chiefly with the dying till, at the very end, I caught it myself. And hospitals, camps and colleges rapidly grew empty.

From these years, I think I learnt chiefly four things. First, that any day can be made to last thirty-six hours, all of them filled. Feverish or selfish work are bad for body and soul : hard work and even impossible work do one good. Second, I came to know intimately and love vast numbers of men from Australia and New Zealand of which so far I knew nothing. These hilarious, robust and consecrated friendships proved almost the dearest thing in my life ; and when, after ten years, I went to those lands, I found there a welcome which suggested that not one day had intervened. Third, I learnt still better by direct experience the infinite value and lovableness, indeed the intelligence and the long-suffering, of the "ordinary man": difficulties arose only when you encountered pretentiousness. But on the whole, armoured self-protection had been smashed away : the best and the worst in a man lay raw : but almost always you would find that what rose in strong pure jets from the soul's unsuspected depths was wholly, almost terribly, good. In the case of Catholics, the Sacraments cemented and consecrated such friendships : in other cases, "implicit" faith, contrition and charity hardly needed to be *elicited*, so spontaneous a reaction were they when you *expected* them. Finally, I have not been willing to indicate what I had been learning, I trust, in terms of the Incarnation—our incorporation into the mystical Body of Christ, the indwelling of the Holy Spirit, *vivificans*, and consequently the presence and operation of "eternal life" within us *now*. But it would have been anomalous had not all this at least led towards that total abdication of self-will which alone leaves God free to act through men's work : of what St. Bernard calls the *curva voluntas*, the will bent back selfward ; of what medieval and later writers call *proprietà*, *propriété* ; all will to *possess* even one's own life, let alone the affection, the self-hood, of others, or to dictate what shall be God's action upon souls. All the above would have been waste of words had it not indicated the necessity of assimilating the doctrine as of St. Ignatius, so of St. John of the Cross.

Till 1927 I remained at Oxford, though travelling in vacations to all, I think, of the universities of this island, for Catholic societies were being formed in all of them and were in fact federated, I being the Federation's very incompetent president. This taught me how utterly untrue was the description of post-war youth as degenerate, whatever temptation to disillusionment, pessimism and apathy politicians might supply them with. A good supplement to this acquaintance with studious youth in the younger universities —themselves a good corrective to the two older ones—was provided by numerous retreats to working-men, not least to miners. But we were also seeking contact with Catholic youth abroad and an association called Pax Romana was formed into the vicissitudes of which I need not go: enough to say that it and our Federation at home have not only survived the Second World War, but have enormously developed, not least in the United States. This took me not only to Rome, but to Berlin, Warsaw, twice to Budapest (whither I went twice more later on), to Zagreb, Ljubljana, Innsbruck, and elsewhere nearer home. This intensified and widened the affection for other nations that the war had so rapidly developed : I hardly like to say that Hungary and Poland became especially dear to me, lest I should seem to be *excluding* other nations. Yet I found a deep melancholy growing on me— men were so good (despite their personal and national temperaments, which might become almost exasperating at times to a foreigner like me, as our own would to them)—and were so horribly treated by financiers and politicians too often the slaves not only of ambition and suspicion, of fear and vengefulness, but of base cupidity. It was not among the rulers that I found honour.

Then suddenly, 1928, I was invited to the International Eucharistic Congress (I was on the permanent committee of these congresses) at Sydney, spending first some months in New Zealand. I have tried in *The Risen Sun* to express some of my rapturous happiness in those two countries, and in being on the sea. The sea opened out a whole new world for me ; but there is no space to enlarge on that. However, after ten days in New Zealand I was involved in a very bad motor smash, which left enduring effects, substantial but without interest, save that by 1930 it was necessary for me to seek the sun, and this brought about many months in South Africa and Southern Rhodesia, chiefly away from white men—or all but —in missionary stations. Still, I think I learnt something of the South African temperament in the southern cities, but especially in Kimberley and Johannesburg ; it was strange to be under the Southern Cross and find something so totally different from Australia. As for what I learnt from natives, I have tried to express it in *African Angelus*, a book snobbishly full of statistics (lest it should appear mere tourist-impressionism) and so quite out of date. Still, this was my first acquaintance with a different *race* ; I can only hope to have inherited some vague "sense" of India from my Father, whose many invitations thither I never could accept. Am I deluding myself if I think I caught a "sense" even of South America, during a Eucharistic Congress that took me via Rio to Buenos Aires, and thence, with one friend, by a very special train, across the continent to Mendoza, and thence, by a cavorting aeroplane, over the Andes to Santiago, Valparaiso, then up to Antofagasta, Lima, Guayaquil, and once more to Panama and once more to New Zealand in a ship full of seamen who remembered me from that old *Rotorua* in which I had travelled six whole years before? Be all that as it may, I was welcomed at Wellington by cries of "Welcome *home*!" And Australia—this time after no motor smash nor influenza nor pneumonia—was equally a "home." Can you wonder if I have learnt the simplest of lessons, gratitude? And finally, in 1937, I went to the Philippines (which meant, on my way home, a fourth visit to Ceylon) ; and I was in Rome at the time of Hitler's visit and the Anschluss and went on to Budapest, knowing very well as I flew homewards that I was saying goodbye to a whole world.

After this, I was almost constantly ill and in and out of hospitals, but in the spring of 1940 was invited to give some lectures in

Copenhagen and other Danish towns. I was quite sure I would not return ; but every ministry in London assured me that there was not the slightest chance of an invasion, so I went there on April 6, and on April 9 the Germans arrived. I propose to say nothing of the next five years, save that to spend so long doing nothing, saying nothing, able to believe nothing, and above all having to black out all imagination and speculation (for it would have meant mere waste of nerve tissue, there being no usable evidence), quite apart from considerable illness due to the appalling winter of 1940–41, had a curious effect upon the mind. Deliberately thus to arrest all emotional and mental processes, and not least to refuse one instant of repining because one had hoped for so much happy hard work such as had filled the previous war years, was all too successful : it had a paralysing effect upon memory and inhibited all *recollection* : it prevented concentration or the acquisition of new ideas : it deadened all appetite. Yet, suspended thus between two worlds, one felt as if one's outlook were clarified. Sadly enough, even before Munich, I had ceased to believe in political promises : nor could I believe in paper programmes, nor in disinterested economics ; and the moment "national interests" were mentioned, I lost heart. Even allowing for all the heroism, the sublime self-sacrifice, the humorous endurance, the pathetic hopes, the grandiose visions, I was far more anxious about the after-war than the war. I was quite prepared for shiftings of centres of gravity much farther than from Europe to the U.S.A.; I had often said, not quite frivolously, that I foresaw a Pope, someday, reigning from Tibet. Certainly I foresaw revolutions, civil wars, tyrannies and everywhere secularist States with Governments at least would-be-omnipotent. What distressed me was, far less that Russia had a plan, bad though it were, than that the Allies had none, or none they were convinced about. A grave authority has stated that whatever Parliament may decree, is legal, renouncing thus not only the Law of God as revealed, but that of God expressing Himself in Nature, in conscience. The only check on such legislation, it was admitted, was popular opinion which might render a law abortive. Lenin once said to an acquaintance of mine : "You are an emotional revolutionary :

that is no good to us. We need cold brains." *We* seemed to me to have doctrinaires in plenty, but spiritual principles? No.

One upshot of those five years was to accelerate my reluctance to read books or listen to arguments; to dissect and analyse, though so much more material for that was being supplied. Whatever truth I met was already included in the universal embrace of the Catholic Faith—all truths appear to me to exist there, unified, pure and supernaturalized. I cannot say that "life" has "taught" me this, though experience has constantly ratified, amplified and elevated what seems to me to have been "given" in childhood itself. I am not all the while consciously reflecting on my Faith any more than I am on my beating heart or my breathing lungs. But in proportion as that Faith is operative in me, I live: if my "charity," due to it, grows cold, I know that I am dying.

I regard it, then, as a great grace of God that He should have shown me so many things, and in them, so much beauty and goodness; and that I have been continuously aware that I cannot even begin properly to appreciate the beauty of one petal of one flower, and that there is here no question of thoughts that lie too deep for tears, but of a perception too deep for thoughts. And when you come to Man—what *then*? If, touching a flower, you truly touch the hem of God's garment; if you can never venerate and love it as He does—for He who is preserving it (who, if I may so put it, *invented* it) sees His own reflection in it infinitely better than we do or can—what, when you touch a soul? Intelligence; freedom; immortality—the worth that *God* sees in each soul, a worth to be estimated by the fact of the Incarnation, the Death and Resurrection of the Son of God made man. It will surely be understood that the nearer you approach perception of this, the less you put any *trust* in literature, art, argument, writing or talking, however much you must make use of all these—"use *all* our 'pieces' (as in chess)," said St. Francis de Sales—and the more you fall back upon the Holy Spirit who alone can plunge into the watery chaos and turn it not only into order, and life, but into a Font wherein the whole course of human history may be baptized. Therefore, once more, I would prefer to say, not that Life has taught me anything, but that God has taught me partly by means of experiences, interior and outward, and has enabled me to live within the *Res Catholica*, and to wish to love and serve God better, and my fellow man for His sake. Therefore I am free to look at these pages, too, with friendly mockery, leaving them wholly to God, whether they are to have any value, or be just waste paper.

It has, however, been suggested that before I take my leave of the reader I should add a few lines about the "lessons" of illness. Perhaps: (1) "Fret not thyself." I am an extremely good patient so long as I am allowed to do exactly what I like. But when coerced, I must not "fret" (e.g. about illness interfering with plans) : fretting retards recovery. (2) Be patient with doctors. They are amazingly nice when tamed. Realize the terribly tedious, often ungrateful, often repulsive, often exhausting work that nurses have to do (one may admire them even when they are officially cheerful, clean and healthy and call one "we"). It depends a lot upon the patient if a nurse feels her work to be a vocation and not merely a profession. As regards surgeons, a certain meek adaptability is doubtless indicated. (3) During convalescence you will probably feel melancholy and fractious and far worse than when ill. Don't *hustle* your convalescence through a desire to get back to work. Perhaps, quite suddenly, you will feel : "Hullo! I am better!" On no account instantly do as much as you feel you can. Because you can't. (4) You often realize that people do *not* realize what you are feeling like. Don't spend time distressing, or boring, them by prolonged descriptions of your experiences : but learn that ten to one, when they are ill, you will not appreciate what *they* are going through : be imaginative enough to sympathize : courageous enough not to be soft : humble enough not to exhort them to exasperating forms of courage, etc. You may even be privileged to help them by taking some of their pain across into yourself. Some visitors are fountains of peace ; others are vampires. (5) When ill, one can quite well learn that pain may be the opposite of pleasure, but not, by any means, of happiness. If one has not provoked one's illness (and even if one has, but is sorry), much healing serenity is produced by the certainty that God does not *want* one to be other than docile for a time—I mean, does not want active work, or the solution of problems or any choice save the one choice—to be ill properly and "according to God." Finally, the Christian who believes himself united supernaturally with Christ, and living in and by means of Him, can unite himself with Gethsemane and Calvary, for the purposes for which those were endured. But this leads us towards considerations here, perhaps, out of place.

SIR SEYMOUR HICKS

Born in 1871 at St. Heliers, Jersey. The son of an Army officer, he himself was originally intended for a military career, but chose the Stage instead at an early age and became equally distinguished as actor, manager and writer. He married Ellaline Terriss, with whom he acted for many years, and took a prominent part in organizing entertainment for the Forces in both World Wars. Was knighted in 1935.

IN THE spring of 1941, a season of by no means pleasant memories for Britain, I decided that as my war work obliged me to proceed in convoy to the Middle East, a journey, in all probability, bristling with torpedoes, mines, bombs and raiders, it would be a wise precaution to take out a new insurance policy on my life. This I may say was not solely for the benefit of my heirs, executors and assigns, but also for the protection of those many trusting merchants to be found in all great cities, who are not averse to encouraging extravagance on the part of those of their customers whose financial year begins every day. Feeling extremely fit, and quite unlike many of my friends who are often only five minutes ahead of one, I took coach, as that most worthy of civil servants Mr. Samuel Pepys might have said, and drove to an imposing looking building, ornate without and chromium-plated within, the home of experts who amass fortunes by feeding fat upon the gullible millions who have been convinced by the vendors of patent medicines, that rheumatoid arthritis and Pagets disease can in ninety-nine cases out of a hundred be traced to the common cold, and that a maidenly blush is undoubtedly "tick-de-la-roo" in holiday attire. Eager and willing to pay any premium in reason, my surprise may well be imagined, when, on being asked by one of the "Dicers with Death" how old I was and replying that seventy wintry British summers had passed me lightly by, he informed me that it would be quite impossible to consider my application. "As you see," he smiled benignly, "at the age of three score years and ten, medically, you are dead."

The reader may not unreasonably inquire what this disconcerting piece of news has got to do with a question framed with the object of discovering "What Life has taught me." May I say in answer to such a query that there are one or two very good reasons for my drawing attention to the fact that I am well on the way to becoming an October geranium, as the schoolboy described his eighty-year-old grandfather, the principal of these being that having refused several times to enter a social confessional box at the peak hours of my gay fifties, I saw no reason to risk becoming a trifle pompous as the sun was setting on a not very distant horizon.

Then again this seemingly simple inquiry was on reflection by no means so easy to deal with as it appeared. It is true that my career of more than sixty working years had been crowded with adventure, a cup full to overflowing, but how best to marshal facts and from them deduce something really worth while to interest or amuse without floundering in platitudes or discovering the obvious, seemed a task impossible for so ordinary a person as I know myself to be. However, that a humble chronicler be bidden attend a feast at which I realized every dish would be garnished with the wit and wisdom of brilliant literary chefs was so signal an honour that to be obliged to refuse such a charming invitation was truly regrettable, and it was with sorrow that I was about to post my tactfully expressed excuses in a nearby pillar box when it suddenly struck me that were I to substitute the word "theatre" for that of "life" I might, without disgracing myself, occupy a seat below the salt and introduce a very beautiful lady in the person of Dame Thespis to the assembled company.

Taking my courage in both hands, therefore, I made up my mind to thank my mistress publicly and very gratefully for the many smiles she had showered upon me, though at times they had been bestowed after slaps of by no means a gentle kind. At the outset of my career she had placed in my hands a jewel more priceless even than the one that somewhat dreary and often troublesome Bourbon family never tired of informing the world they had lost. This was a volume entitled *Human Nature* written by herself, containing tabloid characterizations of all sorts and conditions of men. As she gave it me she whispered: "Between the covers of this strange work you will find detailed descriptions of the often fantastic creatures you will be called upon to portray. Let nothing, however, of apparently little value concerned with many of these unbelievable types escape your notice or seem too small for profound thought and consideration. Remember that the methods, the motives and the manners of your fellow men are the tools of the actor's trade and without an intimate knowledge of how they should be used dismal failure must be the player's lot, or, what is even worse, a niche reserved for him in the hall of pleasant mediocrity."

Had I not obeyed her wise command I should never have learned, among numerous other things, one of the greatest of all lessons: "How to laugh at life." The doctor, the cleric, and the legal light, doubtless possess an extraordinary knowledge of mankind, for it is they who comfort and advise in the hours before what may appear a hopeless dawn. But however careful a study they make of those who seek their aid they do not absorb like the successful actor, and it is not necessary that they should, the reasons for the often extraordinary behaviour of the world's marionettes, who dance on strings held by a hidden hand it is not permitted shall ever be seen.

Oh, yes, there is endless amusement to be got out of a profession which demands a microscopic examination of the minds of men. How then can any exponent of the actor's art, equipped with a sense of humour which should be his most treasured possession, fail to see the humorous side of the desperate struggle everywhere to gain what the Bard of Avon describes as "the bubble reputation even at the cannon's mouth."

Dipping one's hand into the world's bag of all sorts, and pulling out at random a few odd specimens of its fun-makers who so unconsciously teach us to laugh comes first and foremost "the lover," with his passionate longings, his agonies of jealousy, his despair and perhaps ultimate triumph, often to be followed by complete disillusionment. Who more ridiculous to watch than the complacent husband who would look upon the present of a pair of spectacles as an affront, or the impoverished citizen content to believe implicitly in politicians who bake their promises in a pastrycook's oven. Here, too, we see the pompous ass, that purse-proud mountain of avoirdupois sublimely ignorant that he is the biggest bore unhung, cheek by jowl with the miser and the money lender, neither of these worthies with all their cunning seeming conscious of the fact that not even the smallest pocket is to be found in the largest asbestos shroud. Rivalling them as a fun maker also may be seen that charlatan of charlatans, the brave atheist who on his death bed screams aloud to Heaven for mercy.

These, of course, are but a fraction of the models which Nature has manufactured for the enjoyment of the earnest student. Her unbroken mould turns out with few exceptions a host who make for merriment in all walks of life.

Is it to be wondered at then that I am grateful to a profession which has taught me to laugh?

But in having tried, and I hope succeeded, to a small extent in getting beneath the skin of characters as wide apart as the poles, I would not have it thought that all my profession has taught me was how to become a laughing cavalier, for this would indeed be tantamount to saying that a beautiful calling was one incapable of little else, whereas I rank it second to none in its power of appreciating to the utmost the innumerable lovely things which are the gifts Providence offers Man. If it be true, as a brilliant acquaintance of mine once remarked, that he had never known what life meant till he had seen it through the eyes of Corot and the heart of Gissing, then how grateful should the player be that he has been privileged to see it through the master minds of the great literary figures who throughout the centuries have so ungrudgingly given their all to a Cinderella who loved her children none the less, that being servants of many a monarch they have been known "as rogues and vagabonds."

If we feel that the poet is a trifle optimistic in saying that there are "books in the running brooks," still I heartily agree with him when he continues and sings there is "good in everything," reading "everything" as "everybody."

The analysing of character which is the actor's very definite concern has taught me that it is not only in the best brand of human being that good is to be found, for if we trouble to search diligently there are few, even among those who have declared war on society, who are without some redeeming feature.

This I know is a monumental platitude, my reason for mentioning anything so obvious is to make it abundantly clear that for the purpose of his work the actor gains a deeper insight into character than the ordinary man of the world however observant. It is through my work I have learned that a kindly approach to the most difficult people seldom fails to break down an apparently unsurmountable barrier, and so I am beholden to many a brilliant author for shining a light into the darkness of the evil-doer which more often than not discloses some much to be applauded quality.

From my Pandora Box which holds memories of small achievement the word "luck" must not be eliminated. In my own case it is written large. First in the possession of the most wonderful of partners, who in addition to being adored by all those to whom she has given her friendship was one of the most beloved and brilliant artistes of her day, a woman who guided me with her calm and unerring judgment through the shoals and quicksands of many a hazardous adventure. As this is in no sense a biographical effort I do not pursue a tribute I have never failed to pay, and I approach the "luck" which came my way from a purely professional standpoint.

It was towards the end of 1889 that at the age of nineteen, having earned a somewhat precarious livelihood as an actor for some four years, I found myself practically starving in London. For six weeks I had haunted agents' offices in the hope of obtaining work, but without success, when on a bleak October day fate stepped in, having come to the conclusion, I suppose, that ill-fortune had dogged my footsteps long enough. During this particular afternoon I had visited various theatres and tramped along the Strand, then the hub of the theatrical universe, in the hope of hearing of any work that might be going, when at last hungry and weary I turned up Bedford Street to trudge my way to my lodgings in the Earls Court Road. I had not gone far when for some unaccountable reason I retraced my steps and was about to turn the corner into the Strand again when I came face to face with a friend of my own age in the person of an afterwards well-known actor, Mr. Sam Sothern, the son of the famous Sothern who had made two continents laugh at his impersonation of Lord Dundreary and taken London by storm as David Garrick. "Where are you going to?" my friend inquired. "Nowhere in particular," I replied. "Then come and dine with me across the way at Simpson's," said he. As cups of tea and bread and butter in the morning had been my only fare for many a long day it is not difficult to explain how readily I accepted his invitation. What that meal meant to me Sothern never guessed, but when not so many years afterwards I engaged him to act in *The Catch of the Season* at the Vaudeville Theatre, his salary being £40 a week, and I told him of the plight I was in when unknowingly he took pity on a penniless youth he seemed mightily surprised, as never having been in straitened circumstances himself such a contingency arising as a friend wanting for food had never occurred to him. Had we parted directly after dinner that historic night, a much wanted repast might have been my principal memory of a happy reunion, but far from my good-natured companion wishing to end his hospitality with the paying of the bill, he said that as he had been given two seats for the Court Theatre would I like to come with him and see Mr. and Mrs. Kendal act? What greater pleasure could anyone be offered, so off we went by the stifling old Underground to Sloane Square. Little did I dream what was in store for me. Between the acts I was introduced to the manager of the theatre, a friend of Sothern's. He asked Sothern if I was on the stage, and on hearing that I had been in the profession for nearly five years he rather embarrassed me by inquiring if I could act! ! ! Gathering from his manner that he had some good reason for putting the question, I swallowed twice and with all the confidence of youth replied, "Oh yes, rather."

At this my new friend seemed highly amused, and then astonished me by saying, "Well, perhaps you may be exactly what they want. I'll take you round at the end of the play and introduce you to Mrs. Kendal." When I heard why he proposed to do this I could hardly believe my ears. It appeared that the Kendals, who were on the eve of going to the United States for a long tour, had on this very evening received news that the young man who had been engaged to play a number of most important juvenile parts had been taken dangerously ill, and consequently would be unable to leave England. I sat and watched the rest of the performance in a dream, and when the curtain fell and I saw the very greatest of actresses taking call after call as the house shouted itself hoarse, I was terrified at the thought that in a few minutes I should be in the presence of this dominating personality whom I had watched compel laughter or tears at will and leave the audience spellbound.

It is not unnatural I suppose for a boy to be awestruck when confronted with someone whose name is a household word, but I can never remember at any time being so less myself as when I saw a pair of small piercing brown eyes looking me through and through, and heard a voice saying, "Oh! so I hear you think you can act. What's your name?" "Hicks," I bleated. "Hicks? not a very pretty name," snorted Madge Robertson Kendal (snorting being a trick she indulged in, I was afterwards to learn, when pleased, amazed or angry). "Very well, Hicks—you will meet me here tomorrow morning at ten-thirty, and you must show me how to act. Good night." Glad to escape I hurried out of her room and was handed the boy's part in that famous comedy, *The Scrap of Paper*, being told by the stage manager to get as much as possible of it into my head. Need I say that I sat up half the night and arrived the next day to all intents and purposes word perfect? No ordeal by fire could have been more awful than the two hours I spent knowing that my possibilities were being weighed up by a lady who held my immediate future in her hands, and whom I sensed, and afterwards knew to be, one of the most difficult women in the world. The rehearsal over, I am not exaggerating when I say that I could hardly hold the pen I was given when asked to sign a year's contract at a salary of six pounds a week.

From that extraordinary genius I learned all I know of my profession. For fifty years I was her grateful friend; but I never knew her. She was always helpful and fond of me, and although she sent for me two days before her death to open her heart to me in a way I don't think she had ever opened it before to anyone, I still felt I did not know her. This amazing lady was a lonely woman in her latter years, and though admiration and respect were hers, it was a tragedy that she deliberately thrust away the abundant love which could so easily have surrounded her. Many people, and I am one of them, are unshakable in their belief that there is "a divinity that shapes our ends, rough-hew them how we will." Had I ever been tempted to challenge Shakespeare's considered judgment on the point, the inexplicable impulse which made me retrace my steps towards a thoroughfare which all day long had been one holding out no hope of any kind, would surely have convinced me it was "a sign" from which I was to learn that even the most insignificant of mortals are not destined to struggle on unaided. As a natural corollary I learned that no one need fear that prayers for help will remain unanswered when difficulties and disaster seem overwhelming.

In writing this I hope it will not be thought I have taken the lease of a pulpit in my old age, for I am well aware that no one has less right to do so than I, but as so many undeserved blessings have come my way, I feel there is no reason why I should not tell my fellow man-in-the-street that these have often been answers to very definite appeals in times of grave anxiety. In using the word "anxiety" I naturally do so in reference to the greater things of life compared with which the ordinary worries connected with our present-day struggle to exist (I had almost written "to live") mean nothing at all. But as troublesome business problems beset each and all of us, here let me say that my profession soon taught me that with the exception of deliberate gambling there is no more hazardous undertaking than the running of a theatre. Although profound knowledge, the experience of a lifetime and untiring labour are allied for the presenting of what is considered by experts to be a work worthy in every way, success or failure is still dependent on the toss of that coin which the public takes with it to the first performance of every new play, and it therefore behoves the Keepers of the Temple of Thespis to count their blessings gratefully. This was brought home to me very forcibly early in my life as a manager by a theatrical colleague who remarked one night that I seemed a trifle nervy. I explained that I had good reason to be, since not only had I played with two understudies who were incredibly bad, but from early morning everything seemed to have gone wrong at the office over the plans for a forthcoming production. "Everything gone wrong my dear fellow?" he laughed. "Is that all that's the matter? You seem to have got hold of the wrong end of the stick altogether. You ought never say everything has gone wrong. Ask yourself if *one* thing has gone right and if you find yourself in that much to be envied position, thank God, jump into bed and go to sleep hoping that you will be half as lucky on the morrow."

One thing I have never learned is how it comes about that the playgoing public, who take such a tremendous interest in everything connected with their favourites and the parts in which they appear, do not seem to have the remotest idea of the difficulties and pitfalls which beset them at every turn. Even the ever-increasing number of amateur actors and actresses appear to imagine that the professional player dwells in a kingdom of gilded content and that their club is a gateway to it, through which they have only to step to find prizes awaiting them.

In writing like this it must not be thought that I am pointing to a notice board on which is printed, "No Thoroughfare," or crying from the housetops, "Abandon hope." Far from it, I am simply drawing the attention of the youth who hopes to gain fame in my profession to the fact that the apparently placid and beautiful sea on which he is so eager to launch his frail dramatic craft, holds many an uncharted tide and whirlpool, with which the inexperienced navigator will have to cope if he would avoid disaster on a cruel and rocky coastline.

Like "Lear" to his Cordelia, I am asking him to "Think again;" that's all. How helpful it would be if I could say with certainty to Mr. Jones : "It is no good your going on the stage. I know your friend Mr. Smith has been most successful, but he has something you have not. Magnetism. That illusive something, impossible to describe and impossible to acquire." In the art of the Theatre the power to appraise the value of the uncut stone is given to few. Even the mighty Garrick was hopelessly at fault, for it must be remembered that on seeing the equally mighty Mrs. Siddons when she first came to London, he thought nothing of her.

Alas! as there is no Golden Test by which it may be determined whether Mr. Jones or Mr. Brown should be admitted into the charmed circle of His Majesty's Servants, there is nothing to stop the halt and the lame from suffering bitter disappointment in an art which, unlike painting or music, leaves neither visible nor oral record of their iniquities. Mr. Jones and Mr. Brown may ask why I myself went on the stage at the age of fifteen and had the impertinence to think I could act. To this very legitimate inquiry I have no answer, except to say that I humbly apologize for having dared to do so, and that it is true that on November 11, 1887, I started my work-life as a callboy. I have had the most wonderful time and after sixty years of happy "ups and downs," I find that I have no longer a desire to hear a brother callboy shouting "Overture and Beginners"—as, oddly enough, I know most of the overtures and cannot by any stretch of the imagination be called a beginner.

It has been a long, long journey, full of exciting memories—one of the two most vivid being that of a rather exuberant young gentleman at the old Gaiety Theatre singing "Her golden hair was hanging down her back," and the other is the picture of a bewitchingly beautiful person binding great audiences to her with "A Little Bit of String."

SIR GEORGE DYSON

Born in 1883 in Yorkshire. Studied at the Royal College of Music from 1900–04. Was Director of Music at the Royal Naval College, Osborne, and at Marlborough before the First World War and at Wellington and Winchester after the war. Has been Director of the Royal College of Music since 1937, and is the composer of several major works, of which "The Canterbury Pilgrims" is perhaps the best known.

THE MUSICAL faculty is one of those gifts which nature bestows on us to a degree far beyond what we need for the ordinary circumstances of life. It is important that we should be able to hear the sounds which help us to interpret the outside world and to move more safely in it, and we have also learnt to make and use sounds as a means of communicating with one another. But it is not necessary to have what we call a musical ear in order to live comfortably, nor are the sounds we use in speech especially musical. Why, then, should so many of us show such extraordinary sensitiveness to tones and intervals which serve no practical purpose and have no intelligible meaning?

A dog hears sounds that we miss. A bird produces notes far more musical than our speech. Yet the dog has not developed a language, nor do birds produce more than a few reiterated phrases. It is man alone that both speaks and sings, and develops both these faculties far in excess of their immediate usefulness. Man alone is what we call an artist; a being, that is, who builds on a foundation of sensitiveness a whole world of special idioms and values. And within this framework, which he himself makes, he creates ever more fruits of his fantasy and imagination. His final product is a mature art, astonishing equally in its extent, its complexity, and its power to move us. All the arts create these new orders of value, which our own human faculties add to the world of nature. They develop special associations and conventions, and the musician's sphere is but one of these structures of the imagination, through which we learn to express our own and interpret the thoughts and feelings of others.

The musical gift is innate. It can be cultivated and trained, but we vary enormously in our initial sensitiveness. When I was four years old, musical notes were to me already quite fixed and exact. I could find on our piano a note heard outside, without searching for it. I was only a very childish beginner, but I could think notes exactly, and play what I thought. I cannot remember the time when I could not read music, but I believe I could think it before I could read it, and my thinking was instinctive and effortless. I had what is called absolute pitch, and to this day I cannot imagine how complicated music can be grasped without it. There are many gifted musicians, including distinguished composers, whose sense of pitch is only relative, but their methods of thought puzzle me. My mental note A is A and nothing else, my C major is C major, whether heard or imagined.

Yet there are children with absolute pitch whose musical sense does not develop, just as there are individuals highly sensitive to shape and colour who do not become artists. Some women can go into a shop and match from memory a delicate shade of silk or wool. Some men can tell us the year of a vintage wine by tasting it. Tea-tasters have a similar faculty. All these are examples of the kind of exceptional intuition on which the arts are built. Some artists draw from memory. Some need a model. But all must have that instinctive discrimination without which advanced training is impossible.

Equal in importance to the initial gift is the environment in which it occurs. When I was a boy there were no gramophones, no wireless music. I lived in an industrial town in Yorkshire, where music was represented by the cottage piano, the church or chapel organ and choir, the occasional group of amateur orchestral players, and the popular brass band. Very few were the visits of a professional orchestra or a famous soloist. We made our day-to-day music ourselves. As a promising child I was given lessons, but my musical education could not go beyond my immediate surroundings. I knew the Beethoven sonatas, the Bach organ works, some standard anthems, a few oratorios, and various "arrangements" of overtures and symphonies. I had a boy friend who played the violin. We occasionally played the whole eleven Beethoven violin sonatas, lasting about five hours, at one sitting. We devoured everything we could get hold of. I sang in a choir and played in a chapel. There were no other ways of obtaining musical experience. We had to make our own.

I came to London at seventeen, and my four years as a student there were exciting beyond description, both musically and mentally. Then for the first time I lived amid the wealth of orchestral music, of drama and opera. To a provincial student these were all major events, stimulating to a degree hardly possible now. Young people today have listened, if they wished, to broadcast performances of a thousand great works. The concert hall may give them an added thrill, but it is not the complete revelation it was to us. Our experience was much more restricted, but it was extraordinarily vivid and exact. I could recall and rewrite, note for note, scores of substantial works I played as a boy. Present students have covered vastly more ground than we could, but I doubt whether they know their music as intimately as did those of us who had to do our own exploring.

The main patterns of a musical mind are indelibly affected by its earliest impressions. What we learn in youth becomes our intuitive standard of value. I cannot accept equally all styles and all innovations. I was taught in London by eminent men who were both masters of their art and sympathetic to their pupils, but I learnt still more from my fellow students. I believe that to be true of all education. It is far better to be thrown among students of one's own age, and of similar gifts, than to be the isolated pupil of even the best possible teacher. It is the clash and competition of minds of the same age and outlook which is the most stimulating form of education.

After London I lived for four years abroad. I had a travelling scholarship, very modest in amount, which compelled me to live as the native students lived. I picked up two or three languages, heard and saw all that a student could, and stayed long enough to become at home in European surroundings. It is a moot point whether absence for so long is good for a young musician. Music is a universal language, but it is not necessarily a cosmopolitan language. Many elements in it are common to all European countries, but there is also a strong national flavour in all music of permanent rank. Every composer of distinction is in a very real sense the child of a particular tradition and environment. We think of Beethoven as belonging to us all, and so in great measure he does, but he is in essence as definitely German as Purcell is English and Verdi Italian. Cosmopolitan music has no flavour, and fades as fashion changes. Only a native speech can feed a great literature. There is no polyglot art that can long survive.

I saw the native enthusiasm of Italy and its extreme vagaries of taste. I saw the end of the century and a half during which German music was supreme, and I met its last representative, Richard Strauss. Prussianism was then already hardening the fibres of life and art. I enjoyed the wonderful expansion of Russian creative genius, and was fascinated by the sensitiveness of France. But it was not until I returned to England that I fully realized how superior was the music of London in at least two respects. In the first place there was and is in London far more music, and of far greater variety, than in any other single capital of Europe. And secondly, there was and is a school of composers of greater range and vigour, and more genuinely creative, than that of any other western nation. I would go further, and say that spontaneous inspiration has now greatly diminished in Europe, because it is impossible to create freely without freedom of thought and intercourse. Looking eastward is now looking backward. The present is in England, the future here and in America. Art is an intensely individual pursuit. Politicians can stage a spectacle, but only the men of second rank will take part in it. Genius cannot be produced by propaganda.

It is now nearly forty years since I returned from my student wanderings. During most of that time I have been concerned with musical education. A gap of six years, from 1914 to 1920, in the Army and Air Force, seemed at the time to be the end of my music, but I survived uninjured and resumed my profession with a new and permanent zest. I do not regret my share in those war years, because I believe that the arts and those who serve them must not stand aloof from the dangers and upheavals of our corporate life. I would not exempt any class of men from the social duties demanded of their fellows.

There are two reasons for this. It is an insufferable presumption to pretend that any profession has an absolute value above all other services to the community. Genuine service must be prepared, in the last resort, to sacrifice even itself. Half the troubles of the world are due to the apathy of men in face of social problems they avoid or ignore. The artist is particularly liable to this temptation. His specialized talent and outlook may turn him into a parasite on the civilization of his time. He may try to save his art at the expense of his humanity, and risk the loss of both. And the converse of this is also true. An art which is not an integral part of the life of a community becomes a barren and exotic pursuit. The artists of the Renaissance, like the Elizabethan poets, were ready if need be to become soldiers in any compelling crusade. The background of all great literature is social faith, which infers or involves effective social action. The art of the ivory tower immolates both itself and its worshippers.

I have no belief whatever in democratic art in the creative sense. Art is produced by individuals, or by the direction of individuals. The world as a whole cannot be more than a sympathetic spectator. But it follows from this that the arts must never despise their public, because there is a two-way traffic in which the spectator or listener is just as essential as the architect or musician. The actual work of an artist must be created in isolation, but his ears and eyes must be open to the sounds and sights of his environment. He must crystallize the impressions and emotions of real passions and real events.

In the interest and variety of my own personal experience I have been very fortunate. I have been able to play, conduct, lecture and compose, and I have had close relations with pupils, institutions and the general public. I have written books and music, but I have also had church services, chamber music, choral societies and orchestras to handle, and a good deal of administrative work as well. My field may have been even too wide, and I might have done more concentrated work of smaller range, but if the arts are to be a normal and natural part of our social life, then musicians must be ready to accept these obligations, even if they involve some restriction of the more purely personal use of a talent.

As so often happens, my main sphere of work came to me by accident. Returned from my travels, I had a few very lean months, and then two possible posts came together. Both were modest, but one was in London, where every ambitious young man wants to be, and one was far from London and very uncertain in its prospect. It was Sir Hubert Parry, then Director of the Royal College, who persuaded me to take the latter. He told me to go where there was no music and make some, rather than join the crowd of competitors in London. I took his advice and began my career as a school music-master. It was a new appointment with no guarantee, present or future. I had to create the post. By a combination of work and good fortune I enlisted the good will even of those who were not very sympathetic to my subject, and the generous help of those who were. In three years my own position and the musical repute of the school were assured. And I have since passed from one appointment to another, until I am now occupying that very chair from which Sir Hubert launched me on my voyage.

Except for the war years, all my main activities have been connected with what are somewhat illogically called "public" schools, Osborne, Marlborough, Rugby, Wellington and Winchester, in that order. All such schools have much in common, but they also have marked differences, and the first thing one has to learn in that world is never to apply a uniform pattern. Each school has its own tradition, and therein lies its strength. There is no subject in which outsiders flounder more hopelessly than in discussing such schools. In one sense they are narrow and exclusive. They look critically both at strangers and at one another. Yet in another sense they are miniature universities. They hold every type of character and every degree of talent. And owing to the fact that the boys live day and night in the unrelenting company of each other, there is a concentration of influence which, for good or evil, is extraordinarily powerful. They pool their habits, their knowledge, their tastes, and their social experience.

Their corporate knowledge is encyclopædic. To give an example in my own subject, there is no music of fair repute, classical or modern, which is not known to some of the boys in any mature school audience. There is no standard book which some boy has not read, nor any important facet of any subject, literary, historical, scientific or æsthetic, which no boy has touched. I learnt to take more pains to get my facts scrupulously correct, when talking to my boys about music, than when I was talking to a more professedly musical audience. When I was working at Winchester College I also taught one day a week at the Royal College of Music. My London pupils had exceptional talent, but often a very defective background of knowledge. My Winchester boys were only amateur musicians, but they had a remarkably wide discrimination. Enlightened homes, broadcasting, gramophones, reading, and the general pooling of experience in hourly contacts, can give the boys of a boarding school an astonishing equipment of accurate and informed taste.

The same holds good in other spheres of thought. A school may appear to be encrusted with age and tradition. But inside it there may be a range and freedom of outlook not easy to find elsewhere. A clever boy's mind is open, is hungry for facts and arguments, and in the company of his fellows there are no barriers. He either explores himself or is subjected to the explorations of others. This is the essential educational value of a boarding school. There are from time to time tragic misfits, but so there are in any system. The Shelleys of the world are no more amenable out of school than in it, and even for them there are worse fates than a prefect's discipline.

All schools should be miniature universities, where every subject appropriate to a child's age and talent can be pursued without limit. Boarding schools offer the added experience of living in groups and learning to organize and regulate corporate needs and activities. This is their distinctive contribution to education. The world will always need men who instinctively recognize and accept social obligations, who will try to bring order into daily life by understanding and reconciling the infinite varieties of human interest and temperament. A boarding school is the best institution yet devised for practising these social duties, on a small scale and at an early age. Our public schools, whatever faults they may have, are nurseries of that sense of responsibility which is ready both to exert authority and to accept it, to the end that community life may be reasonably ordered.

One story in my own experience will illustrate this attitude which, in a good school, by generations of trial and tradition, becomes second nature. During the war of 1914 to 1918, so many masters were away in the Forces that the provision of substitute teachers was an insoluble problem. Some of these substitutes were quite unfitted to handle boys in the mass, and discipline had to be maintained, if at all, by the senior boys themselves. In one such school the prefects met and posted in their respective houses the following notice: "Boys are reminded that though permanent masters are fair game, there must be no ragging of substitutes."

The phrase "fair game" is an epitome of schoolboy ethics, both with respect to behaviour and property. Some things are "not done." The dividing lines may seem to an outsider somewhat arbitrary or illogical, but they are genuine and spontaneous regulations which do in the main enforce tolerable conduct and rough justice. And this natural growth of a social conscience and discipline can be harnessed to all kinds of corporate activity, material, intellectual, æsthetic, or purely recreational. The ablest boys learn instinctively to organize themselves and their fellows, and they apply these methods when they have to assume responsibilities in after life. They develop a code of behaviour which, however arbitrary or imperfect, is at least a foundation for social order and good faith. They may appear to be cushioned and protected as a class, but they also learn to take hard knocks without losing their sense of proportion. I am not myself a public-school product, but many years of work in that environment have convinced me that it is one of the most effective trainings for the give and take of social life that we have yet devised.

The immediate problem of the universities, and of specialist colleges like my own, is how to provide for the masses of would-be graduates, without neglecting the pursuit of the sciences and arts for their own sake. We are faced with an overwhelming number of candidates, most of whom claim and deserve financial help to an extent which makes them belong to the scholarship class of students ; but many of them look no further than the degree or diploma which will qualify them for a profession. They are not scholars in the old sense of the word.

The days are gone when comparatively idle young men went to a university to amuse themselves and scrape through a pass degree, and nobody wants those days to return. But the system also included the more select few whose talents were outstanding, and to whom learning and research were a vocation. We must not allow the new entrants of average capacity, keen and industrious though they are, to divert our universities from their primary pursuit of knowledge as such. If more and more of our young people are to continue their education to the standard of a university degree, it is inevitable that this university stage must prepare them for many professions, for industry and commerce, and for technical employment in which book-learning plays a comparatively small part. They cannot all go into those few public services where languages and literature, law, history and philosophy are an appropriate background. Nor can many of them become research scientists or creative artists. Ideally we need universities of two kinds, one for the rank and file of students whose university studies are a prelude to the technical and practical professions, the other for those to whom study and research are to be the main purpose of their lives. My own institution, the Royal College of Music, illustrates both these tendencies.

In my college we do at least know that our students wish to be musicians, and they are selected for this particular talent. We are not concerned with the large numbers of students, found in all universities, who do not know what kind of employment awaits them and who, therefore, have to qualify vaguely for whatever may turn up. We are spared this uncertainty of aim. But even so, our problem is not simple, because music and the profession of music can mean so many things. Are our students going to create music, or interpret it, or teach it? Those are the broad divisions of the art, and each of these divisions is highly specialized. In the general structure of our national education, music is now accepted as one of the desirable arts, and there is therefore a pressing demand for those who can teach it. Were we to concentrate on meeting this demand, our college could become in the main a training ground for teachers, and the creative side of our work would inevitably suffer. What policy are we to pursue?

Music begins with the composer. Without him there is no music at all. It is true that the composers of the past have left us a legacy of so much music that we can employ large numbers of musicians to interpret and teach it, just as we can use large numbers of scientists to teach science. But science is discovery, not teaching, and music is fundamentally creation, not interpretation. And if a college of music does not aim first at creating music, where else is that basic purpose to be fulfilled? Composers are few, and of those few only one here and one there may write a masterpiece. Research scientists are also few, and only occasionally may they make a revolutionary discovery. But without them there would be no exact knowledge of any kind, and we provide them with leisure and laboratories so that pure knowledge may grow. In the same way the environment of a musical institution must provide the setting and stimulus for musical composition.

Composition is not confined to works of large scale. There can be genuine and creative artistry in a modest school song. We use an enormous amount of music. We ought always to create a substantial portion of it. All the classics were contemporary in their day. They were not written for posterity. Time has winnowed the field, and preserved the best, but there would have been no best to preserve had not the habit of creation been spontaneous and widespread. There are today many fields in which new music is used for what appear to be occasional and ephemeral purposes, but this was always true. It is out of this fertile background that the greater works will emerge, if they are to emerge at all. And a musical institution should put this creative purpose in the forefront of its educational designs.

After composition comes interpretation, and the selection and training of that executive skill which makes adequate interpretation possible. Music is dead until someone performs it, and the quality of performance must be equal to the quality of composition, which means that the mind of the performer must grasp even the highest thoughts of both past and present creation, and his technical command must be adequate to their statement. We must, therefore, think of the arts of playing and singing as vocations having standards without limit. It is the function of professors and teachers to find and encourage this superlative talent. They cannot make it, but they can provide the soil in which it may grow, and they can preserve the atmosphere of unlimited endeavour which is its proper aim and purpose.

Only when these two needs have been satisfied, the creative and the interpretative, and both at the highest possible level, can we turn to the more pedagogic features of artistic education, the provision of those teaching services which are to minister to the average talent or sensitiveness of amateur performers and listeners, young or old. A great many of our music students will eventually find their life's work in this sphere, and no work is better worth doing, but even they should be educated in an environment which stresses to the full the supreme importance of creative and executive gifts. One of the reasons why students so often think of teaching as a distasteful prospect, is because so much so-called teaching of the arts is concerned with lecturing and class discipline, rather than with the provision of living artistic performances by teachers and students alike. Music is peculiarly liable to mechanical reproduction, textbook analysis, and historical gossip, and it can therefore be made into a class subject containing very little incentive to active and personal experience and participation. If the conditions under which music is taught in schools were such as to employ the executive gifts of the teacher more fully, it would be easier to recruit talented students for that branch of the profession.

The contemporary world of music is expanding and changing

in many ways. The technical competence of performers improves from year to year, so that the gap between the professional and the amateur widens constantly. This is in some part due to broadcasting, which has provided searching standards both for the performer and the listener. Listeners become more and more familiar with the classics and therefore ask for more and more commanding performances of them. This is not all gain, because it forces the singer or player to make a reputation, not by the extent and enterprise of his repertoire, but by some new interpretation or meticulous polish of well-known items. As the wireless public grows its level of taste becomes less adventurous, and programmes tend to be confined to music which has a wide appeal.

In the concert hall the limelight has moved appreciably from the singer to the player, and from the player to the conductor. The ascendancy of the prima donna has gone. Her place was first usurped by the player of international repute. But even he is now overshadowed by the orchestral conductor. The spectacle of a man handling large masses of singers and players impresses our new audiences profoundly. He focuses their attention and is credited not only with his own skill but with the combined accomplishments of the musicians he directs. He in his turn is to a great extent influenced by the public he serves. He, too, finds that a spectacular rendering of a familiar work brings more applause than the most devoted interpretation of a novelty. He must provide entertainment as well as artistry. Symphonies with quiet endings and restrained gestures are not popular.

One other new feature of our time deserves special attention. Music now plays so large a part both in education and recreation that the organizing of all this effort is becoming a profession in itself. Educational authorities are appointing musical officers to supervise the teaching of music in state-aided schools, and these appointments often include the official encouragement of amateur youth and adult music as well. It is administrative work which only a musician can adequately perform, but it demands the sacrifice of the musician's own personal and executive gifts in favour of the day-to-day devising of administrative machinery. At the more public level the Broadcasting Corporation and the Arts

Council of the Ministry of Education employ what is in fact a musical civil service, whose duty it is to plan and administer musical enterprises and programmes of the most varied and comprehensive character. This service needs wide musical knowledge and judgment, but it offers no prospect of personal musical distinction, and the more gifted musicians hesitate to join it.

We shall have to develop a new class of men who, though capable of a distinguished practical career, are prepared to forgo this for the public service. The same need exists in other spheres. My namesake, Sir Frank Dyson, the late Astronomer-Royal, once told me that in his position it was virtually impossible to be a practical astronomer, yet no man who was not an astronomer could do his administrative work. My own position is somewhat similar, and there will be more and more of these administrative posts as the public use and practice of music widens. It is part of the price we must pay for official recognition and public financial help.

The days of private patronage are gone. So are the days when the arts could be managed by amateurs giving their spare time to the task. The whole sphere of artistic endeavour is now a vast democratic field which has to be cultivated by an expert system of public administration and assistance. Two things are necessary for success. We must persuade a sufficient number of talented musicians to accept and perform these administrative tasks with the sympathy and enlightenment which only a high cultivation and practical experience can bring, and we must also contrive to find, within this strenuous and busy field of public endeavour, a few quiet and secluded corners where the most gifted artists of all may have means and leisure to study, create, and beautify their own original work, in peace.

GEORGE LYNDON CARPENTER

Born in Australia in 1872. Joined the Salvation Army in 1892 and was trained at the Melbourne Training College. From 1911 to 1927 was on the staff of the International Headquarters in London, and later was in control of the Salvation Army in South America and Canada. General of the Salvation Army from 1939 to 1946.

MY FATHER, an Australian working man, whilst registered as Anglican, did not follow any religion, though a man of high principle and generous impulse. My mother, nominally Methodist, was not actively associated with her church ; still, she sent her children to Sunday school. Both parents were later brought into vital Christian experience in the Salvation Army.

It was the desire of my parents that I should follow the teaching profession. My preference, however, was for an industrial calling, and I was apprenticed to the printing trade, on a country newspaper in New South Wales. Apart from my trade, and a lively interest in politics, I learned little the other youths did not learn.

Religion, with the passing of the years, less and less interested me. Increasing in godlessness, I became involved in a way of life that could have led to complete moral undoing. At nineteen years of age, however, I was induced by a friend to accompany him to a mission service in the Methodist chapel. Strangely, and without premeditation, that night I was converted. This meant for me facing my life in the light of eternity. Forsaking evil, I submitted myself to God, and what I felt to be His way of life. The change was, in my circumstances, as radical as that of Saul's Damascus Road experience; a complete right about face!

Everything I have learned subsequently has in large measure

been related to that vital spiritual change. With it I received a new spirit, enabling me to perceive truth ; a new direction in life which has taken me into experiences unknown and unknowable to the godless ; a new standard of values, by which to judge not only myself but, as with a yard-stick, to measure men and affairs ; also to evaluate thought, motive and plan. Never do I cease to wonder at the fact of my conversion. Before, I was probably no better or worse than my associates; immediately following, I found myself entirely different, in intention and behaviour.

The inward change of which I was conscious was not the result of much knowledge, but has resulted in much knowledge. Up to that time I knew little of God ; and practically nothing of the Bible. In a hazy way I believed that there was a God, or some originating Power at the centre of the Universe—a kind of final arbiter ; still, remote from day-to-day happenings. By an act of faith and surrender I made contact with that little-apprehended Being. This act carried me over my first important lesson. Faith in the fact of God was confirmed by experience of His power coming into my life. Exercising what faith I had, I received a sense of assurance and a gradually growing experience of the Divine life.

I began to read the Bible, and then to take it as my textbook for life. Through prayer I learned of God by direct personal experience, and through the Bible I was taught increasingly about Him about myself, and about life. The Bible has gradually become more and more satisfying to my spirit and indispensable as a guide to conduct. I cannot overestimate the influence the study of the Bible has had in the fashioning of my life. For more than fifty years it has been bringing to bear upon my thought the compelling influence of absolute standards. Daily I have been testing it as a textbook in the laboratory of life ; relating its message to the hard facts of day-to-day experience ; conducting experiments with its teachings, its promises, its warnings. In the same way I have been examining the fact of God, of Christ, until now well past the normally allotted span of life, to me, my Maker and my Saviour are as real as my own existence, also increasingly a source of certainty and peace.

With these fundamental factors entering every thought and

purpose and judgment, I have learned many valuable lessons as I have been privileged to observe life amongst peoples of many lands.

For the purpose of this paper I will set forth under the following headings some of the most important lessons that life has taught me : About God ; about Myself ; Sin ; Prayer ; Providences ; Life's major problem and its solution.

About God. In my youth I vaguely thought of God as a Judge—a Being to inspire fear and dread. What I mainly recall of religious teaching was largely concerned with rewards for the good and punishments for the bad. There was little emphasis upon the desirability of worship, or the wonder of the Creator's beneficent purposes towards His creatures ; little about God seeking to make Himself known to men or of His purpose to make a people like in spirit unto Himself.

My observation leads me to feel there is of recent years less blatant atheism amongst men. Yet there appears to be in most western lands a larger proportion of those who, without denying the existence of God, imagine Him to be unknowable ; outside the range of human understanding. This tendency, I have come to feel, confronts the Church with a serious challenge and a great opportunity.

Nothing, in my understanding, is comparable with the privilege of personal experience of God, the pursuit of which has become to me the primary quest of life. No plans, either material or spiritual; no purpose in any way related to me or mine, are seriously entertained without first considering their appropriateness to His Kingdom. Indeed, I cannot contemplate my life today apart from its subordination to a Divine purpose.

Just forty-eight years ago, I was moved to enter into a life covenant which, in a word, was, Never to leave my room in the morning without "waiting" for the realization of the presence of God, there with me and possessing me. This daily "practising the presence" of God has, amongst the multitudinous claims of a busy life, been of the utmost value to me. The practice has led to the recognition of the Divine presence at any hour of the twenty-four.

But my knowledge of God is not confined to personal experience.

What I have witnessed of Divine power in other lives—sometimes in the sudden and complete transformation of vicious men and women—further attests the truth.

Of many scores of examples, personally known to me, I might cite that of an American friend who passed away a few days ago. One-time editor of a famous New York daily newspaper, he, through drink and other evils, became a loathsome outcast—declared by a high medical authority to be an incurable alcohol addict. Converted in the Salvation Army he gradually regained his place in society ; became widely known as an evangelist and was used in the reclamation of hundreds of victims of vice such as he himself had been.

I discern also convincing evidence of God's dealings with tribes and individuals back into the distant annals of the race. Further, I see the wonder of His hand powerfully influencing national life. For instance, in great movements that have contributed to human well-being in many lands. One example will suffice—that of Wesley of the eighteenth century. The mighty spiritual awakening associated with his work influenced not only the Old World, but considerable bodies of people in the New also. The movements were not confined to normal evangelism merely ; they inspired ideals that led to important developments in social reform. Impressive examples in Britain are the industrial reforms resulting from the work of Lord Shaftesbury, who drew his inspiration from the Evangelical Revival ; also the changed prison conditions brought about by the concern and practical labours of Elizabeth Fry. Then there were world-wide missionary enterprises and the great British and Foreign Bible Society alike inspired in a large measure by the same Evangelical Movement. They had a share, too, in the emancipation of millions of human beings held in slavery. In these and similar ministries I see the power of God at work on the human level.

When I made my great life decision I had little or no real understanding of Christ the Son of God. But as I have moved forward with increased knowledge, the fact of Christ and the power of His redemption, have become to me an increasing and grateful wonder, binding me more consciously in love and devotion to

God and His will. I stand amazed in contemplation of the extraordinary implications of that truth : "God was in Christ reconciling the world unto Himself."

About Myself. One immediate result of conversion and the growing experience of God, was a new conception of *Myself* in relation to life as a whole.

Multitudes, I have discovered, never reach any real understanding of themselves, of the high meaning of life, its possibilities, and of its significance to God and their fellows. Consequently, there is no sense of wonder within their breasts, nor are they incited to noble purpose in the use of life. I can understand their condition. There is a downward pull that needs correction, and a blindness that must be enlightened, before they can be gripped by the grandeur and the responsibility of life. As for myself before conversion, I became conscious of evil forces in my nature that were, at times, bewildering. They discouraged hope for a better way. The struggle toward the right seemed unequal. Almost unconsciously I gave it up, and for a time lived in some respects, like many are doing today, with little aspiration higher than that of a superior animal. Increasingly I became conscious of the powerlessness of myself to master these forces.

Conversion opened to me a totally new outlook. Soon after this took place there began to dawn the realization that even my small being had a significance beyond anything I had before imagined. I came to understand that my life meant something to God. What Jesus said (Matthew's Gospel) about God and the falling sparrow quickened in me a sense of the wonder of human personality. Whether any life succeeds or fails is of concern to Him. With growing realization of God's interest in me, it seemed wholly unfitting that so precious a gift as life should be devoted to anything but the highest.

Let it not be thought that such a conception of oneself disposes toward pride and self-sufficiency. Quite otherwise! The more I have progressed in knowledge of life and in an understanding of the Divine Will, the more clearly have I perceived the inadequacy of mere human powers, for the ordering of the exalted trust ; the more I have realized the necessity for conscious dependence upon God—the simple dependence of child upon father.

Sin. A by-product, so to speak, of knowing myself is knowledge of the subtle workings of a principle of evil affecting the whole human family. In a word it is the *sin of the human heart*! Man's life is a battlefield for the contending forces of good and evil.

The average man adopts a strange attitude toward the truth concerning sin. Whilst few will trouble to object to being classed generally as "sinners," as for example in the Confession in the Church Prayer Book, they react quite differently should some personal guilt be suggested. Man's pride is hurt to acknowledge sin. This is due, probably, to the disposition that associates sin exclusively with vulgar or vicious practices. Life has taught me that sin is something far less manifest outwardly than murder or profligacy and the like: a wrong attitude toward God, neglect or rebellion, selfishness, or acting independently of God. All are grieving to Him since in them is the root of all wrong. The words of Jesus (recorded by Mark in the seventh chapter of his Gospel) can leave no manner of doubt as to what our Lord thought sin to be. Jesus saw murder in anger and adultery in evil thought.

A study of mankind, coupled with my own experience, and what I have discerned of sin in individuals, is sufficient to convince me of the presence and virulence of a malady afflicting the whole race. Sin is fundamental to every individual and collective problem in life ; its solution is to be found only in Christ, the Divine Redeemer.

Prayer. Life has taught me the necessity as well as the high privilege of *prayer* and of fellowship with God. It would be impossible for me adequately to tell of the enrichment of spirit that has come to me through this sacred relationship. Prayer has become to me almost as natural an excercise as breathing.

True prayer is more than asking ; it is submission—it is union with the will and purposes of God. Prayer in this spirit gives poise and confidence to the life, and not least in moments of crisis. It is natural that this should be so, since prayer integrates the human spirit with the spirit of the Eternal. Is not this the whole philosophy of prayer? Such prayer, I have found, is costly —requiring time, also the surrender of the whole being to God.

There are many—quite decent folks in their way—who seem to regard prayer as an exercise to be called into play when in a tight corner. It was not uncommon to hear during the dark days of war some such expression as: "Well, I've done my bit!" The "bit" often meant the speaker had attended one of the many special assemblies for prayer. This idea is largely on all fours with the practice of wearing charms.

All sorts of questions were raised in my mind when I began to take seriously the thought and practice of prayer. Amongst these was how prayer operates, or how the desire and expression of the human heart moves the heart of the Eternal. Frankly I do not profess to know! But I know it does!

Common sense no more requires me, before praying, to understand the processes of prayer than that, before taking food, I must have knowledge of the science that traces the transmuting of food into bone, and blood and muscle. Then in answer to the objection that fixed laws in Nature rule out the validity of prayer, someone has pointed out wisely that prayer is exercised in a realm totally different from that of natural law. No one questions the truth of fixed laws operating in Nature, though physical conditions are often affected by the impact of spiritual forces in answer to prayer. The laws of Nature do not govern in the realm of the spirit. In this realm it is a question of relationship as of the child to the father.

An ungainsayable answer concerning the validity of prayer is the answered prayer itself. Of this truth over long years as a Christian leader, responsible for vast and varied services, I have had many and wholly satisfying evidences. In addition I have personal knowledge of other large missionary and social welfare undertakings at home and abroad, whose maintenance has been forthcoming in response to the prayers of devoted servants of God in many climes. Even apart from the invaluable services they render to multitudes of people, it appears to me the importance of these institutions as present-day witnesses to the practicality of faith and prayer is beyond our power to assess.

During the recent war extraordinary accounts of answers tc prayer were related from time to time by hard-headed men of the world, to some of whom prior to such experiences the very idea of prayer was unreal and unpractical. Outstanding amongst these, perhaps, I need mention only Captain Eddie Rickenbacker, a notable American air ace, and Lieutenant Whittaker of the U.S. Army. Their frank testimony to answered prayers (after drifting weeks in a rubber dinghy in the Pacific) was published very widely in the newspaper press of the world. Later it was given in person to tens of thousands of American workers.

I have observed a good deal of confusion in the minds of many people of undoubted piety in respect of prayer. This is well illustrated in prayer for the sick. In nothing than in such circumstances is it more important to bear in mind the injunction: "Seek first the Kingdom of God." There is ever the danger of being moved primarily by feelings of family affection rather than by desire for Christ and His Kingdom. Some even of eminence in Christian service I have known to be sorely tried in faith when the expected answer has not been received. Maybe there was some failure in the spirit of their approach. An essential in all prayer is that the request is made in conscious submission to the interest of the Kingdom of God. The fine distinction between desires prompted by affection for one's own and love for Christ, is not always perceived. In prayer it is vital that it should be so.

A personal experience will perhaps illustrate what I have in mind. A daughter of ours of seventeen years, a girl of high promise and possessing rare charm of personality, was stricken with typhoid. Naturally my wife and I had recourse to prayer on her behalf. Fondly as we desired her restoration, we found ourselves mysteriously unable to pray for her recovery. In her infancy we had dedicated our child to God and His service. Everything about her in the unfolding of her beautiful life was an unmixed delight to us. And crowning all was when of her own volition she decided her life should be spent as a missionary in the East.

Everything indicated the appropriateness of prayer that her life might be spared, but, as we knelt daily before God in loving reverence, all that we could utter was an echo of the leper's plea to our Lord: "Thou canst, if Thou wilt." We were confident that His touch could raise up our child should He in His wisdom see that would be best for her, and for His Kingdom. For six weeks, with alternating hopes and fears, we watched and laboured, but that precious earthly life flickered out.

For years I had borne in my heart a hidden dread that one or other of our little family might be taken from us. Such a prospect seemed beyond power to endure. And here was that very thing upon us! Waking early in the morning following our daughter's death, I remarked to my wife upon "a strange sense of calm" that was with me. "And with me, too!" was her reply, adding: "This must be the 'peace of God.' "

Whilst for years we had enjoyed a vital spiritual experience with true manifestation of the presence and power of God in our work, never till that sacred hour did we realize so clearly the significance of "the peace of God."

Gracious, indeed, were the enrichings of heart and mind as we bowed before our Heavenly Father in complete submission and trust. Humbly we have been enabled in many lands in the intervening years to minister to stricken hearts, to witness to the all-sufficient grace of God, and by His mercy to help in stimulating the faith of others.

As for the apparent loss of service in the passing of our loved one—we know of a missionary of considerable influence, labouring for Christ in the East, also a Salvation Army officer and others in the homeland, who were influenced to dedicate their lives to the active service of God through the apparent untimely passing of that promising young servant of our Lord.

The Bible, in St. Paul's letter to the Church at Rome, invites me as a Christian to believe an extraordinary declaration about all things working together for good. I am bound to admit that word at one time made tremendous demands upon my credulity. However, I have seen the principle of which it speaks actually at work in the lives of people in my own and other generations. I can well understand something of the problem such a word raises in the mind of the man of the world—one having no background of faith or Christian experience. There are probably circumstances which to him would appear to make the statement little short of nonsense. For example, he sets his heart upon possessing a farm or other desirable object. A disastrous circumstance sweeps it from his grasp. Maybe, the loss of wife or child leaves him entirely bereft in the world. How, he asks, is it possible to reconcile such a statement with his experience of frustration and loss? In his case it is irreconcilable for the reason that the declaration is conditional to "them that love God." In other words, it applies to people whose lives are surrendered to God and His way.

It has been my privilege to observe this truth working effectively in the lives of workaday folk, and not least remarkably in my own. Let me relate one or two examples.

A cultured Australian lady of our acquaintance, suffering the ravages of a mysterious malady, bore, with great fortitude, a series of painful operations. In time these ultimately deprived her of all her limbs excepting a leg. Though confined to her bed and entirely dependent upon others, for more than thirty years she was ever a radiant witness to the truth of this word of God. Not only large numbers privileged with personal contact, but numbers more in many lands were enriched in spirit and stimulated in labour by the story of her triumph in tribulation.

In this connection, the story of Joseph, recorded in the book of Genesis, has had a formative influence upon my thinking. It is crystallized in Joseph's noble words on being made known to his one-time malicious brothers—"Ye meant it for evil ; God meant it for good."

Experience of life convinces me that in a life rightly related to God's will, there is no experience of trial or suffering that can ever be regarded as disastrous. Life has taught me the truth that "all things work together for good to them that love God."

Here I might be permitted in a slight digression, in order to touch upon a subject allied to the foregoing. It concerns what I have learned from the common aspirations and strivings of men for power and status amongst their fellows.

Naturally, I view such strivings in the light of what the Scriptures have to say concerning motive and purpose in all human endeavour. With its unfailing sanity the Bible enjoins that men should in all things seek first the interests of the Kingdom of God. Man's natural disposition is directly otherwise—seeking, first, personal interests and advancement. Between these mutually exclusive ways of life for men, there arises an inner tension which can be removed only by surrender.

Though often more than ordinarily gifted, many examples of the disposition referred to have been sadly lacking in vital personal influence. In their callings they have lacked neither in opportunity nor in industry and enterprise. But their range of interests has been almost wholly concerned with "me" and "mine." It must be admitted they succeed often in pulling things off. Notwithstanding every seeming success, however, they appear disappointed, frustrated men, and never really happy. Their gains are secured frequently at pain to others ; worse, almost invariably, at cost of those finer heart qualities essential to the enjoyment of the really full life. Dominated by the self-motive they become increasingly cramped in spirit and restricted in outlook, thus rendering them incapable of making any worthwhile contribution to the nobility of life or to the well-being of their fellows. And not only so, but frequently they become objects of a pity that is akin to scorn.

On the other hand, I have observed the outworkings in the lives of men of wholly different standards in spirit and behaviour. Moved by the truth that no man is designed to live unto himself ; that man's first obligation is to God and then to his fellows, they have sought consistently and joyously to order their ways according to Divine requirements. Often their achievements in the material realm have been less successful than others ; sometimes, indeed, they have suffered a measure of hardship. Withal, however, they have been preserved in true peace and tranquillity. Further, they have ever carried with them a quality of spirit that endures, and that enriches all of life about them—a true nobility of character. Such men are the salt of their surroundings, and are invariably called for in times of stress—in moments of great need.

After years of observation I am convinced of the practical day-to-day worth of the Scriptural injunction to "seek first the Kingdom of God and His righteousness." To do so ensures quietness of heart and unfailing equipment for the demands of life.

For many years wide international fellowships and contacts have enabled me to make a passing study, at least, of problems affecting the peoples of many climes. I discern, among peoples of sharply differing ideologies, the similarity of pattern that these problems assume. Not less surprising is the fact that so many able minds amongst legislators and others appear incapable of relating effects to seemingly obvious causes. Consequently, in endeavours to rectify what is amiss they appear fated to turn to human devices, the futility of which has again and again been clearly demonstrated. Such a disposition is age-old. An example of it is provided in the Gospel of Matthew. By pronouncing the forgiveness of his sins to a physical wreck, brought to Him for healing, Jesus caused a mild sensation amongst the bystanders. Rightly diagnosing the case, He well knew the poor fellow's physical suffering to be the result of moral failure ; also that until the root cause of his trouble were dealt with, no amount of tinkering with mere physical effects would avail anything.

Among my early recollections is the fervent propagation of the then popular philosophies for putting the world right. The period which I recall was in the decade or two following the introduction of free and compulsory education in English-speaking lands. Popular education was hailed as the great emancipator of the masses. A glorious era would dawn when John Citizen and his wife enjoyed equal rights with all others, in regard to education, the ballot box, etc. Ancient evils would quickly disappear when Bill Brown and Tom Jones had a hand with law-making. We were promised halcyon days of a warless world, of tranquillity and uninterrupted progress when communications between the peoples of the earth made possible better mutual understanding; and a great many other attractive means to ensure human well-being.

The advantages of education have never been so widely enjoyed as now, though there are yet many millions of illiterates in the world. Modern research and the marvels of present-day communication and transport, in annihilating space, have made neighbours of us all. Man has won a freedom for himself, and a growing mastery over the elements, the hinting of which in my youth would have been regarded as fantastic. Conditions of life for many peoples have been enormously improved in recent decades. Much grinding poverty, once all too common, has passed; gone also is the cruel sense of insecurity in social life. The mass of the people are blessed with greater leisure, thus having fuller opportunity for the enjoyment of the fruits of their labours, and of world progress.

Such desirable improvements in material circumstances would suggest a world of undoubted well-being and goodwill. But we find ourselves in a world bewildered and unresting and unpredictable as never before in all history.

Life has taught me a truth that appears to be of particular relevance to this generation in which vaster numbers of people than ever seem to regard material gains—wealth, power, comfort, security—as the great end of human effort. It is this: "Man shall not live by bread alone but by every Word of God" (Matthew's Gospel). All history has been thundering this truth at us. Yet it is widely ignored today and with tragic consequences, just as it was when the truth fell from the lips of Jesus nearly two thousand years ago—and earlier still!

The most widespread and devastating conflict of all time has emphasized this truth afresh, for was not the war itself a product of the material concept of life to which the Master referred?

During the half-dozen years of the struggle more than twenty millions of men, women and children were hurled to an untimely end. Mountains of rubble and twisted steel have replaced costly edifices of proud and ancient cities. The whole economy of populous states has been destroyed, and social orders rendered chaotic. Multitudes of rich and poor, now alike homeless and bewildered wanderers, are compelled to accept any kind of protection that impoverished nations can provide. Multitudes more, doomed to an existence scarcely above starvation point, face life with feelings akin to despair. And worse still, probably, great nations are today in the grip of suspicion and dread of one another instead of dwelling together in unity, in goodwill and progress.

Having regard to the extraordinary capacities with which man is endowed, to the proud civilization he has built up, and to the enlightenment of this age, how do we account for this universal condition of chaos? No sane person could imagine such to be necessary to human progress! Clearly something is wrong with the principles governing the realm in which man exercises so much authority. The truth is that Man is contending with forces beyond his unaided power to control—a truth he refuses to acknowledge. It is equally true, that by the means hitherto adopted Man is unable to rid the world of the scourge of war, and to give to us a reign of right-doing where prevail truth and justice and unselfish service one to another.

Nevertheless, I am far from being without hope. Hopelessness and the Christian faith are wholly incongruous.

Fundamental to the failure of man's endeavours to give us a warless world is faulty diagnosis. War, it is clear, is effect rather than cause. And it is equally clear that it will continue as one of the inevitables until there is a radical change in the heart of mankind.

Due to lack of perception, as is clearly indicated in the Word of God, the materially minded man holding hard by his philosophy of life, is incapable of discerning spiritual truth, and consequently is incapable of discerning where to begin in putting things right. His diagnosis, his approach to the rectification of human ills, leads him again and again to adopt means that are at once ineffective and doomed to disappointment.

Why do these tragic happenings disturb the peace of the world and interrupt human progress? The cause is to be found in man himself. The world's master problem is in the spirit of man. In short, it arises in the sin of the human heart. Every problem of life is related to it. Until this, the basic trouble, is dealt with, and in the right way, mankind will continue to groan in its bondage, in its frustration, and self-destruction. Neither in education, in political systems nor in improved material circumstances is there hope of remedy.

But there is a remedy. It is in the simple truth of Christ the Redeemer. The hope is sure because He conquered death and burst the tomb. Even as He saved me, an irresponsible youth of nineteen, His matchless plan to save the world is by saving men.

And that is the grandest lesson of all that life has taught me.

SIR WILLIAM Y. DARLING

Born in 1885. Educated at Edinburgh and held various business appointments there, in London and overseas up to the outbreak of the First World War. Enlisted in the ranks in 1914 and a varied war experience included the Gallipoli evacuation. Resumed business activities in Edinburgh where he is the proprietor of a departmental store and two bookshops. Is also Chairman of an engineering company, and Bank, Insurance, Milling and Finance Company Director. Was Lord Provost of Edinburgh 1941–44 and is now one of the city's Members of Parliament.

"WISDOM IS the principal thing; therefore get wisdom and with all thy getting, get understanding."

In spite of the fact that two thousand years have passed since these words were first written, they still are the best advice which can be tendered to—and followed by—all who are begotten of woman.

Wisdom is the principal thing and the search for wisdom and the getting of understanding are, even to those who think there is no discoverable meaning in life, the best objectives towards which one may address his days and nights and years.

To learn from life might well be the object of living and if it, indeed, is not the object of living none has put forward any other compelling justification. This riddle of existence—whence we come—why we are—whither we go—can be answered in many ways. The Hedonist answers it by saying that pleasure is the object of existence, that, in the words of Tom Paine, the object of life is to be happy, the time to be happy is now, the place to be happy is here and the way to be happy is by making others happy. The Stoic tells you that the object of life is to bear all, to endure all and that there is one happier day than the day of one's birth and that is the day of one's departure from this place of wrath and tears.

But neither the Hedonist nor the Stoic, nor any other, wholly answers the question and mankind in the main, to its credit, has looked upon life as an opportunity for learning, for acquiring experience, for achieving some purpose, some end or some ambition, and, in general, most of us would agree that that sheer instinct, more profound than any philosophy, is somehow right. The will to live—and live well—is ever with us. It is valuable, then, for all of us to seek and to find and, in this search, it is worth while to know something of and indeed, to study the lives of others.

Benjamin Jowett, who taught statesmen, has written :—

> Human life and conduct are affected by ideas in the same way that they are affected by eminent men. . . . Striking and obvious to the ordinary mind are the examples of great men, who have served their own generation and are remembered by another. Even in our own family circle, there may have been someone, a woman, or even a child, in whose face has shone forth a goodness more than human. The ideal then approaches nearer to us—and we fondly cling to it.

The sheer instinct of most of us to find such a pattern that we can follow—as well as an objective which we would attain—is not to be denied and, indeed, every man would be the better if he took as his guide the history, the story, the biography of some other man who has travelled the road that he is travelling to the end, at which all alike, must ultimately arrive.

This instinct for a pattern is seen in its supreme characteristic in the Christian faith. Men and women throughout the generations have found in the Founder of Christianity a pattern which they may, if they will (for His service is perfect freedom) follow, but, apart from that Supreme Pattern, others have found in lower, lesser ways of life and living a not dissimilar encouragement. A boy finds in his father a pattern of the man he would like to be, a girl in her mother, and, some, as the years widen, a pattern in an admired school-fellow, a beloved teacher or some other personality encountered at university or in the wider business of life. And this is all to the good and it is well that this generation should recapture this following of a pattern.

Ours is an independent, wilful generation. We would blaze our own trail. We see all things new, we imagine. There have been none quite like us! There never have been such times as these and, less modestly, such heroic figures!

A generation ago, we were hero worshippers, not self admirers. Perhaps, the cynic might say, there were heroes in that generation. We certainly found them.

Hero worship was a philosophy of the life of the nineteenth century (the first High Priest was Carlyle) and it might well be said that we in these democratic days—when Jack is as good as his master and all men are equal—have not greatly bettered the tradition of living by the abandonment of hero worship.

The eighteenth and nineteenth centuries are notable for the great biographies, and hero-worshipping Scottish Boswell, who found in Doctor Samuel Johnson the pattern of a man after his own heart, is only one of many examples. Many lesser men have found in the biographies and autobiographies of the great, and the less great, guidance and inspiration, encouragement and solace as they trod the treadmill of the revolving years. Many a man, for example, has found in the *Journal* of Sir Walter Scott the courage to face his own dilemmas and disasters, or in the pages of the *Comments of Bagshot* by Alfred Spender, a level, liberal series of signposts and lights along the road of private duty and public service.

Their name is legion, these guides and mentors who, in autobiography and biography from Doctor Samuel Smiles's *Self Help* down to the *Journals of Arnold Bennett*, mark for others the road they went and which all must travel.

What one learns from life, then, is the impact of a variety of things. One learns from oneself—those curious instincts, predispositions, inclinations, fads and fears—one learns from them in often awesome moments of self-discovery and self-revelation, one learns from the day-to-day association with one's fellows, how strange and incalculable a creature is man.

One learns not least of all from literature, for literature is not life in the laboratory or behind a glass case in a museum. Literature, for those who use it and understand it with feeling and sympathy, is veritably life itself.

If wisdom is the principal thing and with all one's getting one should get understanding—and none will deny it—there is necessarily a further thing, not only life but the inspiration which keeps life going. The wages of going-on are only the daily currency of mere existence, but the drive, dynamic force, gusto which is necessary to bring life to its highest is not found in the day-to-day drawings from the ordinary resources of mere living. Man must find another inspiration and if one looks closely at those who have not only learned most from life, but put their lessons to best advantage, one sees most markedly that courage is not the least of these qualities. James Matthew Barrie, speaking to the students at St. Andrews towards the end of what was a strangely chequered, lonely career, asserted that "Courage is the thing; all goes if courage goes." And Barrie was right.

This courage is the greatest of human virtues and none need be discouraged because he feels that he has not been endowed with it. It is a quality which can be engendered, created, developed and, indeed, worshipped, and without it nothing will be attempted and certainly nothing will be accomplished.

What I have learned from life, then, is this—that wisdom is the principal thing, that one must get understanding, but that one must, too, bring courage to both.

The fears which are natural to all mankind, fears which are rooted deep in the ineffable, inconceivable, terrifying struggle which the race has undergone in its progress from the clogging slime to sublimity—these fears are natural to us. They are our inheritance. None is born without them, but, if one is to make anything of his life at all, he must cast out fear.

The world is full of great encouragers. "Throw not away the hero in your soul," says Emerson. "Sudden the worst turns the best to the brave," said Browning, and James Graham, Marquis of

Montrose, soon on his way to the scaffold tells, imperiously, the generations of the faint-hearted who follow him that:—

> He either fears his fate too much
> Or his deserts are small,
> Who dare not put it to the touch
> To gain or lose it all.

Courage is a lovely virtue, and, looking back over a life of three score and more, I would claim that my greatest good fortune was to learn early to fight my fears and nourish such heroism as I could find in my soul. Such a decision and such a protection took me through as varied a career as many, and with a measure of success even as the world measures these things.

The forward look, the undying hope, these things grow when fear has been faced and it is easy, with the comrades of Ulysses, to remember as the years roll on that there yet may be

> . . . something ere the end,
> Some work of noble note, may yet be done,
> Not unbecoming men that strove with Gods.

Casting out fear, one can answer at any time the call of Ulysses. It is never "too late to seek a newer world"—never too late "to sail beyond the sunset and the baths of the western stars." With courage as companion one is careless that the "gulfs will wash us down." We know we shall reach the Happy Isles. The venturers' life is held fast by

> an equal temper of heroic hearts
> made weak by time and fate but strong in will
> to strive, to seek, to find and not to yield.

These are brave words. None shall underestimate brave words and certainly I do not, but it may not be unhelpful to those who read to add an outline of how brave words, for me, were joined to this pursuit of wisdom and this getting of understanding.

Although born in England, my childhood and boyhood were spent in Edinburgh, that unique and glorious Capital City of Scotland. "We are all nobly born," said Robert Louis Stevenson —himself a man born in Edinburgh—"happy those who remember it." I am happy in being born of this noble city, happy in recollecting that, if further impetus were necessary to the growing vision for lovelier cities, I would add my quota, because I have had the great good fortune to have been reared in a city of such quality.

It is not that my days were spent in the lap of luxury. It was my good luck to be one of a large family; I saw the loving labours and faithful endeavours of father and mother, and the strivings of brothers and sisters. Life, contrary to popular superstition, has never been easy for anyone, and it certainly was not any easier for my family than for the ordinary run of men and women. Neither my father nor my mother had good health. My father was forced to retire from business in early manhood but found, despite all his handicaps, time and inclination to educate his family and take some part in public affairs. He had a love of reading and in his books he found a solace from the disappointments of life. He armoured himself against fate by learning from those who, too, had fronted it at its worst and had not been dismayed.

Most of all, he loved words. He encouraged us to learn great poetry and fine, majestic prose. He filled our minds with noble thoughts and lofty conceptions and gave us a rich vocabulary—an interest in words and their power and pathos—which had been for me the richest of inheritances.

My mother was the good companion alike to her husband and her children. A farmer's daughter, she brought to the town a freshness and a sweetness that never failed. She befriended the friendless, never failed the ne'er-do-weel, comforted the unhappy and was richly rewarded by the love of her family and the devotion of her neighbours. She never complained about anything. "Things might be worse" was her most severe stricture on any happening, no matter how dire and this philosophy—not to expect too much from life—she imparted to her family.

At school at five and leaving school at fourteen, I managed to evade the temptation of mere academic achievement—that is how

I like to put it as I recollect my sole school prize, a copy of *Literary Celebrities*, published by W. and R. Chambers, 3s. 6d., presented to me in 1897 for "General Excellence." No other academic distinctions came my way, and so I was able to resist the temptation of a possible career in the Civil Service or a continued course of study at the university. My mind, because of its deficiencies probably, urged me to test what little knowledge I had in the face of practical realities, and it was my fortune to find myself at fourteen not at the University of Edinburgh, but behind the counter of a drapery emporium where, believe me, in my judgment, as much may be learned of oneself and one's neighbour as may be acquired in a five-year course in any college. There used to be—perhaps there still is—a kind of snobbish contempt for shopmen. I think it unwarranted. The shop is the show-piece of society. It is the place where the arts of men are displayed and, those who serve there, serve civilization. Man would be a poor creature without his clothes and furnishings and woman would be nothing at all for most, without the graces which discriminating dress and adornment confer on her. These the shop supplies, but to those who serve comes a richer experience. They see human nature as nowhere else—they see it in its search for self-expression—they see it in its search for beauty as it conceives it. And if shopfolk learn from their customers, they learn, too, from themselves. Behind the counter there is a fraternity. In the saloon there is a community. Boys and girls, men and women find themselves, discover their personalities serving in shops as in nowhere else. They learn good manners. They practise patience. They acquire taste and judgment and—above all these—they learn the ways of business by which all well-conducted systems of society live and thrive.

Napoleon—no small judge of human nature—called us a nation of shopkeepers. It was a high compliment to an art which I hope will continue to win increasing appreciation as a wider understanding of all its implications and impacts is more generally acknowledged.

Once my apprenticeship was completed I was eager for the larger world, and at eighteen was earning twelve pounds a year, living in, at one of the great London stores. During the following four or five years I had several changes of occupation, some of my own volition, some at the behest of my employer who probably found in me disqualifications to which I, with my self-complacency, was wholly blind.

There are few human experiences more valuable than to be dismissed from employment—to get the sack, as it is called. It takes courage and insight to "welcome each rebuff" as Browning has it, "that turns earth's smoothness rough." Many men owe much to an employer who, to suit his own ends, dismissed them and compelled them to a new stock-taking—forced them apart awhile to seek other roads to fortune.

These misfortunes did not greatly depress me, although they were in those days visited by somewhat harsher experiences than come today. No unemployment insurance in those years dulled the edge of the ordeal of dismissal ; one's service was terminated by a minute's notice on either side ; security of employment, the goal of so many today, was not known to those of us who served the public in the drapery and fashion business at the beginning of the century. Nor were we, it seems to me, any less happy. There was a gaiety, an abandonment, a carelessness and, indeed, a recklessness about drapers in those days which I do not observe in their present-day successors. And I need hardly add that they were none the worse for it!

We dressed for the part as drapers, and although our income might not be more than twenty or thirty pounds a year we wore silk hats, carried neatly rolled umbrellas to match, patent button boots and smart silk lapelled frock coats.

Our bellies might well be empty but our intelligence was acute and our demeanour alert.

During this London period, when I sought for wisdom and aspired to understanding, difficulties and disasters helped to replenish my cruse of oil, helped me to cast out fear.

Having known what looked like the worst, "the key to the street" as it was called, more than once, familiarity robbed it of its terrors and I successively found myself working in the West End of London, in Peckham, and in Woolwich and in Sloane

Square. Interspersed between these, I managed to exist by writing a little, by speaking in public or, on one glorious occasion, establishing a partnership in a travelling piano-organ and, not least of all, by the possession of a street hawker's licence, issued by Sir Edward Henry, then Commissioner of Police at Scotland Yard, for five shillings.

After some years in London, I returned for a brief spell to Edinburgh, where, at the age of twenty-three, I surveyed the world from the height of my newly-found experience and from that survey decided to see more of it.

Walt Whitman gave me words for the mood—his "Song of the Open Road":

> Allons, the road is before us,
> Camarado, give me your hand.
> I give you myself more precious than money,
> Will you give me yourself—
> Will we travel together as long as we live.

These were disturbing, restless thoughts, and they drove me to see the world . . . the world so full of wonderful things.

Within a year I found myself in Ceylon and after some years there, following again a variegated series of callings, I proceeded to Australia and it was only towards the beginning of 1914 that I found myself, after storekeeping and journalism and attempts at fruit farming and business organization, back in London again. In the few months that lay between me and the outbreak of war in 1914, I again found time to follow a number of occupations—speciality salesman of many sorts, insurance and back behind the counter were among my activities and, when August, 1914, came, like most of my generation, I found myself in the Army.

The story can be brought to a close in a few sentences. Soldier in the Black Watch, officer with the Royal Munster Fusiliers in Gallipoli and with the Royal Scots in France, on the Staff in Germany ; thereafter, a space in Scotland and over to Ireland ; from 1922, business as a merchant, and local government, politics and writing bring me to the Second World War as Chief Air

Raid Warden, District Commissioner, City Treasurer, Lord Provost of the City of Edinburgh and, subsequently, Member of Parliament.

These headings cover a lot of living, a lot of ups and downs, marriage and friends, partings and meetings, failures and achievements, disappointments and miseries, hours of self-gratification and hours of self-abasement. They are the stuff of which my life—all life—is inevitably made. There have been victories and defeats, but on balance life has been good to me for I can honestly assert I sought not only to make good but to find life good, too.

Others have not been so fortunate. I have had luck, but then I also acquired the art of looking for the good in the seeming bad—of discovering that nothing comes ill to those who have the faith to believe that all things—in the ultimate summing-up—work together for good. The sceptics scoff at such a view. It is to them the self-complacency of "comfortable moles," and they may be right.

I will not, nevertheless, lower my flag. For the unfortunate and the unhappy, there is a great good in life. I have often read—for the consolation of others rather than for myself it is true—these little-known words of George Adam Smith. He writes of the effect great sorrow and struggle has upon the noble soul:

> Come to the streets, he says and asks: Who are these whom we can so easily distinguish from the crowd by their firmness of step and look of peace . . . holding without rest or haste, the tenor of their way, as if they marched to music heard by their ears alone? These are they which have come out of great tribulation. They have brought back into time the sense of eternity. They know how near the invisible worlds be to this one and the sense of the vast silences stills all idle laughter in their hearts. The life that is to other men, chance or sport, strife or hurried flight, has for them its allotted distance, is for them a measured march, a constant worship. Sorrow's subject, they are our kings : wrestlers with death, our veterans : and to the rabble armies of society, they set the step of a nobler life.

And so for those who, unlike me, cannot transmute the tinsel of success, there is a vast heaven of sober satisfaction. Life however lived is not mocked. It has the indisputable, unmistakable potentialities of greatness. None need surrender. None need cast away the highest. None need find life base or mean or worthless or contemptible, under the stars of high heaven. Man lives by faith—faith in himself—faith in his fellow men—faith in the world —faith in God. *When faith fails man*, his life maintains, says Goethe somewhere, a sham splendour, a sorry victory, but it will pass as all unprofitable, unfruitful things pass. *When man believes*, life becomes splendid, heart elevating and fruitful. The forward look, the undying hope which redeems a man and men, the confidence that the best is yet to be, these I have learned to be the sovereign passports of life today and forever.

This narrative comes to its conclusion, and with the conclusion of the narrative there is, too, the conclusion of this piece of writing. I began by quoting the Book of Proverbs. I would end by saying that what I have learned from life is that, faced with a choice—and perhaps choice will be less available for the generation now with us than it was for my generation—by instinct I always was, fortunately, inclined to choose the more adventurous, the more speculative, the more difficult, the more dangerous.

It will be a pity if in the future the right to take a chance will be denied to the many, but it may well be so in a society which seeks safety first at all costs. In recent years, after two German wars, the name of Frederick Nietzsche, "The Dionysian Spirit of the Age" as Orage called him, has fallen into disrepute, like all the other authoritarians, to the smooth, level waters of egalitarianism, but it might be permissible for me to recall him to a new generation as I have dared to recall Thomas Carlyle and Samuel Smiles from the past. He has something to say of life and what has to be learned from it. He says:

> Life has not deceived me. I find it, on the contrary, year by year more rich, more desirable and more mysterious—ever since the day there came to me the great liberator, the thought

that life might be an experiment for the seeker after knowledge ; not a duty, not a fatality, not a sham and a fraud.

He goes on to say, and with this I will end :

Life as a means to knowledge—with this principle in one's heart, one can not only live bravely but with joy and laughter.

These are the words of those who seek life ever more abundantly and would learn of it.

Nietzsche has been described by one of his biographers as "The greatest European event since Goethe," but there have been other European events since then. Nietzsche was born in Saxony of Polish descent, and we have learned to respect and admire the Poles. His life ended in 1889 and he died a madman, but truth, fortunately, knows no nationality and carries its own passport, and if I were asked to say shortly what I have learned from life, I would find no better expression than these words of Nietzsche, words which offer no comfort to the aimless, the helpless, the hopeless, offer no ease to the half-hearted and the fearful, but sound a clarion call to those who have ears to hear and whose eyes respond to the beckoning of the far horizons.

SIR WILLIAM BEACH THOMAS

Born in 1868 and educated at Shrewsbury and Oxfora (where he became President of the Athletic Club). Was a War Correspondent in the First World War, but has since devoted his pen to English country life.

MY YOUTH was spent in the deep country, though the hamlet was little more than sixty miles from London. The nearest town was nine miles away and that was almost a village. Country houses, so called, were very few, and an enormous proportion of the population consisted of farmers and farm labourers with their families. The isolation was singularly complete, since modes of motion were few and slow. There were no buses, no motors, not even bicycles; no near railways, and no intellectual connection with the world by telephone or wireless. No theatre, and, of course, no film, was within reach. The few evening parties or dances were carefully dated to give the guests the benefit of a full or nearly full moon. Even games had to be adapted, if not invented. The chief game in my case was "going up the brook"!

Now this much of potted biography is an almost necessary preface to any consideration of "the things that matter," or have mattered as I judge the phrase. It is, doubtless, prejudice, due to the vivid memories of youth, but when, if ever, I am disposed to sum up the results of past experience, I seem to discover that this early knowledge of the deep country sets the flourish on a very great deal that has proved best in life, and most fruitful. It is of cardinal importance to be at home in the world, in many senses of the phrase. Wordsworth wrote, "The world is too much with us" ; but he meant the sort of world that is put alongside the flesh and the devil. In a better sense the world is too little with us, if we mean the face of nature or the fellowship of man. The real key to such a faith was put very briefly in a long poem of Wordsworth's. The mind he says is suited to the world, and adds :

How exquisitely, too, . . .
The external world is fitted to the mind. . . .

If you have once found out how to enjoy the presence of sunsets, landscapes, beasts, birds, trees and plants, you can never feel lonely or a stranger. Some people doubtless have gone to lengths that seem to most of us extravagant in the feeling of kinship with all living things and even stocks and stones. St. Francis of Assisi and, say, Richard Jefferies, are rightly put down among the mystics ; and mysticism is not to be understood or indulged, except by a few saints. Nevertheless, the support and happiness and virtue these exceptional characters have sucked from Mother Nature are manifested and have a place in the life of many of the most practical and successful persons. Three examples among those I have met, though I knew none of them very well, may be given : Lord Grey, Field Marshal Smuts and Lord Tweedsmuir.

No one has written a better essay on happiness than Lord Grey. He was a famous naturalist, a champion games player, an ardent sportsman and was Foreign Secretary in long years of crisis. Whatever he did, he did well. He said of two of his forebears, who were at least as distinguished as he was, that they were great statesmen because they always wanted to get away into the country to their home in Northumberland. Grey himself was like that, and even at school at Winchester it was discovered with wonder by his contemporaries that he read poetry and especially delighted in Wordsworth. When he came to look back and to put down his ideas on the things that had especially influenced him, he put Wordsworth's poems in the forefront. And what he liked above all in his favourite's writing was that he continually insisted on "the deep power of joy." If you can delight in the world about you, you are well on the way to happiness, and therefore success ; for there is no greater success than happiness.

Field Marshal Smuts, that great statesman and soldier, said to me once that he could not have gone through the troubles and dangers he went through, if it had not been for his interest in plants. Wherever he was or however pressing the danger he could always get recreation or amusement from studying the botany of the place. He was like a young soldier of my acquaintance who, in the retreat to Dunkirk, for a while forgot all about the bullets that were flying over, in his excitement at watching a hoopoe, a bird he had never seen before.

John Buchan, who became Lord Tweedsmuir, and was Governor-General of Canada, always had a master interest in the country round about one of his northern homes ; and his novels were a great success largely because of his intimate knowledge of country things and his love of them. My conclusion is that nothing is so valuable as a constant country home and a delighted memory of it. It gives a background valuable beyond all estimation.

There are many reasons for this. A happy countryman does not need artificial amusements ; and the worst results of these is that the more you have the more you want. One of the only pious orations that I remember was delivered by an old Cowley Father at Oxford in support of my college's mission in the East End of London. He said : "To seek to attain happiness by a succession of pleasures is as foolish as trying to keep up a light all night by striking successive matches." What everyone most wants is an interest that goes on burning and is there whatever the circumstances may be, at whatever time or place. Such an interest must be more than a hobby, a side amusement for leisure hours. You cannot attain to happiness by collecting stamps or fancying poultry, or playing golf, though you may get a deal of harmless amusement out of any or all. We all need a something that warms life itself.

How are we to find this? Some fortunate people can say thankfully that it is found for them. First of these fortunates are those who began life in a pleasant country home, among well-educated people. They can find in the thought of it all a sort of background that "stays put" and supplies fodder for the future. In the days when London omnibuses were drawn by horses, the companies used on occasion to send the older and more tired horses back to their native meadows ; and within a year or so—such was the common experience—they recovered form and strength : they renewed their youth. It was so with Lord Grey as with his forefathers. He could slip away into Northumberland or the New Forest and within a week or two, not only feel more vigorous, but face problems in his office with more wisdom and certainty of touch. It was like the old classical fable of the man who increased his strength every time he fell down and so came into touch with Mother Earth. My own feeling, or prejudice, is that by far the most effectual interest is a certain knowledge of the natural scene and a deep pleasure in it. The seasons themselves give variety, and even excitement. You can watch them with as untarnished a pleasure as people take a holiday to watch the sea with its tides, its ripples and waves. It is new every morning, and no two sunsets over it are alike. A Jewish author has written of the English as "that great, happy people"; and if we are great and happy, one reason is to be found in England itself. It deserves the description that Lamb applied to his favourite county, Hertfordshire. It is happy and homely. The seasons follow one another in easy gradation and the winter is beautiful in another form than the spring. There is no hobby like knowing England : its little fields and woods, its hedges and homesteads and rivers and bays and gardens at all times of the year, with their various inhabitants and in their varying guises, even its cricket grounds and other playing fields. Here is an interest that lasts and is continuous. It is unhurried. You have only got to "stand and stare," and, be it remembered, that W. H. Davies, the man who wrote this well-known tag, was at one time a tramp. He lived for many years a rough, some would say a rather disreputable life, before he became a notable writer and poet. But while he was tramping, he gave proof of one virtue that is well marked among countrymen, not least among agricultural workers. He wrote a wonderful account of his life as a tramp, and in the course of it mentioned almost casually that he had to jump off a moving train which he had boarded without a ticket ; and in his fall so damaged his foot that it had to be removed. Not a word was there of the pain or the permanent handicap, and the subject is not again referred to. In short, he was utterly free from the weak and miserable frame of mind, known as self-pity. He made the best of things. To the last years of his life, spent in a lovely Gloucestershire village, he was made happy by his delight in birds and flowers and the charm of the country.

It is not a good thing to be very much alone or to avoid people. After all, friendship is the very best of things, though perhaps, as that very wise Greek, Plutarch, argued, to have a few very great friends is much better than to have a multitude of half-friends or acquaintances. Utter solitariness is apt to grow upon people ; and incidentally forced solitariness may produce a state of mind that can scarcely be distinguished from madness. A good many people at various times have tried to make places do instead of people ; but almost all have found that it does not work. Our nature craves companionship and needs it. That queer character and—to my thinking—charming writer, Thoreau, tried it and wrote a whole delightful book to tell the world how charming a lonely life can be in natural surroundings. He built himself a sort of log house in a remote wood and there enjoyed himself and his thoughts immensely, as he tells us. Some of the things he wrote almost persuade us that such retirement is ideal. He lived there in the house he built for about two years ; but that was enough for him, perhaps too much. Friendship must be one of the stays of a useful and happy life ; and no people are more unfortunate than those who have no gift for friendship, because they are too deeply self-conscious or self-centred or self-seeking or selfish or conceited. One of the ablest and quite the most successful man I ever knew—if money and titles spell success—suffered terribly from an utter inability to make real friends. That rather foolish old man, Polonius, in *Hamlet*, gave his son most excellent advice when he said :—

> The friends thou hast, and their adoption tried,
> Grapple them to thy soul with hoops of steel.

I would put friends first of all blessings, friends of our youth, friends of our middle age, friends even of our old age. They increase all pleasure ; and there is no sort of sadness which is not made less if one can speak of it freely and naturally with a friend. Nevertheless, when all is said about the necessity of friendship, I remain not less strongly convinced that one of the most useful accomplishments is to learn to find pleasure in being alone. He loses more than he knows who is unhappy when left to himself; but solitariness is next door to impossible in a town and, if achieved, loses most of its value.

I once met a small farmer in Cumberland who seemed to me to have exactly the right views on this most important question. He went one day to visit a brother, who was a policeman in Liverpool, and afterwards described his feelings. In the noise and rush of people he said: "I *did* feel so lonely. Now when I'm by myself on the fells I never feel lonely, and *what's more, it leaves something behind*." He said on another occasion, when some town-nurtured engineers were put up at his house: "They only spoke what they'd heard someone else say or what they'd seen in the newspapers. They were so ignorant." And he had much more to complain of on the same subject.

For reasons very much the same as his, I must feel that to be at home in the country does something for us that is scarcely possible in a town. What is welcome in the one is disagreeable in the other. In the town we all like some new thing. Change in the day's occupation, or at any rate in the day's pleasure, is the highest ideal. In the country, on the other hand, the supreme and seldom failing pleasure is something very near to monotony or at least repetition. It is not a mere paradox to say that the variety consists in the repetition of the same things, and that surprise consists in the expectation of an old experience. In a town it is only the present thing that matters. In the country at the breaking of the leaf or the arrival of birds or the bearing of the ice or the opening of the view or the shifts of visibility—the present pleasure is vastly increased by remembrance of the past and expectation of the future. The progress of the seasons ensures continuous novelty, but this is built on the foundation of old enjoyment. It is a part of the proper job of man, as of lesser animals and plants and the old revolutionary earth itself, to be a companion of the seasons, to be—let me say it again—at home in the world.

All sorts of writers and philosophers and poets have said this in one form or another, and inarticulate people have felt it. No one has put it in a more direct and challenging form, without any literary affectation, than Charles Kingsley.

> "Monotony is pleasant in itself; morally pleasant, and morally useful. Marriage is monotonous. . . . It is pleasant and good to see the same trees year after year; the same birds coming back in spring to the same shrubs; the same banks covered with the same flowers. . . . Why should one change one's place, any more than one's wife or one's children? Is a hermit crab slipping its tail out of one strange shell into another, in the hopes of it fitting him a little better, either a dignified character or graceful animal? No; George Riddler was a true philosopher:—
>
> Let vules go saarching vur and nigh,
> We bides at whum, my dog and I;
>
> and become there not only wiser, but more charitable; for the oftener one sees, the better one knows; and the better one knows, the more one loves."

It is not, of course, altogether easy for those who have not been lucky enough to enjoy a country home to learn this attitude of mind. I have known scores of men, whose lives have been spent in a variety of urban occupations, who have thought what a good time they would have, how pleasant life would be, when they could retire. Some of them have saved money to the point of meanness in order that they might retire a little earlier and so have a longer enjoyment of the golden days of leisure to come. The blessed freedom had hardly been obtained, when they began to feel unutterably bored. "I daren't retire to the country," one said to me, "because I know I should be continually looking out of the window and at my watch and asking myself how long it was to the next meal." And how many of those who stay in the towns spend a large proportion of their time in bored hours at their clubs! You have to learn to be at home in the world; and if you don't learn this most important lesson when you are at least fairly young, you will find it difficult to learn at all.

In my experience, the English suffer less from this sort of boredom than many other people, especially perhaps than the American business men. They are wont to throw themselves with such zest into business and money-making—and their energy and concentration doubtless are worth the highest admiration—that they have learnt nothing else. On retirement they try all sorts of ways to escape boredom, especially travel. I have met them in Paris, miserable beyond words. They had not learnt to enjoy architecture or pictures or history or anything that travel could offer. Paris was only less dull than the Swiss Alps or the Riviera. They went to see the things that, as they were told, they ought to see, and the only pleasure they extracted was the boast of having "done" them. A singularly charming retired American business man I met in Paris said that the only method he had found of keeping boredom at bay was to learn all the bus routes, and he became an encyclopædia on this thrilling subject! I should doubt if it "left anything behind," compared with the invigorating enjoyment of the Cumberland farmer on his native fell.

Life, of course, is a complicated business. We have got to make a certain amount of money. Our business is not likely to be wholly congenial or capable by itself of providing the something more that we desire. So the idea has grown up that business and leisure have nothing to do with one another, indeed, that the object of leisure is to make us forget business, that the true refreshment is change. It is a false idea. You cannot with any true satisfaction cut up life into separate sections, differently coloured like a Neapolitan ice. The latter part of life is only the other half of the first ; and the two halves are necessary to make up the whole. We must delight in the world in itself, in which both the business hours and the leisure are spent. I cannot but feel that the sharp distinction now being emphasized between work and leisure springs from a wrong idea of life, at any rate, in the countryman's eyes. One of our reformers has gone so far as to argue that bigger villages with factories and films are necessary to free the poor countryman's life from dullness. If this were a right view, cottage gardens would not be as fruitful and bright as they usually are.

Money, of course, is the trouble. There is no use in denying its almost overriding importance to a great many of us. It is very difficult to fulfil the ideal of Robert Burns :—

> To make a happy fireside clime
> To weans and wife
> That's the true pathos and sublime
> Of human life,

unless the supply of cash is adequate. Nevertheless, a great deal too much may be sacrificed to this necessity. I have known two men, of outstanding capacity, who chose to earn a little money and live an unremarkable life, so far as the public was concerned, because they preferred to sacrifice their career to love of the country ; and because of their inward knowledge that its concerns were necessary to their happiness. Both accomplished very considerable successes and indeed earned some international fame in their study of country subjects, especially botany. They were able to exercise their real talents and enjoy at the same time their real pleasures and happiness. No one who knew them could doubt for a moment that in rejecting greater, more immediate wealth and indeed greater reputation, they did the right thing. Contrariwise, I knew a naturalist, of much native and natural gifts, who ruined both his health and happiness and indeed in the sequel his financial prosperity, by accepting, wholly against the grain, an urban occupation that offered more immediate return. He took this wrong choice largely because the business had been developed by his father ; but he never ceased to regret it till the day of his too early death.

There are people calling themselves psychologists who promise to find out for parents what are the true capacities of their children and to choose a profession accordingly. They may have some good ideas ; but the work ought not to be done from outside, we ought to find out what we can do and enjoy doing, for anything is better done if joy goes to the doing of it. Even though we are forced by circumstance to take up a profession which is not wholly congenial or suitable to our talents, there is generally a side occupation to be found which can run concurrently and be continued when the profession comes to an end.

Now life is very various and not only are people very different, but they do enjoy different things at different periods of their lives. I have said that in my country home we had to make our own amusements ; but as I approached my teens a new game, the game of lawn tennis, was invented and introduced to us ; and then began a sort of passion for games of almost every sort ; and I have often thought that they wasted time and energy which might have been much better spent. But I am not sure of this. They brought more than a deal of temporary pleasure. Fair and honest competition in the field, on the track, in the court, supplied something that it is hard to find anywhere else. Someone said of the English that they are a lazy people—and on the whole that is true—and need something vigorous or dangerous to wake them up. This, it was argued, they found in games and sport, which made their sluggish blood flow more quickly and was to them an almost necessary preliminary to energetic action and thought. The English were forced to invent games for the service of this useful work.

A very learned and most unathletic tutor of mine at Oxford was interested in this subject and kept a long record of the achievements of his pupils in the schools. When he came to sum up the result and analyse his figures, he found—perhaps to his surprise—that the more highly accomplished athletes among his pupils had a much higher record in examination than the non-game-players; but that they did not reach the very top. To achieve supreme distinction needed more specialization and study and exclusive energy than the athlete could give. I have sometimes written of "the tyranny of games"—and they can be very tyrannical—and felt regret, as I have said, that so much time and interest had been spent on so many : on football, both rugby and association, on cricket and lawn tennis, and for some youthful years on running. Yet to be quite honest I would confess that the companionship which they bred was invaluable, that they were and have continued to be a source of great pleasure and in general that they did one good. In training for athletics one reaches a height of physical fitness that is in itself a very great pleasure and cause of reasonable pride. A famous don and a very wise man said to one of his pupils who was talking of the duty of making himself fit, "Fit for what?" It was a shrewd question; but to my thinking, not wholly deserved. To be fit is what the Greeks called "an end in itself." The fit man is in a position to do his best in whatever direction circumstances may demand; and the work of getting into good training, as was proved abundantly with the Commandos in the war, needs the highest self-discipline, which again is "an end in itself," something worth having, whatever it leads to or does not lead to.

Of course, it may be overdone. I cannot but feel that many athletes, especially in America, overdo it. They are put into the hands of a trainer, and are not allowed to disobey him in any particular. They are generally limited to one particular feat. By this means records are made, but the element of pleasure is largely cut out and for self-discipline is substituted obedience to authority. One cannot say that such extreme concentration of effort is to be condemned; but it is not the right thing for most of us. There is a satiric definition of an athlete, current at one time in America, that he is a man who cannot do anything else. For myself I got great pleasure from running all sorts of distances and even in practising such side acts as hurdling and weight-putting. Athletics may be made a very good, useful and enjoyable game, like other games, played for its own sake, not for reaching some best-on-record. Some Greek said that what made people useful and happy was "the free play of life" and in that free play of life is included the free play of our limbs. Someone has argued that what most distinguishes man from other animals is the joint of the thumb which enables him to make and use tools and instruments; and my experience is that the handling of an instrument—of a cricket bat or indeed a gun, a golf club or a fishing rod, or for that matter a ball or the reins of a bridle—give more than just mechanical pleasure: they give play to a real part of the nature of man and especially boy. We are not lithe and lissom and handy for nothing.

This litheness, of course, leaves the limbs of elder people, and for this reason I feel, for myself, a certain regret that I never learnt a craft of some sort, which gives occasion for the handling of instruments—other than hoes or mashies—after the years of quick activity. I should say out of my experience that among the most contented of all people are the craftsmen. An acquaintance of mine, who was blinded in the First World War, became an expert cabinet maker, and his skill with his tools was his salvation. That thumb joint given to man has in some small part atoned even for the loss of his eyes. He can say :—

I too can something make
And joy in the making

and that is one of the finest boasts there is. It would be a great addition to anybody, in the latter half of his life anyway, if he had command of some sort of craft or other, as nearly all women have. Even young men, at the top of their form, may find this out, like certain members of a university eight who, as they approached the highest pitch of physical training, were compelled to knit or net or carpenter in order to quieten their nerves and restore their contentment.

While I am on the question of regrets for the things that were left undone—for what the preachers call sins of omission—my old headmaster (for whom, alas, I had no great respect) urged me to keep a diary. I have never obeyed, though given more than sixty years of opportunity. Perhaps a diary, if at all voluminous, may make some people more self-conscious than is good for them ; but memory is a great part of life and the pleasure of it ; and it is terribly easy to forget even the things that we should most like to remember, thoughts and impressions perhaps, as well as names and events, and even people. A very brief diary with just names and facts and an occasional reference to feelings, with a few phrases and quotations that made a particular appeal to our nature, would be a perennial source of renewable pleasure. The old and too little respected headmaster was quite right. It is a grand mistake to forget. Very often the pleasure of the present is so vivid and real that we think at the time it can never grow dim. But it can ; and very quickly. Indeed, I have sometimes thought that the more vivid it has been the more easily is it forgotten, because the mood of it differed by so large a margin from later and duller moods.

To feel thoroughly at home in the external world, where all our senses may be satisfied and where opportunity is offered for physical as well as mental freedom of movement, is likely to prove, as I have emphasized, one of the chief causes of happiness ; but this doubtless is not true of the majority of people, even of English people. In this northern island, where the arc of the sun is low in winter and the world grows dark towards four o'clock, we are compelled to spend many hours indoors, though most of us spend too many. After all a frosty winter night offers a singularly glorious spectacle. The English, more than most people, perhaps, enjoy the winter. Nevertheless, very few enjoy it or profit by it as they might. How few can honestly say : "How well I know what I mean to do, when the long, dark autumn evenings come!" When I look back I see a vast array of hours that might have been doubly satisfactory, if the art of indoor life had been better understood. In school holidays I read through the whole of the Waverley Novels and doubtlessly enjoyed them ; but, when they were finished, my mind was a shapeless medley of romantic incidents, and I could not have given a reasonable account of any one of the novels. They had left very little behind and might have left a very great deal. In the same way the hurried mopping up of articles in magazines and newspapers and the lighter books generally leaves nothing behind. Now very many people have felt what Gibbon said, that books matter supremely; and perhaps they ought to ; but they mean not half what they ought to mean, if they are read in a hurry or not selected with a certain conscious deliberation.

An old schoolmaster of mine, who used to coach cricketers at the nets, was laughed at because he had just one recipe. "Don't hurry ; there's plenty of time." The advice is in itself wholly wise, whether applied to cricket or sport (especially shooting) ; but it is at its truest in the art and pleasure of reading. The reader is a worse offender than the golfer or the marksman if he snatches at his books. We too often read to get to the end, just as American travellers go to see places or pictures or buildings in order to be able to say that they have "done" them. Almost everything should be done for its own sake, even eating and drinking perhaps, within certain limits. It is doubtless better to eat to live than to live to eat; but those who only eat to live make a mistake. The proper savouring of food and drink is almost as much a duty to our body, as the appreciation of language to our minds. It is thoroughly unwholesome to gobble books, though a certain amount of skipping may be justifiable. Now bad books must be gobbled (and are likely, therefore, to be indigestible) because the language and the thoughts are not worth savouring: they are insipid. When I became a journalist—some five years after leaving Oxford—a great historian said to me by way of advice: "Most journalists do not read enough. Now I should advise you to learn a language a year." I failed to learn so much as one language at all properly in sixty years; and his advice was doubtless too stiff for an ordinary mortal; but the general idea was sound enough. It is not only wise to read a deal, but to learn how to read, a lesson that seventy years failed to teach me.

Three things now seem to me important: First, plan your reading so that it leads you somewhere and so that you may have the pleasure of anticipation and can think with gusto, "How well I know what I mean to do," and the rest. That pleasure in a sort of continuous job may be considerable, with the reader, as with the farmer or gardener or any planner. The second is to read slowly and conscientiously enough to appreciate the texture of what you read and to give yourself at least a chance of remembering and judging. Thirdly comes the choice of books; and one of the wisest things said on this subject was said by the poet, Tennyson. "I like large still books," he said; and however much we read in magazines or what not—as a good deal of this sort of stuff must be read by most of us—to open the pages of a good large, quiet, unhurried book is like slipping into a harbour from a choppy sea that had begun to make us a little seasick. There are few more lasting sources of satisfaction than to pile up affectionate knowledge of a few first-class books that are congenial to one's frame of mind. To know anything well—by heart, as we say—is quite invaluable. All sorts of goodish books seem to serve. One friend of mine never parts from a copy of Stevenson's *Wreckers*. Another is familiar with every page of Dickens. Another told me that he could always recover calm and contentment by going back to the sixth book of the Aeneid, which he had by heart. Another could go on quoting Wordsworth for hours; as in an earlier era people could quote Cowper or the Psalms. Reading what you have read before, if it was good, is often more fun than reading what is new, just as each spring is more enjoyable, because it contains the recollection of past springs.

> The world is so full of a number of things
> I'm sure we should all be as happy as kings,

is an admirable sentiment; but as people grow up it is not the number of things that matter, it is the certainty that enough good things are to be had for the asking. Find out the good things—which vary for different minds and characters—is one of the best of mottoes; and no one can tell you which are the best books for you. You must enjoy. Perhaps I may end with a self-made maxim: Seek pleasure, not pleasures.

SIR WILLIAM DOBBIE

Born in Madras in 1879. Educated at Charterhouse and the Royal Military Academy, Woolwich. Served in the Boer War and the First World War. Retired from the Army in 1939, but became famous for his Governorship of Malta from 1940 to 1942.

BEFORE ATTEMPTING to answer the question "What has life taught me?" it is necessary to outline very briefly certain events in my early life which had an outstanding influence on my outlook, and which have deeply affected my understanding of the lessons learned.

In life it sometimes happens that one's education (using the word in its widest sense) is influenced and perhaps upset by some great upheaval in one's circumstances. The upheaval may be on the material plane, such as loss of money—or it may be loss of health, or it may be of a more positive nature, such as the formation of a great friendship. But whatever its precise nature, its effect is great and far reaching. Such an upheaval took place in my life at a fairly early age, though it was of a very different character from any of those mentioned above. My upbringing and career were very normal. At the age of seven, I went to a good preparatory boarding school for six years. I then went for five years to a public school (Charterhouse), before entering the Royal Military Academy, and subsequently gaining my commission at the age of twenty in the Royal Engineers. All this was very normal, very ordinary and even commonplace, and many others were treading those same or similar paths with me. But the upheaval to which I have referred took place when I was at Charterhouse at the age of fourteen. It may have passed unnoticed by others, but it certainly was the turning point in my life, and from that time things have been vastly different from which they could possibly have been otherwise. It was then that I consciously and very definitely came into a new relationship with God through Jesus Christ, as I realized how greatly I needed His salvation from the penalty and power of sin, and gratefully accepted the offer He made to me, and which cost Him His life to make. The transaction which took place at that time without any fuss or emotionalism was a very real thing, and a very practical thing, too, and marked the beginning of a new life for me, with new outlook, new motives and new desires. The reality of that transaction has never left me in the more than fifty years which have elapsed since then, but rather has it become intensified with the passage of time. I mention this matter because it has had an overriding influence on the whole of the rest of my life, and has had a profound and ineradicable effect on my outlook and indeed on my experience.

My subsequent career was not dissimilar to that of any other officers of the Regular Army of my generation. I served in many parts of the world, and saw active service in three wars. I had many and varied experiences, some of them intensely interesting. I carried increasing responsibilities as I rose in rank, culminating in unusually heavy ones. And, because of the great upheaval in my life to which I have referred, my career has provided a background against which the lessons of life stand out with unusual clearness, and for this reason it may be advisable to use it as such here.

The chief and most far-reaching lesson I have drawn from my experience of life is undoubtedly the reality of God. This lesson is so interwoven with and overshadows all the other lessons I have learned that it may be said in a sense to include them all. When I speak of the reality of God I do not mean some Abstract Idea which some people may call God—nor a vague conception such as the Prime Cause, nor Fate, nor any of the other indefinite and impersonal expressions by which men sometimes seek to describe Him. But I mean that I have learned that He is an intensely personal Being, with Whom one may become acquainted and be in close relationship, and Who is interested in me and my affairs,

Who desires my well-being, and plans to use me to fulfil His purposes. This Being has been intensely real to me especially since the great turning point in my life to which I have already referred, and increasingly so as the years have passed. His reality has been so truly part and parcel of my life that it has exerted a controlling influence on it. In fact, apart from such a conception of Him as I have indicated above, I can find no adequate nor satisfying explanation of my life and of its component parts.

His reality has impressed itself upon me in a number of different ways. For instance, as I look back over my life I can see how He has been shaping it from the beginning, and this realization has become increasingly clear as time has passed. My experience disproves most emphatically (at any rate for those to whom God means something) that life is an accident, that its course is fortuitous and is affected by the winds of chance, or that it is a purposeless thing without any order or design. I have learned that God is the designer of one's life, and that His design has a definite purpose in view from the very beginning. Moreover, it is not only in the *general* design of my life and circumstances that I have seen His hand and that His reality has impressed itself on me, but even more so perhaps in the small details, which have fitted into the general design with perfect harmony. This is, of course, what one would reasonably expect. If the premise is true that God has planned my life in its general outline in order that it may fit into His wider purposes, then one can surely expect that He will keep His hand upon the details, so that they may all make their contribution to the attainment of His ends. I, at any rate, have had unmistakable proofs that He has been acting towards me in this way, not only in progressive training, but in eliminating, or trying to eliminate, those things which would hinder His purposes. I say "trying to eliminate," because the success of the process must depend to some extent on my reaction to His efforts, and my non-co-operation may well militate against them, as I fear it has so often done. In fact, I am so conscious of the way my shortcomings have hindered His plans that I am extremely diffident about stating that He has directed my life in accordance with His purposes, and so give the erroneous impression that I have fulfilled His plan for me. I have fallen sadly short of that, but still, in spite of all, I have always been very conscious of His patient and forbearing interest in my affairs, and this has made Him intensely real to me.

An illustration of the way in which I have seen His guiding hand (at any rate in retrospect) may be helpful. For instance, my entrance into the Army may be quoted as a case in point. As most of my relatives and forebears had been in the Army, I naturally desired to follow their steps. But when I was a boy it was discovered that my eyesight was not too good, and it was considered very unlikely that I would pass the medical examination for the Army. Consequently my studies were planned to enable me to enter the Indian Civil Service ; but it was considered that the experience of a public examination would be beneficial to me, and in consequence I sat for the entrance examination to the Royal Military Academy with that object in view and none other. To my surprise, and that of my parents, I passed the medical test, but I had not passed high enough to qualify for a place. But to my further surprise a number of candidates above me were rejected on *medical* grounds, and in due course I was admitted to the Royal Military Academy. Since my parents and I (and no doubt others, too) had made the choice of my career a definite matter of earnest prayer, we had no doubt that God answered these prayers in this quite unexpected way, and that it was His purpose for me that I should follow a military career, and my subsequent consideration of the matter in the light of experience has, so far as I am concerned, fully confirmed that original opinion.

Another instance of the way in which God obviously shaped my career may be of value. Many years after the time referred to above I was a colonel on the General Staff at the War Office, holding an appointment which was intensely interesting, and, I suppose, of considerable importance. The appointment was expected to last for four years, but when I had held it for just over two years I was suddenly and quite unexpectedly moved from it to another, which did not appeal to me nearly so much. I was naturally greatly disappointed, and not a little troubled, though if I had been able to see into the future, I need not have been.

I had not held my new appointment for more than a month or two, when I was offered the command of the Cairo Infantry Brigade. Needless to say, I accepted it with thankfulness. It meant promotion, it meant command of troops, and thus made me eligible for consideration for promotion to general officer's rank, and it actually gave me experiences which were of the greatest value to me subsequently. None of these solid advantages would I have gained if I had stayed on in my original War Office appointment. I may say, moreover, that the Cairo appointment came to me, entirely unsought, and quite unexpectedly. There again, I can only see God's hand at work steering the course of my life, so that it might fit in with His subsequent purposes for me, and while feeling intensely grateful to Him, I cannot but regret that, on my part, I must have constantly disappointed Him.

The practical and intensely real value of prayer in my life as a soldier has, without a doubt, been one of the chief lessons I have learned from life. That Almighty God should be willing that insignificant creatures such as men should make personal contact with Him is, of course, an amazing mystery. But it is none the less literally true, not only because He has declared it to be so in most unmistakable terms over and over again, but also because it is the clear experience of millions of human beings at all times and in all places. It has certainly been my experience : of that I have no doubt, though I am increasingly conscious of the wonderful privilege, and of my unworthiness to enjoy it. Of course, prayer is far more than just asking God to give me something which I think I would like to have. It is not a unilateral but a bilateral business. It is, or should be, having conversation with God, in which He speaks to me just as much as, if not more than, I speak to Him. It is sharing with Him the problems, perplexities, joys and sorrows of life both in small things and in great things. It is also sharing with Him His desires, plans and purposes for individuals and for nations, and learning how one can forward them in one's own small circle. It covers one's professional and official life, just as it does one's intimate personal life. It is indeed a staggering conception, infinite in its implications (but an undoubted fact), and all the more so when one considers the One with whom we thus converse, the One who is infinite wisdom, infinite power, infinite goodness and infinite love. The possibilities of such intercourse are, of course, immeasurable, and the experience of it, even in a small degree, must leave an indelible impression on one's outlook. Looking back over my experiences I cannot but regret that I have so little availed myself of such a privilege, but even so I can but gratefully acknowledge that the help I have received from Him in this way has been very wonderful and very real, so that I have unconsciously formed the habit of taking every problem to Him and enlisting His help before approaching anyone else.

It may help to clarify my meaning, if I give one or two instances taken from my professional life. I choose these rather than the innumerable smaller instances in my private life, not because they are more wonderful, but because they may be of more general interest.

In 1929, while I was commanding the Cairo Brigade, serious disturbances broke out in Palestine where the situation threatened to get completely out of hand. Troops and naval detachments were rushed up to Palestine from Egypt and elsewhere and I was sent up to take command of the forces of the three fighting Services in the country. Before the full reinforcements had arrived and when the troops in Palestine were fully extended, I received a report in my headquarters at Jerusalem that a large force (said to be 5,000) of armed Bedouin was moving on Gaza from the south-east. In Gaza there were many defenceless people, including a British mission hospital with nurses and families. I knew that if the Bedouin force, inflamed as it was with false propaganda, got into Gaza, the place might well become a shambles ; but I had no available forces to send there, all at my disposal being already very fully employed. I sent an engine with two trucks in which a couple of Lewis guns were mounted to patrol the railway to the east of the city, though I realized that the effect they could have would be microscopic. I also ordered some aircraft to go out, locate the Bedouin, and drop bombs in front of them, in the hope of heading them off. They, however, returned at dusk having been unable to locate the Bedouin, who presumably took cover in the wadis with which the country is intersected. But I continued after that to get information from other sources that the Bedouin were continuing to move towards Gaza until they were extremely close. The situation to me seemed pretty desperate, so I did what I had frequently done before in difficult circumstances and sought God's help. I remember kneeling down in my office in Jerusalem and using some such words as these : "Oh God, I have come to the end of my resources. If the Bedouin get into Gaza it seems certain that there will be a massacre ; I cannot stop them : please intervene." The sequel is interesting. I continued to get information for a short time that the Bedouin were continuing to approach Gaza, i.e. in a north-westerly direction. Then suddenly I heard that they had changed direction by a right angle and were moving north-east, i.e. in a direction where there was nothing to matter. They actually spent the night in the open country and did no harm to anyone. Early next morning H.M.S. *Courageous* arrived at Jaffa with a battalion from Malta ; part of the battalion was immediately sent to Gaza and the situation was saved. A British Government official also succeeded in getting in touch with the Bedouin and after some difficulty managed to convince them that they had been misled and persuaded them to return to their homes. I tried to find out afterwards what had caused the sudden change of direction, but no satisfactory explanation was found. I have never doubted that it was a case when God intervened in answer to humble prayer.

Another instance taken from the many that were evident during the Siege of Malta may be of interest, being one which made a deep impression on us all in that beleaguered fortress. In the early days of 1941 a convoy was brought to Malta, escorted by a strong naval force. The convoy reached harbour safely, and the naval escort was out at sea some twenty miles away. In the naval escort was a new aircraft carrier—H.M.S. *Illustrious*, a magnificent ship and an extremely valuable one in view of the serious shortage of that class of ship in the Royal Navy at that time. The German Air Force, which had recently been established in Sicily in considerable strength, went out and attacked the naval escort and concentrated their attacks on H.M.S. *Illustrious*. In spite of heavy losses incurred they pressed their attacks and succeeded in hitting the ship and seriously damaging her. That night *Illustrious* limped into Malta and was taken into the dockyard to be patched up, so that she might go to some other port for proper repair. Next morning the German aircraft came over and saw *Illustrious* in the dockyard. They promptly renewed their attacks and maintained them for some days, with the obvious determination of immobilizing the ship, if not of sinking her. They succeeded in scoring a number of additional hits on her, causing more and more damage, some of it being of a very serious nature, and the prospect of getting the ship to sea seemed to become very remote. At that time the vice-admiral told me that the dockyard authorities estimated that it would need four clear days without any further damage for the ship to be made fit to go to sea. Since the ship had been receiving fresh damage constantly since her arrival in Malta, the condition of four days without damage seemed to be quite unattainable. However, there it was; we realized the paramount importance to the Royal Navy of getting *Illustrious* into active operation again, and a number of persons in Malta definitely asked God in prayer to help us in our great difficulty. I certainly was one of them. The sequel is instructive. Although during the next four days the German attacks were renewed time after time, and although bombs fell near the ship, yet no further damage was done, and after dusk on the fourth day, we watched with thankful hearts that magnificent ship steam out of the Grand Harbour and head for Alexandria, which she reached without mishap. Humanly speaking the chances of *Illustrious* getting away from Malta were negligible, but the impossible happened, and we watched a miracle being enacted before our eyes.

Another episode of a somewhat similar nature occurred some fifteen months later, and served as a reminder to us of God's protecting hand. H.M.S. *Penelope*, a light cruiser, was based on Malta and used for attacking the Axis sea communications with North Africa. Owing to some damage received *Penelope* had to be put into dry dock for repairs to be carried out. The German air force was in Sicily at that time in very great strength, determined to stop the offensive operations being carried out from Malta against its communications. It consequently concentrated its efforts for a time on *Penelope* while she was in the unfavourable position of being in dry dock. *Penelope* was subjected to extremely heavy and sustained attacks. Bombs fell all round her and riddled her hull and upper works with innumerable splinter holes. The superficial damage was very great, and the crew, with their innate sense of fitness, renamed the ship H.M.S. *Pepperpot.* But in spite of it all no vital damage was done—although a very small difference in the position of the strike of a bomb would on a number of occasions have made all the difference. Eventually she got to sea and headed for Gibraltar—1,000 miles away through enemy-infested seas. She was attacked by every conceivable kind of vessel and aircraft, but she won through. On arrival, a thanksgiving service was held on board to thank God for His great deliverances, not only during the voyage, but also during those never to be forgotten days in dry dock in Malta. This episode made a deep impression on us in Malta, as we saw in it the Hand of God.

These episodes were by no means unique in my experience. I have seen God's hand at work in answer to prayer on many other occasions—some of which had undoubtedly far-reaching consequences on the course of important military operations, which affected the well-being of our country and our cause. This brings me to a further lesson I have learned, or perhaps another aspect of the same great lesson—the reality of God. This reality is an unescapable fact not only so far as individuals are concerned, but equally with nations and empires. His hand has been very much in evidence in the history of our Nation and our Empire, especially in the two world wars in which many of us have taken a part. He has shown us very clearly that He and He alone is the giver of Victory, and that He can deliver those who seek His help, however heavy the odds. An instance from the First World War will perhaps make this clear. It may not be remembered that our Nation was not officially called upon by our Government to seek God's help until the summer of 1918, following the great counter-offensive of the Germans which so nearly brought us to irretrievable disaster. From 1914 to July, 1918, on a number of occasions we were within an ace of disaster—but that disaster just failed to materialize altogether. On other occasions we were close to great successes, but we just failed to attain them. Generally speaking, in this period in the main theatre of war the weather was unfavourable to us. It looked as if we were being kept back from success, but at the same time being preserved from complete disaster, until in the middle of July, 1918, our Government called the Nation to prayer. The date fixed was August 4. It is a remarkable fact which did not escape the notice of those in high places that immediately after the decision was made the Germans suffered a very severe defeat between the Marne and the Aisne, and four days after the day of prayer, success far greater than was anticipated crowned our arms in the Battle of Amiens, and for 100 days victory followed victory until the German Army was crushed and the German Government sued for peace. That there was a definite connection with the long-delayed day of national prayer and the amazing victory of the Allied Cause was realized and acknowledged by many who were in the best position to appreciate the facts.

In the Second World War of 1939–45, the Nation was called upon by His Majesty on a number of occasions to seek God's help, and as one looks back over the happenings of those tremendous years we cannot doubt that God in His mercy answered those prayers and gave us His help. We have surely witnessed a succession of miracles not once nor twice but many times, which can only be accounted for satisfactorily by acknowledging that God was the Doer of them. To many, if not most of our Nation, the evacuation from Dunkirk could only be accounted for on that basis. The fact that we succeeded in withdrawing fifteen times as many men as the most sanguine estimate anticipated, forces any thinking person to that conclusion. Again, the Battle of Britain, when the "few did so much for the many," surely was a miracle, if anything was. It is no disparagement to the magnificent valour and devotion of those few to see in the result the Hand of God, and this has been publicly acknowledged by very responsible persons. The Battle of Malta also was another example of the same phenomenon—which I was privileged to witness during the years of siege, 1940–42. In view of the lamentable weakness of the defence, and the enormous resources of the enemy, the fact that Malta remained in British hands is indeed a miracle. In the very beginning of the siege I was voicing the views and wishes of many who were associated with me in the defence of Malta, when I issued a special order of the day to the garrison and to the people. It may be appropriate to quote the former here :—

> The decision of His Majesty's Government to fight on until our enemies are defeated will have been heard with the greatest satisfaction by all ranks of the garrison of Malta. It may be that hard times lie ahead of us, but however hard they may be, I know that the courage and determination of all ranks will not falter, and that with God's help we will maintain the security of this Fortress.
>
> I therefore call upon all officers and other ranks humbly to seek God's help, and then in reliance upon Him to do their duty unflinchingly.

And during those two eventful years we were constantly seeing enacted before our eyes happenings which gave us unmistakable evidence that the Hand of God was at work. That was the only reasonable explanation of what we saw, and this was acknowledged by many. Our Nation and Empire has surely had many opportunities to learn the lesson that God is. It is to be hoped that a lesson learned in such a hard school of experience will not be forgotten, and that God Who undoubtedly delivered us and helped us in our hour of need will not be left out of our plans as we seek to rebuild our shattered economy.

Few would deny that ultimately the Spiritual is more important than the material. But in these days of mechanization, and the replacement of the man by the machine, this fact is apt to be overlooked and forgotten. We are prone to assess our strength and that of our enemies simply in material terms, in spite of the fact of our survival when our material resources were woefully inadequate. But it is still true on the battlefield as elsewhere that it is the spirit of the man that matters, however excellent may be the machines he wields. This again is true for individuals as well as for nations, and it is a lesson which must be learned and acted upon. Material resources, after all, are but temporary things—liable to change and deterioration. Christ described them as "the meat which perisheth" and therefore not worthy of the "labour" we are inclined to expend on them to the exclusion of that which endures. Man needs to be reminded that "he does not live by bread alone."

One other lesson which I have learned from life is the importance of a firm foundation on which to build. One may easily become so engrossed in planning the fair edifice that one forgets the importance of the foundation on which it will rest, and on which it depends for its stability and permanence. This is specially noticeable in these days when the word "reconstruction" is so frequently on our lips. As in the case of the other lessons I have learned, this applies to nations and communities as well as to individuals. And we individuals who long to see our Nation rebuilt on a good foundation on which can rest a beautiful superstructure, sometimes forget that the Nation is composed of individuals, and will only do what we individuals do. It is therefore important that we individually should make sure of the foundation on which we are building. Much of the unrest, sorrow and perplexity which are such prominent features of life today is due to the lack of foundation and firm roots. Uncertainty, instability and doubts which prevent us from being sure of anything are the cause of much of our troubles. But can a foundation be found, on which we can safely and confidently build the fair edifice we desire? Thank God it can, as I have learned. It can be found in God as revealed in the person of Jesus Christ. On Him and on Him alone the individual and the Nation can find firm ground on which to build so that, as in the example quoted by Christ, "when the rains descended and the floods came and the winds blew and beat upon that house, it fell not : for it was founded upon a rock."

In God's mercy to me I have learned that that is true, and that those built upon Christ can face with absolute confidence whatever the future may have in store.

VISCOUNT TEMPLEWOOD

Born in 1880, and educated at Harrow and Oxford. Was Member of Parliament for Chelsea from 1910 to 1944 and, as Sir Samuel Hoare, occupied various positions in the Cabinet from 1923 to 1940. From 1940 to 1944 he was Ambassador to Spain on Special Mission and received his Viscounty in July, 1944. Represented Oxford at tennis and racquets, has taken a special interest in flying, and is now President of the Lawn Tennis Association and Chancellor of Reading University.

GRACIAN, the Montaigne of Spanish literature, has described the three ages of man. In his youth, man talks with his books, in his middle age with his friends, and in his old age with himself. Whilst I am unwilling to divide my life into these three water-tight compartments, I admit that the later chapters of life are the time for self-meditation. Let me then soliloquize for a few moments on myself.

I suppose that, judged by several standards, I can claim that my life has been full and varied. So full and varied, in fact, that never until now have I had time to look back and reflect on the many mistakes that I have certainly made. Even if I had had the time in the past, I would have resisted the temptation of building a retrospect on the back of hypotheses. How easy it is to say that "if I had done this or that, the result would have been so much better," but how easy it is also to weaken one's nerve for the future by these *post facto* inquests.

If, therefore, I now look back over the past, I will try to avoid an attitude of morbid introspection, and to examine my life as dispassionately as a historian who sets out to explain the causes and effects of established facts and influences.

Starting from this point of view, I at once realize that I have been constantly influenced by my family traditions. For generations my ancestors were Quakers and bankers. As Quakers, they were the members of a small community, intent upon Christian service and mundane stability, that maintained its distinctive code and method of life as firmly as a religious order or a regimental unit. The community married within itself. Its successive generations maintained their hereditary avocations, and their unswerving support of such good causes as the abolition of slavery and the reform of the penal laws. Influences such as these created a habit of life that, though its cut has often been changed, has worn well in spite of the changing fashions of the world.

When, as in the case of my own family, the Quakers were also private bankers, the force of tradition became even stronger.

The private banker of the eighteenth and nineteenth centuries was essentially cautious and patient. He did not attempt to make a quick fortune. He knew his clients and between him and them was the mutual trust of an understanding family. He avoided controversy and would never take a case into court that could conceivably be settled outside. Morley's essay on Compromise would have given him a manual of daily conduct, and Walter Bagehot, a fellow private banker, a guide to political action. This double influence of Quaker and private banker has constantly shown itself in my own life, though my family joined the Church of England at the beginning of the nineteenth century and my father gave up banking when I was a baby. Anyone who cared to study in detail my public record would find many instances of this Quaker-banker complex.

The third family influence that has worked upon me is a love of sport and physical exercise. Sport may at first sight appear to be an incongruous taste for Quaker stock. In point of fact, there were no keener sportsmen than my Quaker ancestors. My family records show how, year after year, they went to Norfolk for the shooting season, and how it was the love of sport that interested them in country life and particularly in birds.

When I think of my own past, I put this love of country life and birds as one of its most abiding influences. Since my father's time it has been carried a step further into the field of games and physical exercise. He was the first of the family to be a notable player of games. He was well known as a cricketer, and was one of the pioneers of lawn tennis. His love of games descended upon me. The happiest moments of my life have been connected with games. There is something so concrete and immediately satisfying about a success in them. The offdrive past cover, the half-volley at racquets, the perfect chase at tennis or the passing shot at lawn tennis, the follow-through at golf that seems to put wings to the ball, the poise and control of advanced skating, the rhythm of good dancing—these are things that have given me the most subtle pleasures of my life. Such things, though to many they may seem of little account, have meant for me the secret of balance and rhythm. Furthermore, physical exercise has cleared my head when it was becoming confused. The complete concentration that is needed for success in a sport or game has been excellent training for concentration upon public affairs. The feeling that mind and body are working in harmony upon a given purpose gives assurance to sensitive people like myself who need the encouragement of a certain measure of success. To say, therefore, that sport and games have had a very definite influence on my life is neither to overstate my experience nor to discredit it. I am in good company. Aeschylus asked that his bodily prowess rather than his poetic genius should be remembered on his tomb. The palæstra was as important for the Greeks as the agora. For the love of games and sport I am indebted to my family. I am constantly conscious of the value of the debt that I owe for it.

After tradition come two other influences, books and experience. I cannot place them in order of merit, as they have interacted to such an extent that it is difficult to say where one ends and the other begins. In the matter of books, I have stepped outside the limits set by Gracian. For I have constantly conversed with them throughout the whole of my life. Perhaps I have read too much. Perhaps also, my passion for books has taken me into many culs-de-sac where I have wasted my time and tired my mind. Perhaps also, the reading of so many books has detracted from the abiding influence of the best of them. One thing is certain. It has damaged my style of public speaking. There is all the difference in the world between the written and the spoken word, and it is the written word that has most influenced me.

If I am asked what books have chiefly affected me, I cannot give an answer. There are scarcely any books, good or bad, from which I have not learnt something. Two authors have, however, never left my side.

As an analyst of human nature, I have always kept Stendhal close at hand. For the philosophy of life I have taken Montaigne for my guide. Emile Faguet, the great French critic, whose lectures I once attended at the Sorbonne, used to say that every man should read Montaigne twice in his life, once when he was twenty to learn how to live, and next, towards the end of life to learn how he ought to have lived. As one whom Montaigne has greatly influenced, I commend this advice to the world at large.

Montaigne lived at a moment when the world was in a state of upheaval. The Middle Ages were dissolving into the Renaissance and Reformation. It was a time of disturbing contrasts. Side by side with the revived study of the humanities and the new chapter of great discoveries, religious fanaticism and materialist brutality were running riot. A battle so close that its result could not yet be foreseen was being daily fought between the forces of civilization and the forces of intolerance. It was against this background that Montaigne in his tower in Guyenne impartially analysed his own experiences.

Today, the world is even more bitterly divided between contending forces than in Montaigne's time. On the one hand science has opened out a limitless field of material progress, on the other hand prejudice, intolerance, want and fear have set a wall at its entrance that has not at present been crossed. It is in this riven world that most of my active life has been lived. How different a background from the peaceful landscape of the Quaker bankers who preceded me! To them war was anathema. Many of them, knowing the horrors of war, were for peace at any price. It may be that it was their Quaker influence that has sometimes made me "ingeminate peace" like Falkland at the battle of Newbury, when there was no peace. It may be that their banker influence has made me search for compromises when the two sides were each bent on complete victory. I cannot say. We must all of us, like Borrow's Jaspar Petulengro, fulfil our destiny, and mine was to be a man of peace, and not of war.

My many experiences of public life have confirmed me in this attitude. But whilst they have underlined my inherited propensities, they have taught me many useful lessons and enriched my natural instincts. Patience and tolerance are the two chief legacies that they have left me.

Patience, the most useful but the most difficult of political virtues! How well I remember a conversation that I had with that wise man, Lord Haldane. He told me that he was once walking through St. James's Park with Morley and Elihu Root, the well-known American publicist, when their talk was on the qualities needed for public life. "Eloquence," said one, "Courage," another, but eventually they all agreed that more necessary then either eloquence or courage was patience. Lord Haldane was to find in his own career the truth of this conclusion. Patience, like the steadfast fortitude of Collingwood tossing month after month in the Channel and waiting for an enemy that would not attack, patience like Lord Haldane's own refusal to be deflected from his purpose by disparagement and provocation, and his persistence in working out detail by detail the programme upon which he had decided. How much I needed this patience myself in my long mission in wartime Spain!

Tolerance, how gradually I have learnt its virtue as I have seen more of the world and rubbed shoulders with all sorts and conditions of men and women!

These two, patience and tolerance, come from the major decalogue of experience. But there is another precept that experience has given, a precept, it may be, on a lower scale but none the less useful in the daily round of public and private life—the precept of accuracy. Upon whatever work I have been engaged, I have tried to follow William Blake's injunction "to labour well the minute particulars." My critics have said that this passion for accuracy has given me the precision of a maiden aunt. So far from resenting the criticism, I welcome it. For the more I look upon the troubled world, the more I am convinced that loose thinking and loose talking lead to disillusionment, despair and disaster, and that we must keep William James's precept to "forge every word and act in the teeth of ineluctable and stubborn fact."

The spiritual forces that have worked upon me I have not attempted to describe. I keep them to myself as in the silence of a Quaker meeting. I will only say of them that if I have followed Montaigne along his path of life, I have not forgotten his directions for the path of death. The road to a *bona mors* is often rough and obscure. Overhanging branches that hide the sky and undergrowth of weeds and brambles that catch the feet, make the journey difficult and often laborious. Some, trusting to themselves, want no guide. Others, less assured, need the help of a travel association. I am one of those who require this help. It is on this account that, when in accordance with Gracian's injunction for the later chapters of life I meditate with myself, I strengthen myself with the support of the great and abiding institution of the historic Church.

VISCOUNT JOWITT

Born in 1885 and educated at Marlborough and New College, Oxford. Called to the Bar in 1909, and was a Liberal M.P. from 1922-29. Joined the Labour Party in 1929, and in the same year was made Attorney-General. After holding various Ministerial posts during the Second World War, was created a peer in 1945 and became Lord Chancellor.

THE TEMPTATION to indulge in a few respectable platitudes when asked to write on the theme "What life has taught me," is almost irresistible; and, as has been said by a witty writer, "the only way to be rid of temptation is to yield to it." I feel sure that I shall yield before I finish these few remarks.

I ought to have learnt much more from life than I have in fact learnt. I fear that were I to start life again with my present knowledge, though I should avoid my worst mistakes, I should make very much the same sort of mistakes as I have in fact made. Perhaps this is because my life has been active rather than contemplative and I have had all too little time to sit still and think.

I used to hear it said that youth is the age at which you think of the naughty things you will do; the prime of life is when you do them; and old age is when you wish you had not. I believe all these three statements are profoundly untrue.

Certainly when I was young I lived in the present and spent precious little time contemplating the future, and now that I am old I look back on my past misdeeds with interest and without undue shame; whilst as to my doings in the prime of life, I can here rely on the maxim that no one is obliged to convict himself.

On the whole I would say that I have learnt that the happiness and achievement in life depends upon one's relationship with one's fellow men. After long experience of my fellow men and in spite of the fact that I have seen much of the seamy side of life, I have come to the conclusion that man is a noble animal—far nobler in fact than is generally supposed.

Of course each man has his own individual defects and these defects he is generally only too ready to advertise; but deep down, if you take the trouble to search for it, you will find the pure gold, covered though it may be by some inferior dross.

Life has taught me, therefore, that the right course is to search for the gold in one's fellow men. I believe that the maxim that "the proper study of mankind is man," is profoundly true. By getting to know your fellow men you will discover all sorts of interesting problems and personalities.

The secret of a happy life is to be as interested in other people, and in their problems, as you are in your own. Happiness is an elusive Will o' the Wisp. If you seek to capture it it will surely evade you. If you try to make others happy, happiness will come to you as a sort of by-product.

That I believe to be the principal and the most important lesson I have learnt, but there are two other lessons to which I would like to refer. The first is in reference to the dread which people, and young people in particular, have of being in any way different from their associates. I remember well the agony through which I used to pass if I went to a party in an inappropriate dress. I think this is due to the fact that we are apt, particularly when we are young, to imagine that all the casual acquaintances we meet in a room are taking a profound interest in us, whereas, as a matter of fact, it is probably more true to say that most of them do not care two pins whether we are alive or dead. I think the knowledge of this fact, which is acquired in later life, makes these small matters absolutely unimportant.

A sense of humour, a sense of proportion and a sense of detachment are most valuable qualities. If we could sometimes watch ourselves as though our life were being portrayed on the stage and we ourselves were momentarily sitting in the stalls at the same time, we could acquire the necessary detachment. A sense of detachment shows us that our misfortunes and apparent disasters are generally not quite so crushing as they seem to be at the moment.

The next lesson I have learnt is that as we get older we get more tolerant. Tolerance is by no means necessarily a virtue. If and in so far as it springs from indifference, it is indeed rather a discredit. The tolerance that is worth while is the tolerance which enables a man to listen quietly to points of view with which he violently disagrees.

I think that as a man gets older he is rather more ready to make allowances for other people and he realizes that defects which they frequently show have a cause. If, on occasions, a particular person shows himself to be irritable and cantankerous the young tend to write him down as a person normally possessed of these characteristics. But the older man realizes that those defects are very likely due to the fact that that person has got some trouble at home or that he has got toothache or some other pain or worry which is affecting him at that particular moment of time. It is easier to make allowances in mature life. Youth is apt to be intolerant.

Perhaps this is a variant of my first theme in that it is all part of the advice that the secret of life is the getting to know one's fellow men, and success in this makes it easier to make allowances.

Finally, I remember a quotation which was written up on the fireplace of my classroom at school. I am not sure where the quotation comes from, but it was as follows:

"Money lost, little lost,
Honour lost, much lost,
Heart lost, all lost."

Life has taught me that these statements are true.

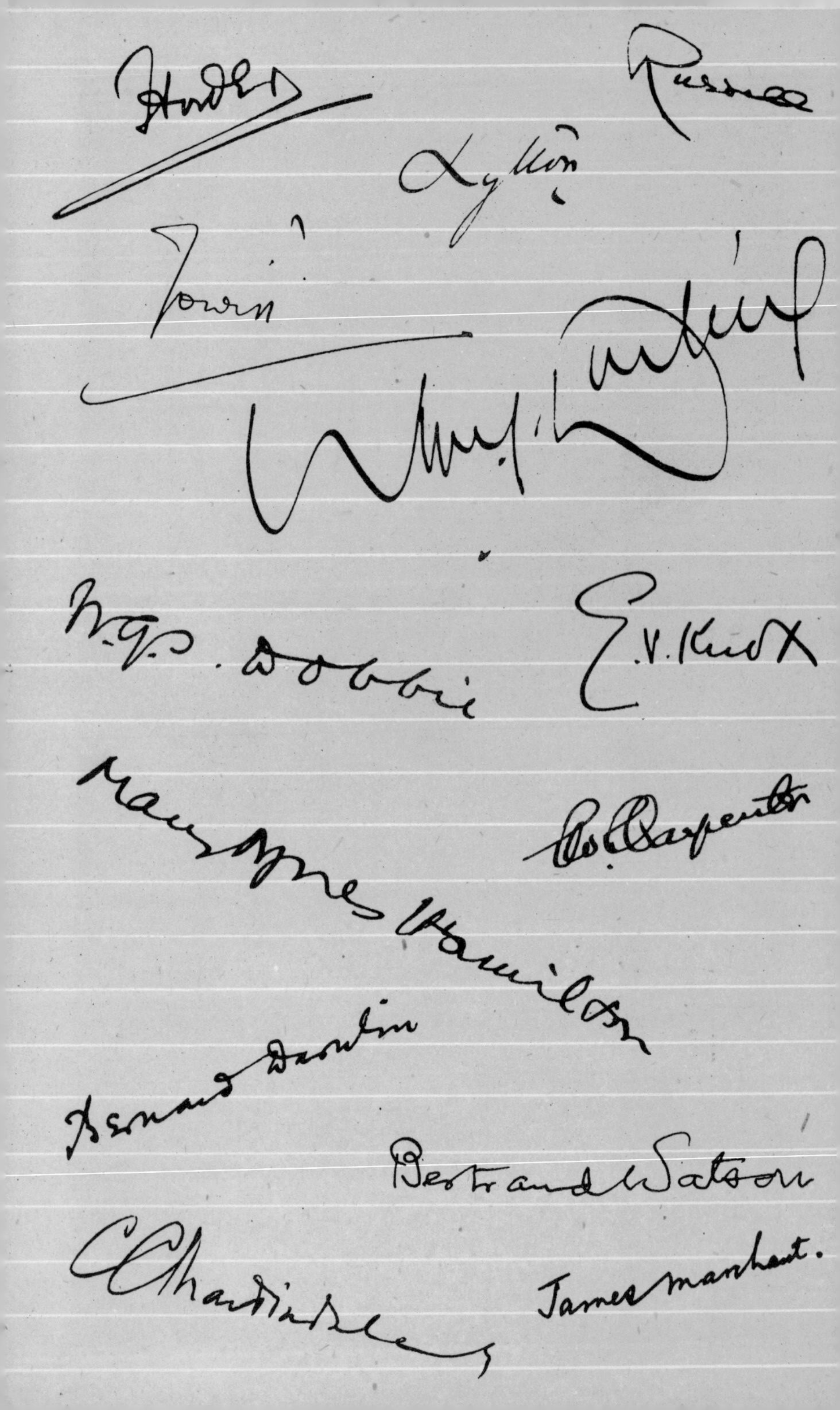

Russell

Lytton

W. G. S. Dobbie

E. V. Knox

Mary Agnes Hamilton

Bernard Darwin

Bertrand Watson

James Marchant.